ALSO BY RAYMOND SMULLYAN

THE LADY
OR THE TIGER?

◆ ◆ ◆

THE LADY
OR THE TIGER?

and Other Logic Puzzles

INCLUDING A MATHEMATICAL NOVEL

THAT FEATURES GÖDEL'S

GREAT DISCOVERY

BY

Raymond Smullyan

TIMES BOOKS

The problems in Chapter 3, "The Asylum of Doctor Tarr
and Professor Fether," originally appeared
in *The Two-Year College Mathematics Journal*.

Library of Congress Cataloging-in-Publication Data

Smullyan, Raymond M.
The lady or the tiger? : and other logic puzzles, including a
mathematical novel that features Gödel's great discovery / by
Raymond Smullyan. — 1st ed.
p. cm.
Originally published: New York : Knopf, 1982.
ISBN 0-8129-2117-8 (pbk.)
1. Puzzles. 2. Mathematical recreations 3. Philosophical
recreations. I. Title.
[GV1493.S626 1992]
793.73—dc20   92-53887

Manufactured in the United States of America

9 8 7 6 5 4 3 2

Contents

CONTENTS

Preface

Among the numerous fascinating letters I have received concerning my first puzzle book (whose name I can never remember!), one was from the ten-year-old son of a famous mathematician who was a former classmate of mine. The letter contained a beautiful original puzzle, inspired by some of the puzzles in my book which the boy had been avidly reading. I promptly phoned the father to congratulate him on his son's cleverness. Before he called the boy to the phone, the father said to me in soft conspiratorial tones: "He is reading your book and loves it! But when you speak to him, don't let him know that what he is doing is math, because he *hates* math! If he had any idea that this is really math, he would stop reading the book immediately!"

I mention this because it illustrates a most curious, yet common, phenomenon: So many people I have met claim to hate math, and yet are enormously intrigued by any logic or math problem I give them, provided I present it in the form of a puzzle. I would not be at all surprised if good puzzle books prove to be one of the best cures for so-called "math anxiety." Moreover, any math treatise *could* be written in the format of a puzzle book! I have sometimes wondered what would have happened if Euclid had written his classic *Ele-*

ments in such a format. For example, instead of stating as a theorem that the base angles of an isosceles triangle are equal, and then giving the proof, he could have written: *"Problem:* Given a triangle with two equal sides, are two of the angles necessarily equal? Why, or why not? (For the solution, see page —.)" And similarly with all the rest of his theorems. Such a book might well have become one of the most popular puzzle books in history!

In general, my own puzzle books tend to be different from others in that I am primarily concerned with puzzles that bear a significant relation to deep and important results in logic and mathematics. Thus, the real aim of my first logic book was to give the general public an inkling of what Gödel's great theorem was about. The volume you are now holding goes still further in this direction. I used the manuscript of it in a course entitled "Puzzles and Paradoxes," where one of the students remarked to me: "You know, this whole book—particularly parts Three and Four—has much the flavor of a mathematical novel. I have never before seen anything like it!"

I think the phrase "mathematical novel" is particularly apt. Most of this book is indeed in the form of a narrative, and a good alternative title for it would be "The Mystery of the Monte Carlo Lock," since the last half concerns a case in which Inspector Craig of Scotland Yard must discover a combination that will open the lock of a safe in Monte Carlo to prevent a disaster. When his initial efforts to crack the case prove unsuccessful, the inspector returns to London, where he serendipitously renews acquaintance with a brilliant and eccentric inventor of number machines. Together they team up with a mathematical logician, and soon the three find themselves in ever-deepening waters that flow into the very heart of Gödel's great discovery. The Monte Carlo lock, of course, turns out to be a "Gödelian" lock in disguise, its *modus operandi* beautifully reflecting a fundamental idea of Gödel's that has basic ramifications in many scientific theories dealing with the remarkable phenomenon of self-reproduction.

As a noteworthy dividend, the investigations of Craig and his friends lead to some startling mathematical discoveries hitherto unknown to either the general public or the scientific community. These are "Craig's laws" and "Fergusson's laws," which are published here for the very first time. They should prove of equal interest to the layman, the logician, the linguist, and the computer scientist.

This whole book has been great fun to write, and should be equal fun to read. I am planning several sequels. Again I wish to thank my editor, Ann Close, and the production editor, Melvin Rosenthal, for the wonderful help they have given me.

RAYMOND SMULLYAN

Elka Park, N.Y.
February 1982

PART ONE

◆◆◆

THE
LADY
OR THE
TIGER
?

◆ 1 ◆

Chestnuts—
Old and New

I would like to begin with a series of miscellaneous arithmetical and logical puzzles—some new, some old.

1 ◆ How Much?

Suppose you and I have the same amount of money. How much must I give you so that you have ten dollars more than I? (Solutions come at the end of each chapter.)

2 ◆ The Politician Puzzle

A certain convention numbered one hundred politicians. Each politician was either crooked or honest. We are given the following two facts:

(1) At least one of the politicians was honest.

(2) Given any two of the politicians, at least one of the two was crooked.

Can it be determined from these two facts how many of the politicians were honest and how many were crooked?

3

3 ◆ Old Wine in a Not-so-new Bottle

A bottle of wine cost ten dollars. The wine was worth nine dollars more than the bottle. How much was the bottle worth?

4 ◆ How Much Profit?

The amazing thing about this puzzle is that people always seem to fight over the answer! Yes, different people work it out in different ways and come up with different answers, and each insists his answer is correct. The puzzle is this:

A dealer bought an article for $7, sold it for $8, bought it back for $9, and sold it for $10. How much profit did he make?

5 ◆ Problem of the Ten Pets

The instructive thing about this puzzle is that although it can easily be solved by using elementary algebra, it can also be solved without any algebra at all—just by plain common sense. Moreover, the common-sense solution is, in my judgment, far more interesting and informative—and certainly more creative—than the algebraic solution.

Fifty-six biscuits are to be fed to ten pets; each pet is either a cat or a dog. Each dog is to get six biscuits, and each cat is to get five. How many dogs and how many cats are there?

Any reader familiar with algebra can get this immediately. Also, the problem can be solved routinely by trial and error: there are eleven possibilities for the number of cats (anywhere from zero to ten), so each possibility can be tried until the correct answer is found. But if you look at this problem in just the right light, there is a surprisingly simple solution that involves neither algebra nor trial-and-error. So, I urge even those of you who have gotten the answer by your own method to consult the solution I give.

6 ◆ Large Birds and Small Birds

Here is another puzzle that can be solved either by algebra or by common sense, and again I prefer the common-sense solution.

A certain pet shop sells large birds and small birds; each large bird fetches twice the price of a small one. A lady came in and purchased five large birds and three small ones. If, instead, she had bought three large birds and five small birds, she would have spent $20 less. What is the price of each bird?

7 ◆ The Disadvantages of Being Absent-minded

The following story happens to be true:

It is well known that in any group of at least 23 people, the odds are greater than 50 percent that at least two of them will have the same birthday. Now, I was once teaching an undergraduate mathematics class at Princeton, and we were doing a little elementary probability theory. I explained to the class that with 30 people instead of 23, the odds would become enormously high that at least two of them had the same birthday.

"Now," I continued, "since there are only nineteen students in this class, the odds are much *less* than fifty percent that any two of you have the same birthday."

At this point one of the students raised his hand and said,

"I'll bet you that at least two of us here have the same birthday."

"It wouldn't be right for me to take the bet," I replied, "because the probabilities would be highly in my favor."

"I don't care," said the student, "I'll bet you anyhow!"

"All right," I said, thinking to teach the student a good lesson. I then proceeded to call on the students one by one to announce their birthdays until, about halfway through, both I and the class burst out laughing at my stupidity.

The boy who had so confidently made the bet did not know the birthday of anyone present except his own. Can you guess why he was so confident?

8 ♦ Republicans and Democrats

In a certain lodge, each member was either a Republican or a Democrat. One day one of the Democrats decided to become a Republican, and after this happened, there was the same number of Republicans as Democrats. A few weeks later, the new Republican decided to become a Democrat again, and so things were back to normal. Then another Republican decided to become a Democrat, at which point there were twice as many Democrats as Republicans.

How many members did the lodge contain?

9 ♦ A New "Colored Hats" Problem

Three subjects—A, B, and C—were all perfect logicians. Each could instantly deduce all consequences of any set of premises. Also, each was aware that each of the others was a perfect logician. The three were shown seven stamps: two

6

red ones, two yellow ones, and three green ones. They were then blindfolded, and a stamp was pasted on each of their foreheads; the remaining four stamps were placed in a drawer. When the blindfolds were removed, A was asked, "Do you know one color that you definitely do not have?" A replied, "No." Then B was asked the same question and replied, "No."

Is it possible, from this information, to deduce the color of A's stamp, or of B's, or of C's?

10 ◆ For Those Who Know the Rules of Chess

I would like to call your attention to a fascinating variety of chess problem which, unlike the conventional chess problem—White to play and mate in so-many moves—involves an analysis of the past history of the game: how the position arose.

Inspector Craig of Scotland Yard,* whose interest in this type of problem was equal to that of Sherlock Holmes,† once walked with a friend into a chess club, where they came across an abandoned chessboard.

"Whoever played this game," said the friend, "certainly doesn't know the rules of chess. The position is quite impossible!"

"Why?" asked Craig.

"Because," replied the friend, "Black is now in check from both the White rook and the White bishop. How could White possibly have administered this check? If he has just

* Inspector Craig is a character from my previous book of logic puzzles, *What Is the Name of This Book?*
† My book *The Chess Mysteries of Sherlock Holmes* contains many puzzles of this genre.

moved the rook, the Black king would already be in check from the bishop, and if he has just moved the bishop, the king would already be in check from the rook. So, you see, the position is impossible."

Craig studied the position for a while. "Not so," he said, "the position, though exceedingly bizarre, is well within the bounds of legal possibilities."

Craig was absolutely right! Despite all appearances to the contrary, the position really is possible, and it can be deduced what White's last move was. What was it?

◆ SOLUTIONS ◆

1 ◆ A common wrong answer is $10. Now, suppose we each had, say, $50. If I gave you $10, you would then have $60 and I would have only $40; hence you would have $20 more than I, rather than $10.

The correct answer is $5.

2 ◆ A fairly common answer is "50 honest and 50 crooked." Another rather frequent one is "51 honest and 49 crooked."

Both answers are wrong! Now let us see how to find the correct solution.

We are given that at least one person is honest. Let us pick out any one honest person, whose name, say, is Frank. Now pick any of the remaining 99; call him John. By the second given condition, at least one of the two men—Frank, John—is crooked. Since Frank is not crooked, it must be John. Since John arbitrarily represents any of the remaining 99 men, then each of those 99 men must be crooked. So the answer is that one is honest and 99 are crooked.

Another way of proving it is this: The statement that given any two, at least one is crooked, says nothing more nor less than that given any two, they are not both honest; in other words, no two are honest. This means that at most one is honest. Also (by the first condition), at least one is honest. Hence exactly one is honest.

Do you prefer one proof to the other?

3 ♦ A common wrong answer is $1. Now, if the bottle were really worth a dollar, then the wine, being worth $9 more than the bottle, would be worth $10. Hence the wine and bottle together would be worth $11. The correct answer is that the bottle is worth 50¢ and the wine is worth $9.50. Then the two add up to $10.

4 ♦ Some argue as follows: After having bought the article for $7 and sold it for $8, he has made a dollar profit. Then, by buying the article back for $9 after having sold it for $8, he loses a dollar; hence at this point he is even. But then (the argument continues) by selling for $10 what he has bought for $9, he has made a dollar again; therefore, his total profit is $1.

Another argument leads to the conclusion that the dealer broke even: When he sold the article for $8 after having bought it for $7, he made $1 profit. But then he loses $2 by buying back for $9 the item for which he originally paid $7, and so at this point he is $1 in the hole. Then he gets back the dollar by selling for $10 the article for which he last paid $9, and so now he is even.

Both arguments are wrong; the correct answer is that the dealer made $2. There are several ways to arrive at this—one such goes as follows: First, after selling for $8 the article for which he has paid $7, he has clearly made $1. Now, suppose that instead of buying back the *same* article for $9 and then selling it for $10, he were to buy a *different* article for $9 and sell it for $10. Would this really be any different from a purely economic point of view? Of course not! He would obviously, then, be making another dollar on the buying and selling of this second article. Thus, he has made $2.

Another and very simple proof: The dealer's total outlay is $7 + $9 = $16, and his total return is $8 + $10 = $18, giving a profit of $2.

For those not convinced by these arguments, let us suppose that the dealer has a certain amount of money—say, $100—at the opening of the day and that he makes just these four deals. How much will he have at the close of the day? Well, first he pays $7 for the article, leaving him with $93. Then he sells the article for $8, giving him $101. Next he buys the article back for $9, bringing him down to $92. Finally, he sells the article for $10 and thus winds up with $102. So he has started the day with $100 and ended it with $102. How, then, could his profit be anything other than $2?

5 ◆ The solution I have in mind is this: First feed five biscuits to each of the ten pets; this leaves six biscuits. Now, the cats have already had their portion! Therefore, the six remaining biscuits are for the dogs, and since each dog is to get

one more biscuit, there must be six dogs, and thus four cats.

Of course, we can check out the solution: Six dogs each getting six biscuits accounts for thirty-six biscuits. Four cats each getting five biscuits accounts for twenty biscuits. The total (36 + 20) is 56, as it should be.

6 ◆ Since each large bird is worth two small birds, then five large birds are worth ten small birds. Hence five large birds plus three small birds are worth thirteen small birds. On the other hand, three large birds plus five small birds are worth eleven small birds. So the difference between buying five large and three small birds or buying three large and five small birds is the same as the difference between buying thirteen small birds and buying eleven small birds, which is two small birds. We know that the difference is $20. So two small birds are worth $20, which means one small bird is worth $10.

Let us check: A small bird is worth $10, and a large bird $20. Therefore, the lady's bill for five large and three small birds was $130. Had she bought three large and five small birds, she would have spent $110, which is indeed $20 less.

7 ◆ At the time I accepted the bet from the student, I had totally forgotten that two of the other students, who always sat next to each other, were identical twins.

8 ◆ There were twelve members: seven Democrats and five Republicans.

9 ◆ The only one whose color can be determined is C. If C's stamp were red, then B would have known that his stamp was not red by reasoning: "If my stamp were also red, then A, seeing two red stamps, would know that his stamp is not red.

But A does not know that his stamp is not red. Therefore, my stamp cannot be red."

This proves that if C's stamp were red, then B would have known that his stamp was not red. But B did not know that his stamp was not red; therefore, C's stamp cannot be red.

The same argument, replacing the word *red* with *yellow*, shows that C's stamp cannot be yellow either. Therefore, C's stamp must be green.

10 ♦ It is not given which side of the board is White and which side is Black. It may well *appear* that White is moving up the board, but if he really were, then the position *would* be impossible! The truth is that White must be moving down the board, and that before the last move, the position was this:

The circle on the lower left-hand square represents some Black piece (either a queen, rook, bishop, or knight; there is no way to know which). The White pawn then captures this Black piece and promotes to a rook, bringing the game to the present position.

Of course, one might well ask: "Why did White promote to a rook instead of a queen; is this not highly improbable?" The answer is that indeed it is highly *improbable*, but that any other last move is not merely improbable but impossible, and as Sherlock Holmes so wisely said to Watson: "When we have eliminated the impossible, whatever remains, however improbable, must be the truth."

◆ 2 ◆

Ladies or
Tigers?

Many of you are familiar with Frank Stockton's story "The Lady or the Tiger?," in which the prisoner must choose between two rooms, one of which contains a lady and the other a tiger. If he chooses the former, he marries the lady; if he chooses the latter, he (probably) gets eaten by the tiger.

The king of a certain land had also read the story, and it gave him an idea. "Just the perfect way to try my prisoners!" he said one day to his minister. "Only, I won't leave it to chance; I'll have signs on the doors of the rooms, and in each case I'll tell the prisoner certain facts about the signs. If the prisoner is clever and can reason logically, he'll save his life—and win a nice bride to boot!"

"Excellent idea!" said the minister.

THE TRIALS OF THE FIRST DAY

On the first day, there were three trials. In all three, the king explained to the prisoner that each of the two rooms contained either a lady or a tiger, but it *could* be that there were tigers in both rooms, or ladies in both rooms, or then again, maybe one room contained a lady and the other room a tiger.

1 ◆ The First Trial

"Suppose both rooms contain tigers," asked the prisoner. "What do I do then?"

"That's your hard luck!" replied the king.

"Suppose both rooms contain ladies?" asked the prisoner.

"Then, obviously, that's your good luck," replied the king. "Surely you could have guessed the answer to that!"

"Well, suppose one room contains a lady and the other a tiger, what happens then?" asked the prisoner.

"In that case, it makes quite a difference which room you choose, doesn't it?"

"How do I know which room to choose?" asked the prisoner.

The king pointed to the signs on the doors of the rooms:

I	II
IN THIS ROOM THERE IS A LADY, AND IN THE OTHER ROOM THERE IS A TIGER	IN ONE OF THESE ROOMS THERE IS A LADY, AND IN ONE OF THESE ROOMS THERE IS A TIGER

"Is it true, what the signs say?" asked the prisoner.

"One of them is true," replied the king, "but the other one is false."

If you were the prisoner, which door would you open (assuming, of course, that you preferred the lady to the tiger)?

2 ◆ The Second Trial

And so, the first prisoner saved his life and made off with the lady. The signs on the doors were then changed, and new occupants for the rooms were selected accordingly. This time the signs read as follows:

I	II
AT LEAST ONE OF THESE ROOMS CONTAINS A LADY	A TIGER IS IN THE OTHER ROOM

"Are the statements on the signs true?" asked the second prisoner.

"They are either both true or both false," replied the king. Which room should the prisoner pick?

3 ◆ The Third Trial

In this trial, the king explained that, again, the signs were either both true or both false. Here are the signs:

I	II
EITHER A TIGER IS IN THIS ROOM OR A LADY IS IN THE OTHER ROOM	A LADY IS IN THE OTHER ROOM

Does the first room contain a lady or a tiger? What about the other room?

16

THE SECOND DAY

"Yesterday was a fiasco," said the king to his minister. "All three prisoners solved their puzzles! Well, we have five trials coming up today, and I think I'll make them a little tougher."

"Excellent idea!" said the minister.

Well, in each of the trials of this day, the king explained that in the lefthand room (Room I), if a lady is in it, then the sign on the door is true, but if a tiger is in it, the sign is false. In the righthand room (Room II), the situation is the opposite: a lady in the room means the sign on the door is false, and a tiger in the room means the sign is true. Again, it is possible that both rooms contain ladies or both rooms contain tigers, or that one room contains a lady and the other a tiger.

4 ◆ The Fourth Trial

After the king explained the above rules to the prisoner, he pointed to the two signs:

I	II
BOTH ROOMS CONTAIN LADIES	BOTH ROOMS CONTAIN LADIES

Which room should the prisoner pick?

5 ◆ The Fifth Trial

The same rules apply, and here are the signs:

I	II
AT LEAST ONE ROOM CONTAINS A LADY	THE OTHER ROOM CONTAINS A LADY

6 ◆ The Sixth Trial

The king was particularly fond of this puzzle, and the next one too. Here are the signs:

I	II
IT MAKES NO DIFFERENCE WHICH ROOM YOU PICK	THERE IS A LADY IN THE OTHER ROOM

What should the prisoner do?

7 ◆ The Seventh Trial

Here are the signs:

I	II
IT DOES MAKE A DIFFERENCE WHICH ROOM YOU PICK	YOU ARE BETTER OFF CHOOSING THE OTHER ROOM

What should the prisoner do?

8 ◆ The Eighth Trial

"There are no signs above the doors!" exclaimed the prisoner.

"Quite true," said the king. "The signs were just made, and I haven't had time to put them up yet."

"Then how do you expect me to choose?" demanded the prisoner.

"Well, here are the signs," replied the king.

```
THIS ROOM
CONTAINS
A TIGER
```

```
BOTH ROOMS
CONTAIN
TIGERS
```

"That's all well and good," said the prisoner anxiously, "but which sign goes on which door?"

The king thought awhile. "I needn't tell you," he said. "You can solve this problem without that information.

"Only remember, of course," he added, "that a lady in the lefthand room means the sign which should be on that door is true and a tiger in it means the sign should be false, and that the reverse is true for the righthand room."

What is the solution?

THE THIRD DAY

"Confound it!" said the king. "Again all the prisoners won! I think tomorrow I'll have *three* rooms instead of two; I'll put a lady in one room and a tiger in each of the other two rooms. Then we'll see how the prisoners fare!"

"Excellent idea!" replied the minister.

"Your conversation, though flattering, is just a bit on the repetitious side!" exclaimed the king.

"Excellently put!" replied the minister.

9 ◆ The Ninth Trial

Well, on the third day, the king did as planned. He offered three rooms to choose from, and he explained to the prisoner that one room contained a lady and the other two contained tigers. Here are the three signs:

I	II	III
A TIGER IS IN THIS ROOM	A LADY IS IN THIS ROOM	A TIGER IS IN ROOM II

The king explained that at most one of the three signs was true. Which room contains the lady?

10 ◆ The Tenth Trial

Again there was only one lady and two tigers. The king explained to the prisoner that the sign on the door of the room containing the lady was true, and that at least one of the other two signs was false.

Here are the signs:

I	II	III
A TIGER IS IN ROOM II	A TIGER IS IN THIS ROOM	A TIGER IS IN ROOM I

What should the prisoner do?

11 ◆ First, Second, and Third Choice

In this more whimsical trial, the king explained to the prisoner that one of the three rooms contained a lady, another a tiger, and the third room was empty. The sign on the door of the room containing the lady was true, the sign on the door of the room with the tiger was false, and the sign on the door of the empty room could be either true or false. Here are the signs:

I	II	III
ROOM III IS EMPTY	THE TIGER IS IN ROOM I	THIS ROOM IS EMPTY

Now, the prisoner happened to know the lady in question and wished to marry her. Therefore, although the empty room was preferable to the one with the tiger, his first choice was the room with the lady.

Which room contains the lady, and which room contains the tiger? If you can answer these two questions, you should have little difficulty in also determining which room is empty.

THE FOURTH DAY

"Horrible!" said the king. "It seems I can't make my puzzles hard enough to trap these fellows! Well, we have only one more trial to go, but this time I'll *really* give the prisoner a run for his money!"

12 ◆ A Logical Labyrinth

Well, the king was as good as his word. Instead of having three rooms for the prisoner to choose from, he gave him nine! As he explained, only one room contained a lady; each of the other eight either contained a tiger or was empty. And, the king added, the sign on the door of the room containing the lady is true; the signs on doors of all rooms containing tigers are false; and the signs on doors of empty rooms can be either true or false.

Here are the signs:

I THE LADY IS IN AN ODD-NUMBERED ROOM	II THIS ROOM IS EMPTY	III EITHER SIGN V IS RIGHT OR SIGN VII IS WRONG
IV SIGN I IS WRONG	V EITHER SIGN II OR SIGN IV IS RIGHT	VI SIGN III IS WRONG

VII	VIII	IX
THE LADY IS NOT IN ROOM I	THIS ROOM CONTAINS A TIGER AND ROOM IX IS EMPTY	THIS ROOM CONTAINS A TIGER AND VI IS WRONG

The prisoner studied the situation for a long while.

"The problem is unsolvable!" he exclaimed angrily. "That's not fair!"

"I know," laughed the king.

"Very funny!" replied the prisoner. "Come on, now, at least give me a decent clue: is Room Eight empty or not?"

The king was decent enough to tell him whether Room VIII was empty or not, and the prisoner was then able to deduce where the lady was.

Which room contained the lady?

◆ SOLUTIONS ◆

1 ◆ We are given that one of the two signs is true and the other false. Could it be that the first is true and the second false? Certainly not, because if the first sign is true, then the second sign must also be true—that is, if there is a lady in Room I and a tiger in Room II, then it is certainly the case that one of the rooms contains a lady and the other a tiger. Since it is not the case that the first sign is true and the second one false, then it must be that the second sign is true and the first one false. Since the second sign is true, then there really is a lady in one room and a tiger in the other. Since the

first sign is false, then it must be that the tiger is in Room I and the lady in Room II. So the prisoner should choose Room II.

2 ◆ If Sign II is false, then Room I contains a lady; hence at least one room contains a lady, which makes Sign I true. Therefore, it is impossible that both signs are false. This means that both signs are true (since we are given that they are either both true or both false). Therefore, a tiger is in Room I and a lady in Room II, so again the prisoner should choose Room II.

3 ◆ The king must have been in a generous mood this time, because both rooms contain ladies! We prove this as follows:

Sign I says in effect that *at least* one of the following alternatives holds: there is a tiger in Room I; there is a lady in Room II. (The sign does not preclude the possibility that both alternatives hold.)

Now, if Sign II is false, then a tiger is in Room I, which makes the first sign true (because the first alternative is then true). But we are given that it is not the case that one of the signs is true and the other one false. Therefore, since Sign II is true, both signs must be true. Since Sign II is true, there is a lady in Room I. This means that the first alternative of Sign I is false, but since at least one of the alternatives is true, then it must be the second one. So there is a lady in Room II also.

4 ◆ Since the signs say the same thing, they are both true or both false. Suppose they are true; then both rooms contain ladies. This would mean in particular that Room II contains a lady. But we have been told that if Room II contains a lady, the sign is false. This is a contradiction, so the signs are not

true; they are both false. Therefore, Room I contains a tiger and Room II contains a lady.

5 ◆ If the first room contains a tiger, we get a contradiction. Because if it does contain a tiger, then the first sign is false, which would mean that neither room contains a lady; both rooms would contain tigers. But we have been told that a tiger in the second room indicates that the second sign is true, which would mean that the other room contains a lady, contrary to the assumption that the first room contains a tiger. So it is impossible for the first room to contain a tiger; it must contain a lady. Therefore, what the second sign says is true, and the second room contains a tiger. So the first room contains a lady and the second room contains a tiger.

6 ◆ The first sign says, in effect, that either both rooms contain ladies or both contain tigers—that is the only way it could make no difference which room is picked.

Suppose the first room contains a lady. Then the first sign is true, which means the second room also contains a lady. Suppose, on the other hand, the first room contains a tiger. Then the first sign is false, which means that the two occupants are not the same, so again the second occupant is a lady. This proves that Room II must contain a lady regardless of what is in Room I. Since Room II contains a lady, Sign II is false and Room I must contain a tiger.

7 ◆ The first sign says in effect that the two occupants are different (one a lady and the other a tiger), but doesn't say which room contains which. If Room I's occupant is a lady, the sign is true; hence Room II must contain a tiger. If, on the other hand, Room I's occupant is a tiger, then the first sign is false, which means that the two occupants are not really dif-

ferent, so Room II must also contain a tiger. Therefore, Room II definitely contains a tiger. This means that the second sign is true, so a lady must be in the first room.

8 ◆ Suppose the top sign, THIS ROOM CONTAINS A TIGER, were on the door of Room I. If a lady is in the room, the sign is false, violating the conditions given by the king. If a tiger is in the room, the sign is true, which again violates the king's conditions. So that sign can't be on the first door; it must be on the second. This means the other sign is to be put on the first door.

The sign belonging on the first door thus reads: BOTH ROOMS CONTAIN TIGERS. So the first room can't contain a lady, or the sign would be true, which would mean that both rooms contain tigers—an obvious contradiction. Therefore, the first room contains a tiger. From this it follows that the sign is false, so the second room must contain a lady.

9 ◆ Signs II and III contradict each other, so at least one of them is true. Since at most one of the three signs is true, then the first one must be false, so the lady is in Room I.

10 ◆ Since the sign of the room containing the lady is true, then the lady certainly can't be in Room II. If she is in Room III, then all three signs must be true, which is contrary to the given condition that at least one sign is false. Therefore, the lady is in Room I (and sign II is true and sign III is false).

11 ◆ Since the sign on the door of the room containing the lady is true, then the lady cannot be in Room III.

Suppose she is in Room II. Then sign II would be true; hence the tiger would be in Room I and Room III would be empty. This would mean that the sign on the door of the tiger's room would be true, which is not possible. Therefore, the lady is in Room I; Room III must then be empty, and the tiger is in Room II.

12 ♦ If the king had told the prisoner that Room VIII was empty, it would have been impossible for the prisoner to have found the lady. Since the prisoner did deduce where the lady was, the king must have told him that Room VIII was not empty, and the prisoner reasoned as follows:

"It is impossible for the lady to be in Room Eight, for if she were, Sign Eight would be true, but the sign says a tiger is in the room, which would be a contradiction. Therefore, Room Eight does not contain the lady. Also, Room Eight is not empty; therefore, Room Eight must contain a tiger. Since it contains a tiger, the sign is false. Now, if Room Nine is empty, then Sign Eight would be true; therefore, Room Nine cannot be empty.

"So, Room Nine is also not empty. It cannot contain the lady, or the sign would be true, which would mean that the room contains a tiger; this means Sign Nine is false. If Sign Six is really wrong, then Sign Nine would be true, which is not possible. Therefore, Sign Six is right.

"Since Sign Six is right, then Sign Three is wrong. The only way Sign Three can be wrong is that Sign Five is Wrong and Sign Seven is right. Since Sign Five is wrong, then Sign Two and Sign Four are both wrong. Since Sign Four is wrong, then Sign One must be right.

"Now I know which signs are right and which signs are wrong—namely:

"1 – Right	4 – Wrong	7 – Right
2 – Wrong	5 – Wrong	8 – Wrong
3 – Wrong	6 – Right	9 – Wrong

"I now know that the lady is in either Room One, Room Six, or Room Seven, since the others all have false signs. Since Sign One is right, the lady can't be in Room Six. Since Sign Seven is right, the lady can't be in Room One. Therefore, the lady is in Room Seven."

◆ 3 ◆

The Asylum of Doctor Tarr and Professor Fether

Inspector Craig of Scotland Yard was called over to France to investigate eleven insane asylums where it was suspected that something was wrong. In each of these asylums, the only inhabitants were patients and doctors—the doctors constituted the entire staff. Each inhabitant of each asylum, patient or doctor, was either sane or insane. Moreover, the sane ones were *totally* sane and a hundred percent accurate in all their beliefs; all true propositions they knew to be true and all false propositions they knew to be false. The insane ones were totally inaccurate in their beliefs; all true propositions they believed to be false and all false propositions they believed to be true. It is to be assumed also that all the inhabitants were always honest—whatever they said, they really believed.

1 ◆ The First Asylum

In the first asylum Craig visited, he spoke separately to two inhabitants whose last names were Jones and Smith.

"Tell me," Craig asked Jones, "what do you know about Mr. Smith?"

"You should call him *Doctor* Smith," replied Jones. "He is a doctor on our staff."

Sometime later, Craig met Smith and asked, "What do you know about Jones? Is he a patient or a doctor?"

"He is a patient," replied Smith.

The inspector mulled over the situation for a while and then realized that there was indeed something wrong with this asylum: either one of the doctors was insane, hence shouldn't be working there, or, worse still, one of the patients was sane and shouldn't be there at all.

How did Craig know this?

2 ◆ The Second Asylum

In the next asylum Craig visited, one of the inhabitants made a statement from which the inspector could deduce that the speaker must be a sane patient, hence did not belong there. Craig then took steps to have him released.

Can you supply such a statement?

3 ◆ The Third Asylum

In the next asylum, an inhabitant made a statement from which Craig could deduce that the speaker was an insane doctor. Can you supply such a statement?

4 ◆ The Fourth Asylum

In the next asylum, Craig asked one of the inhabitants, "Are you a patient?" He replied, "Yes."

Is there anything necessarily wrong with this asylum?

5 ♦ The Fifth Asylum

In the next asylum, Craig asked one of the inhabitants, "Are you a patient?" He replied, "I believe so."

Is there anything necessarily wrong with this asylum?

6 ♦ The Sixth Asylum

In the next asylum Craig visited, he asked an inhabitant, "Do you believe you are a patient?" The inhabitant replied, "I believe I do."

Is there anything necessarily wrong with this asylum?

7 ♦ The Seventh Asylum

Craig found the next asylum more interesting. He met two inhabitants, A and B, and found out that A believed that B was insane and B believed that A was a doctor. Craig then took measures to have one of the two removed. Which one, and why?

8 ♦ The Eighth Asylum

The next asylum proved to be quite a puzzler, but Craig finally managed to get to the bottom of things. He found out that the following conditions prevailed:

1. Given any two inhabitants, A and B, either A trusts B or he doesn't.

2. Some of the inhabitants are *teachers* of other inhabitants. Each inhabitant has at least one teacher.

3. No inhabitant A is willing to be a teacher of an inhabitant B unless A believes that B trusts himself.

4. For any inhabitant A there is an inhabitant B who trusts all and only those inhabitants who have at least one teacher who is trusted by A. (In other words, for any inhabitant X, B trusts X if A trusts some teacher of X, and B doesn't trust X unless A trusts some teacher of X.)

5. There is one inhabitant who trusts all the patients but does not trust any of the doctors.

Inspector Craig thought this over for a long time and was finally able to prove that either one of the patients was sane or one of the doctors was insane. Can you find the proof?

9 ♦ The Ninth Asylum

In this asylum, Craig interviewed four inhabitants: A, B, C, and D. A believed that B and C were alike as far as their sanity was concerned. B believed that A and D were alike as far as their sanity was concerned. Then Craig asked C, "Are you and D both doctors?" C replied, "No."

Is there anything wrong with this asylum?

10 ♦ The Tenth Asylum

Inspector Craig found this case particularly interesting, though difficult to crack. The first thing he discovered was that the asylum's inhabitants had formed various committees. Doctors and patients, he learned, could serve on the same committee and sane and insane persons might be on the same committee. Then Craig found out the following facts:

1. All patients formed one committee.

2. All doctors formed one committee.

3. Each inhabitant had several friends in the asylum, and among them one who was his best friend. Also, each inhabitant had several enemies in the asylum, and among them one called his worst enemy.

4. Given any committee, C, all inhabitants whose best friend was on C formed a committee, and all inhabitants whose worst enemy was on C also formed a committee.

5. Given any two committees—Committee 1 and Committee 2—there was at least one inhabitant, D, whose best friend believed that D was on Committee 1 and whose worst enemy believed that D was on Committee 2.

Putting all these facts together, Craig found an ingenious proof that either one of the doctors was insane or one of the patients was sane. How did Craig know this?

11 ◆ An Added Puzzle

Craig lingered for a while in this last asylum, because certain other questions caught his theoretical fancy. For example, he was curious to know whether all sane inhabitants formed a committee and all insane inhabitants formed a committee. He could not settle these questions on the basis of facts 1, 2, 3, 4, and 5, but he was able to prove—and just on the basis of 3, 4, and 5—that it was not possible for *both* of these groups to have formed committees. How did he prove this?

12 ◆ Another Puzzle About the Same Asylum

Finally, Craig was able to prove something else about this same asylum. He regarded it as quite significant, and in fact it simplified the solutions of the last two problems. It is, namely, that given any two committees—Committees 1 and 2—there must be an inhabitant E and an inhabitant F who believe as follows: E that F serves on Committee 1, and F that E serves on Committee 2. How did Craig prove this?

13 ◆ The Asylum of Doctor Tarr and Professor Fether

The last asylum Craig visited he found to be the most bizarre of all. This asylum was run by two doctors named Doctor Tarr and Professor Fether. There were other doctors on the staff as well. Now, an inhabitant was called *peculiar* if he believed that he was a patient. An inhabitant was called *special* if all patients believed he was peculiar and no doctor believed he was peculiar. Inspector Craig found out that at least one inhabitant was sane and that the following condition held:

Condition C: Each inhabitant had a best friend in the asylum. Moreover, given any two inhabitants, A and B, if A believed that B was special, then A's best friend believed that B was a patient.

Shortly after this discovery, Inspector Craig had private interviews with Doctor Tarr and Professor Fether. Here is the interview with Doctor Tarr:

Craig: Tell me, Doctor Tarr, are all the doctors in this asylum sane?

Tarr: Of course they are!

Craig: What about the patients? Are they all insane?

Tarr: At least one of them is.

The second answer struck Craig as a surprisingly modest claim! Of course, if all the patients are insane, then it certainly is true that at least one is. But why was Doctor Tarr being so cautious? Craig then had his interview with Professor Fether, which went as follows:

Craig: Doctor Tarr said that at least one patient here is insane. Surely that is true, isn't it?

Professor Fether: Of course it is true! All the patients in this asylum are insane! What kind of asylum do you think we are running?

Craig: What about the doctors? Are they all sane?

Professor Fether: At least one of them is.

Craig: What about Doctor Tarr? Is he sane?

Professor Fether: Of course he is! How dare you ask me such a question?

At this point, Craig realized the full horror of the situation! What was it?

(Those who have read "The System of Doctor Tarr and Professor Fether," by Edgar Allan Poe, will probably guess the solution before they prove it is correct. See remarks following the solution.)

✦ SOLUTIONS ✦

1 ✦ We will prove that either Jones or Smith (we do not know which) must be either an insane doctor or a sane patient (but again we don't know which).

Jones is either sane or insane. Suppose he is sane. Then his belief is correct; hence Smith really is a doctor. If Smith is insane, then he is an insane doctor. If Smith is sane, then his belief is correct, which means that Jones is a patient and hence a sane patient (since we are assuming Jones to be sane). This proves that if Jones is sane, then either he is a sane patient or Smith is an insane doctor.

Suppose Jones is insane. Then his belief is wrong, which makes Smith a patient. If Smith is sane, then he is a sane patient. If Smith is insane, then his belief is wrong, which makes Jones a doctor, hence an insane doctor. This proves that if Jones is insane, then either he is an insane doctor or Smith is a sane patient.

To summarize, if Jones is sane, then either he is a sane patient or Smith is an insane doctor. If Jones is insane, then either he is an insane doctor or Smith is a sane patient.

2 ✦ Many solutions are possible. The simplest I can think of is that the inhabitant said, "I am not a sane doctor." We then prove that the speaker must be a sane patient as follows:

An insane doctor could not hold the true belief that he is not a sane doctor. A sane doctor could not hold the false belief that he is not a sane doctor. An insane patient could not hold the true belief that he is not a sane doctor (an insane patient is in fact *not* a sane doctor). So the speaker was a sane patient, and his belief that he was not a sane doctor was correct.

3 ✦ One statement which would work is: "I am an insane patient." A sane patient could not hold the false belief that he is an insane patient. An insane patient could not hold the true belief that he is an insane patient. Therefore, the speaker was not a patient; he was a doctor. A sane doctor could never believe that he is an insane patient. So the speaker was an insane doctor, who held the false belief that he was an insane patient.

4 ✦ The speaker believes that he is a patient. If he is sane, then he really is a patient; hence he is a sane patient and

shouldn't be in the asylum. If he is insane, his belief is wrong, which means that he is not a patient but a doctor; hence he is an insane doctor and shouldn't be on the staff. It is not possible to tell whether he is a sane patient or an insane doctor, but in neither case should he be in this asylum.

5 ♦ This is a very different situation! Just because the speaker *says* that he believes he is a patient does not necessarily mean that he *does* believe he is a patient! Since he says he believes he is a patient, and he is honest, then he *believes* that he believes he is a patient. Suppose he is insane. Then his beliefs are all wrong—even those about his own beliefs—so his believing that he believes he is a patient indicates that it is false that he believes he is a patient, and therefore he actually believes that he is a doctor. Since he is insane and believes he is a doctor, then he is in fact a patient. So if he is insane, he is an insane patient. On the other hand, suppose he is sane. Since he believes that he believes he is a patient, then it is true that he believes he is a patient. Since he believes he is a patient, then he is a patient. So, if he is sane, then again he is a patient. We see, therefore, that he could be either a sane patient or an insane patient, and we have no grounds for finding anything wrong with this asylum.

More generally, let us note the following basic facts: If an inhabitant of this asylum believes something, then that something is true or false depending on whether the believer is sane or insane. But if an inhabitant believes that he believes something, then the something must be true, regardless of whether the believer is sane or insane. (If he is insane, the two beliefs cancel each other, analogously to the negative of a negative making a positive.)

6 ♦ In this case, the speaker didn't claim that he was a patient nor that he believed he was a patient; he claimed that

he believed that he believed he was a patient. Since he believed what he claimed, then he believed that he believed that he believed that he was a patient. The first two beliefs cancel each other out (see last paragraph of the solution to the last problem), so in fact he believed that he was a patient. The problem then reduces to that of the fourth asylum, which we have already solved (the speaker must be either a sane patient or an insane doctor).

7 ♦ Craig had A removed. *Reason:* Suppose A is sane. Then his belief that B is insane is correct. Since B is insane, his belief that A is a doctor is wrong, so A is a sane patient and should be removed. Suppose, on the other hand, that A is insane. Then his belief that B is insane is wrong, so B is sane. Then B's belief that A is a doctor is correct, so in this case A is an insane doctor who should be removed.

Nothing at all can be deduced about B.

8 ♦ By condition 5, there is an inhabitant—call him Arthur—who trusts all patients but no doctors. By condition 4, there is an inhabitant—call him Bill—who trusts just those inhabitants who have at least one teacher who is trusted by Arthur. This means that for any inhabitant X, if Bill trusts X, then Arthur trusts at least one teacher of X, and if Bill doesn't trust X, then Arthur trusts no teacher of X. Since being trusted by Arthur is the same thing as being a patient (by condition 5), then we can rephrase the last sentence as follows: For any inhabitant X, if Bill trusts X, then at least one teacher of X is a patient, and if Bill doesn't trust X, then no teacher of X is a patient. Now, since this holds for *every* inhabitant X, then it also holds when X is Bill himself. Therefore, we know the following:

(1) If Bill trusts himself, then Bill has at least one teacher who is a patient.

(2) If Bill doesn't trust himself, then no teacher of Bill is a patient.

There are two possibilities: either Bill trusts himself or he doesn't. Let us now see what is implied by each case.

Case 1—Bill trusts himself: Then Bill has at least one teacher—call him Peter—who is a patient. Since Peter is a teacher of Bill, then Peter believes that Bill trusts himself (this according to condition 3). Well, Bill does trust himself, so Peter believes truly and is sane. Therefore, Peter is a sane patient and should not be in this asylum.

Case 2—Bill doesn't trust himself: In this case, none of Bill's teachers is a patient. Yet Bill, like every other inhabitant, has at least one teacher—call him Richard. Then Richard must be a doctor. Since Richard is a teacher of Bill, then Richard believes that Bill trusts himself. His belief is wrong; therefore Richard is insane. So Richard is an insane doctor and shouldn't be on the staff.

To summarize: if Bill trusts himself, then at least one patient is sane. If Bill doesn't trust himself, then at least one doctor is insane. Since we don't know whether Bill trusts himself or not, we don't know just what is wrong with this asylum—whether there is a sane patient or an insane doctor.

9 ◆ We shall first prove that C and D are necessarily alike as far as their sanity is concerned.

Suppose A and B are both sane. Then B and C are really alike, and A and D are really alike. This implies that all four are sane; hence in this case C and D are both sane, and thus alike. Now suppose A and B are both insane. Then B and C are different, and so are A and D; hence C and D are both sane, and so again alike. Now suppose A is sane and B is insane. Then B and C are alike, so C is insane, but A and D are different, which means D is also insane. Lastly, suppose A is insane and B is sane. Then B and C are different and so C is insane, but A and D are alike; hence D is also insane.

In summary, if A and B are alike, then C and D are both sane; if A and B are different, C and D are both insane.

Thus, we have established that C and D are either both sane or both insane. Suppose they are both sane. Then C's statement that he and D are not both doctors was true, which means that at least one is a patient, hence a sane patient. If C and D are both insane, then C's statement was false, which means they are both doctors, hence both insane doctors. Therefore, this asylum contains at least one sane patient, or else at least two insane doctors.

10, 11, 12 ✦ First read problems 11 and 12, because the easiest way to solve Problem 10 is to start with Problem 12.

Before we begin, let me point out a useful principle: Suppose we have two statements, X and Y, which are known to be either both true or both false. Then any inhabitant of the asylum, if he believes one of the statements, must also believe the other. *Reason:* If the statements are both true, then any inhabitant who believes one of them must be sane, hence must also believe the other, which is also true. If the statements are both false, then any inhabitant who believes one of them must be insane, and must also believe the other, since it is also false.

Now let us solve Problem 12: Take any two committees, Committee 1 and Committee 2. Let U be the group of all inhabitants whose worst enemy belongs to Committee 1, and let V be the group of all inhabitants whose best friend belongs to Committee 2. According to Fact 4, both U and V are committees. Therefore, according to Fact 5, there is some inhabitant—call him Dan—whose best friend—call him Edward—believes Dan is on U, and whose worst enemy—call him Fred—believes Dan is on V. Thus, Edward believes Dan is on Committee U and Fred believes Dan is on Committee V. Now, by the definition of U, to say that Dan is on U is to say that his worst enemy, Fred, is on Committee 1; in other words, the two statements "Dan is on U" and "Fred is on Committee 1" are either both true or both false. Since Edward believes the one—namely, that Dan is on U—then he must also believe the other—namely, that Fred is on Committee 1 (recall our preliminary principle!). So Edward believes Fred is on Committee 1.

Fred, on the other hand, believes that Dan is on Committee V. Now, Dan is on V only if his friend Edward is on Committee 2 (by the defintion of V); in other words, these two facts are either both true or both false. Then, since Fred believes Dan is on V, Fred must also believe that Edward is on Committee 2.

Thus we have two inhabitants, Edward and Fred, with these beliefs: Edward that Fred is on Committee 1, and Fred that Edward is on Committee 2. This solves Problem 12.

To solve Problem 10, let us now take as Committee 1 the group of all patients and as Committee 2 the group of all doctors, which are committees according to Facts 1 and 2. According to the solution of Problem 12, there exist inhabitants—Edward and Fred—who believe the following: Edward, that Fred is on Committee 1 of all patients; and Fred, that Edward is on Committee 2 of all doctors. In other words, Edward believes that Fred is a patient and Fred believes that Edward is a doctor. Then, according to Problem 1 (using the names *Edward* and *Fred* rather than *Jones* and *Smith*), one of the two, Edward or Fred (we don't know which), must be either an insane doctor or a sane patient. So something is definitely wrong with this asylum.

As for Problem 11, suppose that the group of all sane inhabitants and the group of all insane inhabitants *are* both committees, Committees 1 and 2 respectively. Then, according to Problem 12, inhabitants Edward and Fred would believe: (a) Edward, that Fred is sane—in other words, a member of Committee 1; (b) Fred, that Edward is insane—and thus a member of Committee 2. This is impossible, because if Edward is sane, his belief is correct, which means Fred is sane; hence Fred's belief is correct, which means Edward is insane. So if Edward is sane, he is also insane, which is impossible. On the other hand, if Edward is insane, his belief about Fred is wrong, which means Fred is insane; hence Fred's belief about Edward is wrong, which means Edward is sane. So if Edward is insane, he is also sane, which again is impossible. Therefore, the assumption that the group of sane inhabitants and the group of insane inhabitants are *both* committees leads to a contradiction. Therefore, it cannot be that both these groups are committees.

13 ♦ What Craig realized, to his horror, was that in this asylum, all the doctors were insane and all the patients were sane! He reasoned this out in the following manner:

Even before his interviews with Doctor Tarr and Professor Fether, he knew that there was at least one sane inhabitant, A. Now let B be A's best friend. By Condition C, if A believes that B is special, then A's best friend believes that B is a patient. Since A's best friend is B, then if A believes that B is special, B believes that B is a patient. In other words, if A believes that B is special, then B is peculiar. Since A is sane, then A's believing that B is special is tantamount to B's actually being special. Therefore, we have the following *key fact:*

If B is special, then B is peculiar.

Now, either B is peculiar or he isn't. If he is peculiar, then he believes he is a patient, and therefore (see Problem 4) he must be either an insane doctor or a sane patient; either way, B shouldn't be in the asylum. But suppose B is not peculiar, what then? Well, if B is not peculiar, he is not special either, because, in accordance with the "key fact," B can only be special if he is also peculiar. So B is neither peculiar nor special. Since he is not special, then the two assumptions that all patients believe he is peculiar and that no doctor believes he is peculiar cannot both be true, which means that at least one of them is false. Suppose the first assumption is false. Then at least one patient, P, does not believe that B is peculiar. If P were insane, then he would believe that B is peculiar (since B isn't); therefore, P is sane. This means that P is a sane patient. If the second assumption is false, then at least one doctor, D, believes that B is peculiar. Then D must be insane (since B is not peculiar); so D is an insane doctor.

To summarize: If B is peculiar, then he is either a sane patient or an insane doctor. If B is not peculiar, then either some sane patient, P, doesn't believe that B is peculiar, or some insane doctor, D, does believe B is. Therefore, this asylum must contain either a sane patient or an insane doctor.

As I said, Craig realized all this before his interviews with Doctor Tarr and Professor Fether. Now, Doctor Tarr believes that all the doctors are sane, and Professor Fether believes that all the patients are insane. They cannot both be right (as we have proved); hence at least one of them is insane. Also, Professor Fether believes that Doctor Tarr is sane. If Professor Fether is sane, he has to be right, and Doctor Tarr would also be sane, which we know is not true. Therefore, Professor Fether must be insane. Then his belief that Doctor Tarr is sane is wrong, so Doctor Tarr is also insane. This proves that Doctor Tarr and Professor Fether are both insane.

Since Doctor Tarr is insane and believes that at least one

patient is insane, then in fact all the patients must be sane. Since Professor Fether is insane and believes that at least one doctor is sane, then in fact all the doctors are insane. This proves that all the patients are sane and all the doctors are insane.

Remarks: This puzzle, of course, was suggested by Edgar Allan Poe's story "The System of Doctor Tarr and Professor Fether," in which the patients of a lunatic asylum managed to overcome all the doctors and staff, put them, tarred and feathered, in the patients' cells, and assumed their rôles.

◆ 4 ◆

Inspector Craig
Visits
Transylvania

A week after these last adventures, Craig was preparing to return to London when he suddenly received a wire from the Transylvanian government, urgently requesting him to come to Transylvania to help solve some baffling cases of vampirism. Now, as I explained in my previous book of logic puzzles, *What Is the Name of This Book?*, Transylvania is inhabited by both vampires and humans; the vampires always lie and the humans always tell the truth. However, half the inhabitants, both human and vampire, are insane and totally deluded in their beliefs (just like the mad inhabitants of the asylum of Doctor Tarr and Professor Fether)—all true propositions they believe false and all false propositions they believe true. The other half of the inhabitants are completely sane and totally accurate in their judgments (just like the sane inhabitants of the asylums in Chapter 3)—all true statements they know to be true and all false statements they know to be false.

Of course, the logic of Transylvania is much more complicated than that of the lunatic asylums, because in the latter, the inhabitants are at least honest and make false statements only out of delusion, never out of malice. But when a Transylvanian makes a false statement, it could be either out of delusion or out of malice. Sane humans and insane vampires both make only true statements; insane humans and sane vampires make only false statements. For example, if you ask a Transylvanian whether the earth is round (as opposed to flat), a sane human knows the earth is round and will truthfully say so. An insane human believes the earth is not round, and will then truthfully express his belief and say it is not round. A sane vampire knows the earth is round, but will then lie and say it isn't. But an insane vampire believes the earth is not round and then lies and says it is round. Thus an insane vampire responds the same way to any question as a sane human, and an insane human the same way as a sane vampire.

It was fortunate that Craig was as well versed in vampirism as in logic (the general range of Craig's interests and knowledge was quite remarkable altogether). When he arrived in Transylvania, he was informed by the authorities (all of whom were sane humans) that there were ten cases with which they needed help, and he was requested to take charge of the investigations.

THE FIRST FIVE CASES

Each of these cases involved two inhabitants. In each case, it was already known that one of them was a vampire and the other was human, but it was not known which was which (or perhaps I should say, which was witch). Nothing was known, except in Case 5, about the sanity of either.

1 ✦ The Case of Lucy and Minna

The first case involved two sisters named Lucy and Minna, and Craig had to determine which one of them was a vampire. As indicated above, nothing was known about the sanity of either. Here is the transcript of the investigation:

Craig (to Lucy): Tell me something about yourselves.

Lucy: We are both insane.

Craig (to Minna): Is that true?

Minna: Of course not!

From this, Craig was able to prove to everyone's satisfaction which of the sisters was the vampire. Which one was it?

2 ✦ Case of the Lugosi Brothers

The next case was that of the Lugosi brothers. Both had the first name of Bela. Again, one was a vampire and one was not. They made the following statements:

Bela the Elder: I am human.

Bela the Younger: I am human.

Bela the Elder: My brother is sane.

Which one is the vampire?

3 ✦ The Case of Michael and Peter Karloff

The next case involved another pair of brothers, Michael and Peter Karloff. Here is what they said:

Michael Karloff: I am a vampire.

Peter Karloff: I am human.

Michael Karloff: My brother and I are alike as far as our sanity goes.

Which one is the vampire?

4 • The Case of the Turgeniefs

The next case involved a father and son whose surname was Turgenief. Here is the transcript of the interrogation:

Craig (to the father): Are you both sane or both insane, or are you different in this respect?

Father: At least one of us is insane.

Son: That is quite true!

Father: I, of course, am not a vampire.

Which one is the vampire?

5 • The Case of Karl and Martha Dracula

The last case of this group involved a pair of twins, Karl and Martha Dracula (no relation to the count, I can assure you!). The interesting thing about this case is that not only was it already known that one of them was human and the other a vampire, but it was also known that one of the two was sane and the other insane, although Craig had no idea which was which. Here is what they said:

Karl: My sister is a vampire.

Martha: My brother is insane!

Which one is the vampire?

FIVE MARRIED COUPLES

The next five cases each involved a married couple. Now (as you may or may not know), in Transylvania it is illegal for humans and vampires to intermarry, hence any married couple there are either both humans or both vampires. In these cases, as in Problems 1 through 4, nothing was known about the sanity of either person.

6 ◆ The Case of Sylvan and Sylvia Nitrate

The first case in this group was that of Sylvan and Sylvia Nitrate. As already explained, they are either both humans or both vampires. Here is the transcript of Craig's interrogation:

Craig (to Mrs. Nitrate): Tell me something about yourselves.

Sylvia: My husband is human.

Sylvan: My wife is a vampire.

Sylvia: One of us is sane and one of us is not.

Are they humans or vampires?

7 ◆ The Case of George and Gloria Globule

The next case involved the Globules.

Craig: Tell me something about yourselves.

Gloria: Whatever my husband says is true.

George: My wife is insane.

Craig did not feel that the husband's remark was overly gallant; nevertheless, these two testimonies were sufficient to solve the case.

Is this a human or a vampire couple?

8 ◆ The Case of Boris and Dorothy Vampyre

"It is important," said the Transylvanian chief of police to Inspector Craig, "not to let the last name of the suspects prejudice the issue."

Here are the answers they gave:

Boris Vampyre: We are both vampires.
Dorothy Vampyre: Yes, we are.
Boris Vampyre: We are alike, as far as our sanity goes.
What kind of couple are we dealing with?

9 ✦ The Case of Arthur and Lillian Sweet

The next case involved a foreign couple (foreign to Transylvania, that is) named Arthur and Lillian Sweet. Here is their testimony:

Arthur: We are both insane.
Lillian: That is true.
What are Arthur and Lillian?

10 ✦ The Case of Luigi and Manuella Byrdcliffe

Here is the testimony of the Byrdcliffes:

Luigi: At least one of us is insane.
Manuella: That is not true!
Luigi: We are both human.
What are Luigi and Manuella?

TWO UNEXPECTED PUZZLES

11 ✦ The Case of A and B

Inspector Craig was relieved that all these unpleasant cases were over and was packing his things for his return to London, when quite unexpectedly a Transylvanian official burst into his room, begging him to stay just one more day to help solve a new case that had just come up. Well, Craig certainly did not relish the idea; still, he felt it his duty to assist where possible, and he consented.

It appeared that two suspicious-looking characters had just been picked up by the Transylvanian police. They both happened to be prominent persons, and Craig has requested that their names and sexes be withheld, so I shall just call them A and B. In contrast to the previous ten trials, nothing was known in advance concerning any relationship between them; they might both be vampires or both be human, or one could be a vampire and the other human. Also, they could be both sane or both insane, or one could be sane and the other insane.

At the trial, A stated that B was sane, and B claimed that A was insane. Then A claimed that B was a vampire, and B declared that A was human.

What can be deduced about A and B?

12 ◆ Two Transylvanian Philosophers

Happy that these weird trials were over at last, Craig was comfortably seated in a Transylvanian railroad station awaiting the train that would take him out of the country. He so looked forward to being back in London! Just then he overheard a dispute between two Transylvanian philosophers, who were eagerly discussing the following problem:

Suppose there is a pair of identical Transylvanian twins, one of whom is known to be a sane human and the other an insane vampire. And suppose you meet one of them alone and wish to find out which one he is. Can any amount of yes/no questions suffice to do this? The first philosopher maintained that no number of questions could possibly accomplish this, since either one would give the same answer as the other to any question asked. That is, given any question, if its correct answer is yes, the sane human will know the answer is yes and will truthfully answer yes; whereas the insane vampire will believe the answer is no and then lie and say yes. Similarly, if the correct answer to the question is no, then the sane human will answer no and the insane vampire, thinking the answer is yes, will lie and also say no. Therefore, the two brothers are indistinguishable in their outward verbal behavior, even though their minds work entirely differently. So, the first philosopher argued, no questions could tell them apart—unless, perhaps, given with a lie detector.

The second philosopher disagreed. Actually, he did not present any arguments to support his position; all he said was, "Let me interrogate one of those two brothers, and I'll tell you which one he is!"

Craig was curious to hear the outcome of the dispute, but just then his train pulled in and the philosophers did not board it.

Inspector Craig sat in his carriage for some time pondering as to which philosopher was right. He eventually realized that it was the second philosopher: if you met one of the twins, you could indeed find out by yes/no questions which of them you were addressing, and no lie detector was necessary. This then leaves two problems:

(1) What is the smallest number of questions you need to ask?

(2) More interesting yet, just what is wrong with the first philosopher's argument?

◆ SOLUTIONS ◆

There is a principle that will apply in several of the solutions that follow and which we will establish in advance—namely, that if a Transylvanian says he is human, then he must be sane, and if he says he is a vampire, then he must be insane. The reason is this: Suppose he says he is human. Now, his statement is either true or false. If his statement is true, then he really is human, but the only humans who make true statements are sane humans so in this case he is sane. If, on the other hand, his statement is false, then he is really a vampire, but the only vampires who make false statements are sane vampires (insane vampires make true statements, just like sane humans), so again he is sane. This proves that when a Transylvanian claims to be human, he must be sane, regardless of whether he is really human or not.

Suppose a Transylvanian claims to be a vampire; what follows? Well, if his claim is true, then he really is a vampire, but the only vampires who make true claims are insane vampires. If his claim is false, then he is in fact human, but the only humans who make false claims are insane humans; so in this case he is also insane. Thus, any Transylvanian who claims to be a vampire is insane.

We trust that the reader can verify for himself the fact that any Transylvanian who claims to be sane must in fact be human, and any Transylvanian who claims to be insane must in fact be a vampire.

Now let us turn to the solutions of the problems.

1 ◆ Lucy's statement is either true or false. If it is true, then both sisters are really insane; hence Lucy is insane, and the

only insane Transylvanian who can make a true statement is an insane vampire. So, if Lucy's statement is true, then Lucy is a vampire.

Suppose Lucy's statement is false. Then at least one of the sisters is sane. If Lucy is sane, then, since she has made a false statement, she must be a vampire (because sane humans make only true statements). Suppose Lucy is insane. Then it must be Minna who is sane. Also, Minna, by contradicting Lucy's false statement, has made a true statement. Therefore, Minna is sane and has made a true statement; so Minna is human, and again Lucy must be the vampire.

This proves that regardless of whether Lucy's statement is true or false, Lucy is the vampire.

2 ◆ We have already established the principle that any Transylvanian who says he is human must be sane and any Transylvanian who says he is a vampire must be insane (see discussion prefacing the solutions). Now, both the Lugosi brothers claim to be human; therefore, they are both sane. Therefore, Bela the Elder makes a true statement when he says that his brother is sane. So Bela the Elder is both sane and makes true statements; hence he is human. Therefore, it is Bela the Younger who is the vampire.

3 ◆ Since Michael claims to be a vampire, he is insane, and since Peter claims to be human, he is sane. So Michael is insane and Peter is sane; thus the two brothers are *not* alike as far as their sanity goes. Therefore, Michael's second statement is false, and since Michael is insane, he must be human (insane vampires don't make false statements!). Therefore, Peter is the vampire.

4 ◆ Father and son agree in answering the question about their sanity. This means that they either both make true

statements or both make false statements. But, since only one of them is human and the other is a vampire, they must necessarily be different as regards their sanity: If they are both sane, the one who is human would make true statements and the vampire would make false statements, and they could never agree; if they are both insane, the human would make false statements and the vampire would make true statements, and again they could not agree. Therefore, it is really true that at least one of them is insane. This proves that both of them make true statements. Then, since the father says he is not a vampire, he really isn't. So it is the son who is the vampire.

5 ♦ Suppose Martha is the vampire. Then Karl is human, and also Karl has made a true statement; hence Karl in this case has to be a sane human. This would make Martha an insane vampire, since, as we have been told, Karl and Martha are different as regards their sanity. But then Martha, an insane vampire, would have made a false statement—that Karl is insane—which insane vampires cannot do. Therefore, the assumption that Martha is a vampire leads to a contradiction. So it is Karl who is the vampire.

We can also determine their sanity or lack of it: Karl has made a false statement; hence, being a vampire, he is sane. But then Martha has also made a false statement; hence, being human, she is insane. So the complete answer is that Karl is a sane vampire and Martha is an insane human; Karl is lying when he says that his sister is a vampire, and Martha is deluded when she says that her brother is insane. (Quite a pair, even for Transylvania!)

6 ♦ Now we are in the situation where either both are vampires or both are human. Therefore, the first two statements cannot both be right, nor can they both be wrong (for if they

are both wrong, Sylvan would be a vampire and Sylvia would be human). So one of the two statements is right and one is wrong. This means that one of the two people is sane and the other insane (because if they were both sane, their statements would both be right if they were human, and both wrong if they were vampires). Therefore, Sylvia is right when she says that one of the two is sane and the other insane. This means that Sylvia makes true statements. Therefore her statement that her husband is human is true. This means that they are both human (and, incidentally, Sylvia is sane and Sylvan insane).

7 ◆ Gloria, in saying that whatever her husband says is true, is assenting to his claim that she is insane; in other words, Gloria is indirectly claiming to be insane. Only vampires can make such a claim (as we proved in the discussion preceding the solutions); hence Gloria must be a vampire. Therefore, they are both vampires.

8 ◆ Suppose they are human. Then their statements that they are both vampires are false, which means they are insane humans. That would mean that they *are* alike as far as their sanity goes; hence Boris's second statement is true, which is not possible for an insane human. Therefore, they cannot be human; they are vampires (and insane ones).

9 ◆ Suppose they are human. A sane human couldn't possibly say that he/she and someone else are both insane hence they would both have to be insane humans. Then you would have insane humans making the true statement that they are both insane, which is not possible. Therefore, they cannot be human; they are vampires. (They could be either sane vampires who lie when they say that they are insane, or insane

vampires making the true statement that they are insane. Remember that insane vampires always make true statements, although they don't intend to!).

10 ◆ Luigi and Manuella contradict each other; one of them must be right and the other wrong. Therefore, one of them makes true statements and the other makes false statements. Since they are either both human or both vampires, then it must be true that at least one of them is insane, because if they are both sane, then they would either both make true statements if they were human or both make false statements if they were vampires. So Luigi is right when he says that at least one of the two is insane. Therefore, Luigi makes true statements, and when he says that they are both human, he is right about that, too. This proves that they are both human (and, incidentally, that Luigi is sane and Manuella insane).

11 ◆ Let us call a Transylvanian *reliable* if he makes correct statements and *unreliable* if he makes incorrect ones. Reliable Transylvanians are either sane humans or insane vampires; unreliable Transylvanians are either insane humans or sane vampires. Now, A claims that B is sane, and also that B is a vampire. A's two claims are either both true or both false. If they are both true, then B is a sane vampire, which means that B is unreliable. On the other hand, if A's claims are both false, then B must be an insane human, which again means that B is unreliable. So in either case (whether A's claims are both true or both false), B is unreliable. Hence B's claims are both false and A is neither insane nor human; therefore, A must be a sane vampire. This also means that A is unreliable; so A's claims are both false, which means that B must be an insane human. So the answer is that A is a sane vampire and B is an insane human.

Incidentally, this problem is only one out of sixteen of a similar nature that could be devised and that all have unique solutions. The *combination* of whatever two statements A makes about B (one about his sanity and one about his human or vampire nature) with any two statements of B about A (one about A's sanity and the other about his nature)—and there are sixteen possibilities for these four statements—will uniquely determine the precise character of both A and B. For example, if A says B is human and B is sane, and B says A is a vampire and A is insane, the solution will be that B is a sane human and A is an insane vampire. Again, suppose A says B is sane and B is a vampire, and B says A is insane and A is a vampire. What are A and B? *Answer:* A is a sane human and B is a sane vampire.

Have you seen how to solve each of these sixteen possible problems and why each one must have a unique solution? If not, look at it this way: A can make four possible pairs of statements about B—namely, (1) B is sane; B is human. (2) B is sane; B is a vampire. (3) B is insane; B is human. (4) B is insane; B is a vampire. In each of the four cases, we can determine whether or not B is reliable. In Case 1, B must be reliable regardless of whether A's statements are both true or both false—because if both are true, B is a sane human and hence reliable; if both are false, B is an insane vampire, hence again reliable. Likewise in Case 4, B must be reliable. In Cases 2 and 3, on the other hand, B must necessarily be unreliable. So from A's statements we can always determine the reliability of B. In a similar manner, from B's two statements we can determine the reliability of A. Then, when we know the respective reliabilities of A and B, we know which of all four statements are true and which are false, and the problem is then solved.

I might also remark that if, instead of A and B each making

two statements about the other, each made a *conjunction* of them, the problem would be unsolvable. If, for example, instead of making two separate statements—"B is sane," "B is a vampire"—A said, "B is a sane vampire," we could deduce nothing about the reliability of B; this is because if A's statement is correct, B *is* a sane vampire, but if A's statement is incorrect, B could be either an insane vampire or a sane human or an insane human.

12 ◆ One question is enough! All you need ask him is, "Are you human?" ("Are you sane?" would also work, and "Are you a sane human?" as well.) So suppose you ask him, "Are you human?" Well, if the one you are addressing is the sane human, he of course will answer yes. But suppose you are addressing the insane vampire. Being insane, he will erroneously believe he is human and then, being a vampire, will lie and say no. So the sane human will answer yes and the insane vampire will answer no. Therefore, if you get yes for an answer, you will know that he is the sane human, and if you get no for an answer, you will know that he is the insane vampire.

Now, more interesting yet, what was wrong with the first philosopher's argument? The first philosopher was certainly right in that if you ask the two brothers the same question, you will get the same answer. What the philosopher didn't realize was that if you ask, "Are *you* human?" to each of the two brothers, you are not actually asking the same question but rather two *different* questions, because the question contains the variable word *you*, whose meaning depends on the person to whom the question is addressed! So, even though you utter the same words when you put the question to two different people, you are really asking a different question in each case.

To look at it another way: Suppose the names of the two

brothers are known—John, say, is the name of the sane human, and Jim the name of the insane vampire. If I ask either brother, "Is John human?" both brothers will reply yes because I am now putting the *same* question to each; similarly, if I ask, "Is Jim human?" both brothers will answer no. But if I ask each brother, "Are *you* human?" I am really asking a different question in each case.

◆◆◆

PART TWO

PUZZLES
AND
METAPUZZLES

◆ 5 ◆

The Island of
Questioners

Somewhere in the vast reaches of the ocean, there is a very strange island known as the Island of Questioners. It derives its name from the fact that its inhabitants never make statements; they only ask questions. Then how do they manage to communicate? More on that later.

The inhabitants ask only questions answerable by yes or no. Each inhabitant is one of two types, A and B. Those of type A ask only questions whose correct answer is yes; those of type B ask only questions whose correct answer is no. For example, an inhabitant of type A could ask, "Does two plus two equal four?" But he could not ask whether two plus two equals five. An inhabitant of type B could not ask whether two plus two equals four, but he could ask whether two plus two equals five, or whether two plus two equals six.

1

Suppose you meet a native of this island, and he asks you, "Am I of type B?" What would you conclude?

2

Suppose, instead, he had asked you whether he is of type A. What would you have concluded?

3

I once visited this island and met a couple named Ethan and Violet Russell. I heard Ethan ask someone, "Are Violet and I both of type B?"

What type is Violet?

4

Another time I met two brothers whose first names were Arthur and Robert. Arthur once asked Robert, "Is at least one of us of type B?"

What types are Arthur and Robert?

5

Next I met a couple whose last name was Gordon. Mr. Gordon asked his wife, "Darling, are we of different types?"

What can be deduced about each?

6

Then I met a native whose last name was Zorn. He asked me, "Am I the type who could ask whether I am of type B?"

Can anything be deduced about Zorn, or is this story impossible?

7

Going from the sublime to the ridiculous, I came across a native who asked, "Am I the type who could ask the question I am now asking?"

Can anything be deduced about him?

8

I next came across a couple whose last name was Klink. Mrs. Klink asked her husband, "Are you the type who could ask me whether I am of type A?"

What can be deduced about Mr. and Mrs. Klink?

9

Then I met a couple named John and Betty Black. Betty asked John, "Are you the type who could ask whether at least one of us is of type B?"

What are John and Betty?

Remarks: The last two puzzles remind me of the title of a song I heard many years ago. It was part of a collection of songs all of which were sort of "spoofs" on psychoanalysis. This particular one was titled: "I can't get adjusted to the you who's gotten adjusted to me."

10

The next incident was really a logical tangle! I met three sisters named Alice, Betty, and Cynthia. Alice asked Betty, "Are you the type who could ask Cynthia whether she is the type who could ask you whether you two are of different types?"

As I walked away, I tried to puzzle this out and finally realized that it was possible to deduce the type of only one of the three girls. Which one, and which type is she?

A STRANGE ENCOUNTER

The next three exchanges I witnessed on the Island of Questioners were the most bizarre of all! Three patients from one of the insane asylums of Chapter 3 escaped and decided to pay a visit to the island. We recall that a patient from one of these asylums could be sane or insane and that the sane ones are totally accurate in all their beliefs, and the insane ones totally inaccurate in all their beliefs. We also recall that the patients, whether sane or insane, are always truthful; they never make statements unless they believe them to be true.

11

On the day after their arrival, one of the patients, whose name was Arnold, met a native of the island. The native asked him, "Do you believe I am of type B?"

What can be deduced about the native, and what can be deduced about Arnold?

12

The next day, another of the three patients, Thomas, had a long conversation with one of the natives (if you can call it a conversation—Thomas kept making statements and the native kept asking questions!). At one point the native asked Thomas, "Do you believe I am the type who could ask you whether you are insane?"

What can be deduced about the native, and what can be deduced about Thomas?

13

Several days later, I had a conversation with the third patient, whose name was William. William told me that on the preceding day he had overheard a conversation between Thomas and a native named Hal, in which Thomas said to Hal, "You are the type who could ask whether I believe you are of type B."

Can anything be deduced about either Thomas, Hal, or William?

WHO IS THE SORCERER?

At this point in my adventures, I still did not know whether Thomas was sane or insane, nor did I have much time to find out. The next day all three patients left the island. The last I heard, they had voluntarily returned to the asylum from which they escaped. They were evidently happy there, since they agreed unanimously that life outside the asylum was even crazier than life inside.

Well, it was a relief to have things back to normal on the Island of Questioners. Then I heard a rumor that interested me very much—namely, that there might be a sorcerer on this island. Now, sorcerers have fascinated me since childhood, so I was very anxious to meet a real one, if the rumor was true. I wondered how I could find out!

14

Fortunately, a native asked me a question one day, and then I knew that there must be a sorcerer on the island.

Can you supply such a question?

At this point, the reader might well be wondering how I could possibly have heard a rumor about a sorcerer on the island or, for that matter, heard anything at all about the island, since the inhabitants never make statements but only ask questions. Assuming that the reader hasn't already figured out the answer for himself, the solution to this problem will show exactly how the inhabitants can communicate information just as freely (if somewhat more clumsily) as anyone else.

As you can imagine, I was delighted to find out that there really was a sorcerer on the island. I also learned that he was the island's only sorcerer. But I had no idea who he was. Then I discovered that a grand prize had been offered to any visitor who could correctly guess his name. The only drawback was that any visitor who guessed wrong would be executed.

So I got up early the next morning and walked around the island, hoping that the natives would ask me enough questions to enable me to deduce with certainty who the sorcerer was. Here is what happened:

15

The first native I met was named Arthur Good. He asked me, "Am I the sorcerer?"

Did I have enough information yet to know who the sorcerer was?

16

The next native was named Bernard Green. He asked me, "Am I the type who could ask whether I am not the sorcerer?"

Did I yet have enough information?

17

The next native, Charles Mansfield, asked, "Am I the type who could ask whether the sorcerer is the type who could ask whether I am the sorcerer?"

Do I yet have enough information?

18

The next native was named Daniel Mott. He asked, "Is the sorcerer of type B?"

Do I yet have enough information?

19

The next native was named Edwin Drood. He asked, "Are the sorcerer and I of the same type?"

Eureka! I now had enough pieces to solve the mystery! Who is the sorcerer?

◊ ◊ ◊

Bonus Problem

Are you a good detective? We recall the patient Thomas who visited this island. Is he really sane or insane?

◆ SOLUTIONS ◆

1 ◆ It is impossible for any native of this island to ask you this question. If a native of type A asks, "Am I of type B?," the correct answer is no (since he isn't of type B), but a type A cannot ask any question whose correct answer is no. Therefore, no native of type A can ask this question. If a native of type B asks the question, the correct answer is yes (since he *is* of type B), but a type B cannot ask a question whose correct answer is yes. Therefore, a native of type B cannot ask the question either.

2 ◆ Nothing can be concluded. Any native of this island can ask whether he is of type A, because he is of either type A or type B. If he is of type A, then the correct answer to the question, "Am I of type A?" is yes, and anyone of type A can ask any question whose correct answer is yes. On the other hand, if the inhabitant is of type B, then the correct answer to the question is no, and any inhabitant of type B can ask a question whose correct answer is no.

3 ◆ We must first find out Ethan's type. Suppose Ethan is of type A. Then the correct answer to his question must be yes (since yes is the correct answer to questions asked by those of type A), which would mean that Ethan and Violet are both of type B, which would mean that Ethan is of type B, and we have a contradiction. Therefore, Ethan can't be of type A; he must be of type B. Since he is of type B, the correct answer to his question is no, so it is not the case that he and Violet are both of type B. This means Violet must be of type A.

4 ◆ Suppose Arthur were of type B. Then it would be true that at least one of the brothers was of type B, which would make yes the correct answer to his question, which would mean he is of type A. This is a contradiction; hence Arthur cannot be of type B; he must be of type A. From this it follows that the correct answer to his question is yes, which means that at least one of the two is of type B. Since Arthur is not of type B, this must be Robert. So Arthur is of type A and Robert is of type B.

5 ◆ Nothing can be deduced about Mr. Gordon, but Mrs. Gordon must be of type B. Here are the reasons why:

Mr. Gordon is of either type A or type B. Suppose he is of type A. Then the correct answer to his question is yes, which means the two are of different types. This means Mrs. Gordon must be of type B (since he is of type A and the two are of different types). So, if Mr. Gordon is of type A, then Mrs. Gordon must be of type B.

Now, suppose Mr. Gordon is of type B. Then the correct

answer to his question is no, which means the two are not of different types; they are of the same type. This means that Mrs. Gordon is also of type B. So if Mr. Gordon is of type B, so is Mrs. Gordon.

This proves that regardless of whether Mr. Gordon is of type A or type B, Mrs. Gordon must be of type B.

Another proof—much simpler but more sophisticated—is this: We already know from the first problem that no one on this island can ask whether he is of type B. Now, if Mrs. Gordon were of type A, then for an inhabitant to ask whether he is of a different type from Mrs. Gordon would be equivalent to his asking whether he is of type B, which he cannot do. Therefore, Mrs. Gordon cannot be of type A.

6 ◆ This story is perfectly possible, but Zorn must be of type B. The easiest way to see this is by recalling (Problem 1) that no native of this island can ask whether he is of type B. So when Zorn asks whether he is the type who could ask whether he is of type B, the correct answer is no (since no inhabitant could ask whether he is of type B). Since the correct answer is no, Zorn must be of type B.

7 ◆ Since the native just *did* ask the question, then he obviously *could* ask the question. Hence the correct answer to his question is yes, and he is of type A.

8 ◆ Nothing can be deduced about Mrs. Klink, but Mr. Klink must be of type A. Here are the reasons: Suppose Mrs. Klink is of type A. Then the correct answer to her question is yes, which means that Mr. Klink *could* ask Mrs. Klink if she is of type A. And, since Mrs. Klink is of type A, the correct answer would be *yes*, which makes Mr. Klink of type A. So, if Mrs. Klink is of type A, so is her husband. Now, suppose Mrs.

Klink is of type B. Then the correct answer to her question is no, which means that Mr. Klink is not the type who could ask her if she is of type A. Thus he could not ask a question whose correct answer is no, so he must be of type A. So, Mr. Klink is of type A, regardless of the type of Mrs. Klink.

9 ◆ Suppose Betty is of type A. Then the correct answer to her question is yes; hence John could ask if at least one of them is of type B. But this leads to a contradiction: If John is of type A, then it would be false that at least one of them is of type B. Hence the correct answer to his question would be no, which is not possible for one of type A. If John is of type B, then it would be true that at least one of them is of type B, which makes yes the correct answer to his question. But one of type B cannot ask a question whose correct answer is yes. Thus the assumption that Betty is of type A is impossible; she must be of type B.

Since Betty is of type B, then the correct answer to her question is no, which means that John cannot ask her if at least one of them is of type B. Now, if John were of type A, then he *could* ask that question, because it is true that at least one of them is of type B (namely, Betty). Since he can't ask that question, he must also be of type B.

So the answer is that both of them are of type B.

10 ◆ It is easiest to build the solution of this problem in graded steps. First, we can easily establish the following two propositions:

Proposition 1: Given any inhabitant X of type A, no inhabitant could ask whether (s)he and X are of different types.

Proposition 2: Given any inhabitant X of type B, then any inhabitant could ask whether (s)he and X are of different types.

We have already proved Proposition 1 in the solution of Problem 5, in which we saw that if Mrs. Gordon had been of type A, then Mr. Gordon *couldn't* have asked whether he and Mrs. Gordon were of the same type.

As for Proposition 2, if X is of type B, then the question of whether one is of a different type than X is equivalent to the question of whether one is of type A, and anyone can ask that question, as we saw in the solution of Problem 2. Therefore, anyone can ask X whether (s)he is of a different type, if X is of type B.

Now for the problem: I will prove that the correct answer to Alice's question is no; hence Alice must be of type B. In other words, I will prove that it is *not* possible for Betty to ask Cynthia whether Cynthia is the type who could ask Betty whether Cynthia and Betty are of different types.

Suppose Betty asks Cynthia whether Cynthia could ask whether Cynthia and Betty were of different types. We get the following contradiction: Betty is either of type A or type B. Suppose Betty is of type A. Then by Proposition 1, Cynthia could not ask whether she and Betty are of different types; hence the answer to Betty's question is no, which is impossible since Betty is of type A! On the other hand, suppose Betty is of type B. Then by Proposition 2, Cynthia *could* ask whether she and Betty are of different types, which makes yes the correct answer to Betty's question, which is not possible since Betty is of type B.

This proves that Betty could never ask Cynthia the question which Alice asks Betty whether she could ask, so the correct answer to Alice's question is no, and Alice is of type B. As to the types of Betty and Cynthia, nothing can be determined.

11 ♦ This strikes me as the funniest problem of this chapter, since nothing can be deduced about the native who asked the

question; but as to Arnold, though he never opened his mouth (as far as we know), he must be insane! The fact is that no native could ask a *sane* person whether he believes the native to be of type B, because asking a sane person whether he believes such-and-such to be the case is tantamount to asking whether such-and-such really is the case, and no native can ask whether he is of type B. So no native X could ask a sane person whether he believes X is of type B.

On the other hand (and we need this fact for a subsequent problem), any native X could ask an *insane* person whether he believes X is of type B, because asking that of an insane person is tantamount to X asking whether X is of type A, which, as we have seen, any native X can do.

12 ◆ Nothing can be deduced about Thomas, but the native who asked the question must be of type B. For, suppose he were of type A, then the correct answer to his question is yes, which means that Thomas does believe that the native could ask him whether he is insane. Now, Thomas is either sane or insane. Suppose he is sane. Then his belief is correct, which means that the native could ask him if he is insane. But one of type A can ask a question only if the correct answer is yes, which would mean that Thomas must be insane; so the assumption that Thomas is sane leads to the conclusion that Thomas is insane. Therefore, it is contradictory to assume that Thomas is sane. On the other hand, suppose Thomas is insane. Then Thomas's belief that the native could ask if Thomas is insane is wrong; hence the native couldn't ask him if he is insane. (Thomas would answer no—impossible, given that the native is of type A.) But, given that Thomas is insane, and the native is of type A, then the native *could*, by the rules on the Island of Questioners, ask Thomas if he is insane (since the correct answer would be yes). So it is also contradictory to assume that Thomas is insane.

The only way out of the contradiction is that the native must be of type B rather than type A, and no contradiction arises, regardless of whether Thomas is sane or insane.

13 ◆ I will show that the story which William reported could never really have happened; hence William must be insane to believe that it had.

Suppose the story were true: we get the following contradiction. Suppose Thomas is sane; then his statement is correct, which means that Hal could ask Thomas if he believes that Hal is of type B. But by the solution to Problem 11, this implies that Thomas is insane! So it is contradictory to assume that Thomas is sane. On the other hand, suppose Thomas is insane. Then his statement is false; hence Hal couldn't ask Thomas if he believes that Hal is of type B. But, as we saw in Problem 11, a native *can* ask an insane person whether he believes the native to be of type B; so we also get a contradiction in this case.

The only way out of the contradiction is that Thomas never did ask such a question of any native, and William only imagined he did.

14 ◆ Many questions will do the trick; my favorite one is: "Am I the type who can ask whether there is a sorcerer on this island?"

Suppose the questioner is of type A. Then the correct answer to his question is yes; the questioner *can* ask if there is a sorcerer on the island. Being of type A, he can ask whether there is a sorcerer on the island only if there is in fact a sorcerer on the island (so the correct answer would be yes). Thus, if the questioner is of type A, then there must be a sorcerer on the island.

Suppose the questioner is of type B. Then the correct answer to his question is no, which means that he cannot ask if there is a sorcerer on the island. Now if there *were* no sorcerer on the island, then the questioner (being of type B) *could* ask if there is a sorcerer on the island (since the correct answer would be no). However, since the questioner can't ask this (as we have seen), it follows that there must in fact be a sorcerer on the island. This proves that if the questioner is of type B, there is a sorcerer on the island. So, regardless of whether the questioner is of type A or type B, there must be a sorcerer on the island.

15 ✦ Of course not!

16 ✦ All that can be deduced is that Bernard Green is not the sorcerer (by the same reasoning as in the solution of Problem 14).

17 ✦ All that can be deduced is that the sorcerer is the type who could ask if Charles Mansfield is the sorcerer. (Remember that, as we found out in Problem 11, when a native asks, "Am I the type who could ask such-and-such?" then the such-and-such must in fact be true.)

18 ✦ All that can be deduced is that Daniel Mott is not the sorcerer (because the sorcerer cannot ask whether the sorcerer is of type B; no one can ask whether he is of type B).

19 ✦ It is not possible to deduce who the sorcerer is from what Edwin Drood asks by itself, but from Edwin Drood's question *together with earlier questions*, the problem becomes completely resolved!

What follows from Edwin Drood's question is that the sorcerer must be of type A. For, suppose Edwin is of type A. Then the correct answer to his question is yes; hence he and the sorcerer really would be of the same type; so the sorcerer would also be of type A. On the other hand, suppose Edwin is of type B. Then the correct answer to his question is no, which means that he and the sorcerer would not be of the same type. Since Edwin would be of type B, and the sorcerer would not be of the same type as Edwin, then again the sorcerer must be of type A.

This proves that the sorcerer is of type A. Now, we saw in Problem 17 that the sorcerer could ask if Charles Mansfield is the sorcerer. Since the sorcerer is of type A, then the correct answer to that question is yes; hence Charles Mansfield must be the sorcerer!

Bonus Problem ✦ I told you that Arnold, Thomas, and William were unanimously agreed that life outside the asylum was even crazier than life inside. Since Thomas agrees with Arnold and William, who are insane, then Thomas must also be insane.

◆ 6 ◆

The Isle of
Dreams

I once dreamed that there was a certain island called the Isle of Dreams. The inhabitants of this island dream quite vividly; indeed, their thoughts while asleep are as vivid as while awake. Moreover, their dream life has the same continuity from night to night as their waking life has from day to day. As a result, some of the inhabitants sometimes have difficulty in knowing whether they are awake or asleep at a given time.

Now, it so happens that each inhabitant is of one of two types: *diurnal* or *nocturnal*. A diurnal inhabitant is characterized by the fact that everything he believes while he is awake is true, and everything he believes while he is asleep is false. A nocturnal inhabitant is the opposite: everything a nocturnal person believes while asleep is true, and everything he believes while awake is false.

1

At one particular time, one of the inhabitants believed that he was of the diurnal type.

Can it be determined whether his belief was correct? Can it be determined whether he was awake or asleep at the time?

79

2

On another occasion, one of the natives believed he was asleep at the time. Can it be determined whether his belief was correct? Can it be determined what type he is?

3

(a) Is it true that an inhabitant's opinion of whether he is diurnal or nocturnal never changes?

(b) Is it true that an inhabitant's opinion of whether he is awake or asleep at the time never changes?

4

At one time, an inhabitant believed that she was either asleep or of the nocturnal type, or both. (*Or* means *at least one* or *possibly both.*)

Can it be determined whether she was awake or asleep at the time? Can it be determined what type she is?

5

At one time, an inhabitant believed that he was both asleep and diurnal. What was he really?

6

There is a married couple on this island whose last name is Kulp. At one point Mr. Kulp believed that he and his wife were both nocturnal. At the same instant, Mrs. Kulp believed that they were not both nocturnal. As it happened, one of them was awake and one of them was asleep at the time. Which one of them was awake?

7

There is another married couple on this isle whose last name is Byron. One of them is nocturnal and the other is diurnal. At one point the wife believed that they were either both asleep or both awake. At the same instant, the husband believed that they were neither both asleep nor both awake.

Which one was right?

8

Here is a particularly interesting case: at one time an inhabitant named Edward believed amazingly that he and his sister Elaine were both nocturnal, and at the same time that he was not nocturnal.

How is this possible? Is he nocturnal or diurnal? What about his sister? Was he awake or asleep at the time?

9 ✦ The Royal Family

This isle has a king and a queen and also a princess. At one point the princess believed that her parents were of different types. Twelve hours later, she changed her state (either from sleeping to waking or from waking to sleeping), and she then believed that her father was diurnal and her mother was nocturnal.

What type is the king and what type is the queen?

10 ✦ And What About the Witch Doctor?

No island is complete without a sorcerer or magician, a medicine man or witch doctor, or something like that. Well, this island, as it happens, has a witch doctor and only one witch doctor. Now comes a particularly intriguing puzzle concerning this witch doctor:

At one time an inhabitant named Ork was wondering whether he himself was the witch doctor. He came to the conclusion that if he was diurnal and awake at that point, then he must be the witch doctor. At the same instant, another inhabitant named Bork believed that if he was either diurnal and awake or nocturnal and asleep, then he (Bork) was the witch doctor. As it happened, Ork and Bork were either both asleep or both awake at the time.

Is the witch doctor diurnal or nocturnal?

11 ♦ A Metapuzzle

I once gave a friend the following puzzle about this island:

"An inhabitant believed at one time that he was diurnal and awake. What was he really?"

My friend thought about this for a while and then replied, "You obviously haven't given me enough information!" Of course my friend was right! He then asked me, "Do *you* know what type he was and whether he was awake or asleep at the time?"

"Oh, yes," I replied, "I happen to know this inhabitant well, and I know both his type and his state at the time."

My friend then asked me a shrewd question: "If you were to tell me whether he was diurnal or nocturnal, would I then have enough information to know whether he was awake or asleep at the time?" I answered him truthfully (yes or no), and he was then able to solve the puzzle.

Was the inhabitant diurnal or nocturnal, and was he awake or asleep at the time?

12 ✦ A More Difficult Metapuzzle

On another occasion, I told a friend the following puzzle concerning this island:

"An inhabitant at one point believed that she was both asleep and nocturnal. What was she really?"

My friend immediately realized that I had not given him enough information.

"Suppose you told me whether the lady was nocturnal or diurnal," my friend asked me. "Would I then be able to deduce whether she was asleep or awake at the time?"

I answered him truthfully, but he was *not* able to solve the problem (he still hadn't enough information).

Some days later, I gave the same problem to another friend (without telling him about the first friend). This second friend also realized that I hadn't given him enough information. Then he asked me the following question: "Suppose you told me whether the lady was awake or asleep at the time; would I then have enough information to know whether she was diurnal or nocturnal?"

I answered him truthfully, but he was unable to solve the problem (he too did not have enough information).

At this point, *you* have enough information to solve the puzzle! Was the lady diurnal or nocturnal, and was she awake or asleep at the time?

Epilogue

Suppose there really existed an island of the type described in this chapter, and suppose that I were one of the inhabitants. Would I be the diurnal or nocturnal type? It is really possible to answer this on the basis of things I have said in this chapter!

◆ SOLUTIONS ◆

1, 2, 3 ◆ Let us first observe that the following laws must hold:

Law 1: An inhabitant while awake believes he is diurnal.

Law 2: An inhabitant while asleep believes he is nocturnal.

Law 3: Diurnal inhabitants at all times believe they are awake.

Law 4: Nocturnal inhabitants at all times believe they are asleep.

To prove Law 1: Suppose X is an inhabitant who is awake at a given time. If X is diurnal, then he is both diurnal and awake; hence his beliefs at the time are correct; and he knows he is diurnal. On the other hand, suppose X is nocturnal. Then, being nocturnal but awake at the time, his beliefs are wrong; hence he erroneously believes he is diurnal. In summary, if X is awake, then if he is diurnal, he (rightly) believes he is diurnal, and if he is nocturnal, he (wrongly) believes he is diurnal.

The proof of Law 2 is parallel: If X is asleep, then if he is nocturnal, he (rightly) believes he is nocturnal, and if he is diurnal, he (wrongly) believes he is nocturnal.

To prove Law 3, suppose X is diurnal. While awake, his beliefs are correct; hence he then knows he is awake. But while asleep, his beliefs are wrong; hence he then erroneously believes he is awake. So, while awake he (rightly) believes he is awake, and while asleep he (wrongly) believes he is awake.

The proof of Law 4 parallels the proof of Law 3, and is left to the reader.

Now, to solve Problem 1, it cannot be determined whether his belief was correct. But he must have been awake at the time, for had he been asleep, he would have believed himself nocturnal rather than diurnal (by Law 2).

As for Problem 2, again it cannot be determined if his belief was correct; but the native must have been nocturnal, for were he diurnal, he would have believed himself to be awake rather than asleep (by Law 3).

As for Problem 3, the answer to (a) is no (because by Laws 1 and 2, an inhabitant's opinion as to whether he is diurnal or nocturnal changes from state to state; that is, from the waking state to the sleeping state), but the answer to (b) is yes (by Laws 3 and 4).

4 ✦ You can solve this systematically by considering each of the four possibilities in turn: (1) she is nocturnal and asleep; (2) she is nocturnal and awake; (3) she is diurnal and asleep; (4) she is diurnal and awake. You can then see which of the possibilities is compatible with the given conditions. However, I prefer the following argument:

First of all, could her belief be incorrect? If it is, then she is neither asleep nor nocturnal, which means she is awake and diurnal. However, this is a contradiction, since a person who is awake and diurnal cannot have an incorrect belief. Therefore, her belief cannot be incorrect; it must be correct. This means that she is asleep and nocturnal.

5 ✦ Again, this could be solved by trying each of four answers in turn, but again I prefer a more creative solution.

Could his belief have been correct? If so, then he was really asleep and diurnal, but being asleep and diurnal, he couldn't have a correct belief. Therefore, his belief was wrong. Now, the only occasions on which an inhabitant can have a wrong belief is when he is either asleep and diurnal or awake and nocturnal. If he were asleep and diurnal, then his belief would have been correct (for that is what he believes). Hence he must have been awake and nocturnal.

6 ◆ If you go about solving this puzzle systematically, you will have sixteen cases to consider! (Four possibilities for the husband, and with each of these four possibilities there are four possibilities for the wife.) Fortunately, there is a much simpler method of approaching the problem.

To begin with, since one of the two is asleep and the other awake, and since they believe opposite things, then they must be of the same type (that is, either both diurnal or both nocturnal), because if they were of different types, their beliefs would be opposite when they were both asleep or both awake and would coincide when one was asleep and the other was awake. Since their beliefs when one is asleep and the other awake don't coincide, then they must be of the same type.

Given, therefore, that they are either both nocturnal or both diurnal, let us suppose they are both nocturnal. Then the husband's belief at the time was correct, and since he is nocturnal, he must have been asleep at the time. Now, suppose they are both diurnal. Then the husband was obviously wrong in believing that they were both nocturnal, and since he is diurnal and had a wrong belief, then he must have been asleep at the time. So, whether they are nocturnal or diurnal, the husband must have been asleep at the time and his wife awake.

7 ◆ This is even simpler: Since the husband and wife are of different types, then their beliefs must be opposite when they are in the same state (that is, both awake or both asleep), and their beliefs must be the same when they are in different states (one asleep and the other awake). Since on this occasion their beliefs were opposite, then they were in the same state—both asleep or both awake. Therefore, the wife was right.

8 ◆ Obviously, Edward must have been in an unreliable state of mind at the time to believe these two logically incompatible propositions! So, both of Edward's beliefs must be wrong. Since he believed that he and Elaine were both nocturnal, then they are not both nocturnal. And since he believed he was not nocturnal, then he *is* nocturnal. So he is nocturnal, but they are not both nocturnal, so Elaine is diurnal. Since he is nocturnal and believed falsely at the time, he must have been awake. So, the answer is that he is nocturnal, his sister is diurnal, and he was awake.

9 ◆ Since the princess changed her state, then one of her two beliefs was correct and the other incorrect. This means that of the following two propositions, one is true and the other is false:
(1) The king and queen are of different types.
(2) The king is diurnal and the queen is nocturnal.
If (2) is true, then (1) would also have to be true, but we know that (2) and (1) can't both be true. Therefore, (2) must be false, and hence also (1) must be true. So the king and queen really are of different types, but it is not the case that the king is diurnal and the queen nocturnal. Therefore, the king is nocturnal and the queen is diurnal.

10 ◆ Suppose Ork were diurnal and awake at the time; would it follow from that supposition that Ork must be the witch doctor? Yes it would, by the following argument: Suppose Ork really were diurnal and awake at the time. Then his belief is correct, which means that *if* he is diurnal and awake, then he *is* the witch doctor. But he is diurnal and awake (by supposition); hence he must be the witch doctor (still under the supposition, of course, that he is diurnal and awake). So, the supposition that he is diurnal and awake leads to the conclusion that he is the witch doctor. This, of course, does not prove that the supposition is true, nor that he is the witch doctor, but only that *if* he was diurnal and awake, then he is the witch doctor. So we have established the hypothetical proposition that *if* Ork was diurnal and awake, *then* he is the witch doctor. Well, it was precisely this hypothetical proposition which Ork believed at the time; therefore, Ork's belief was correct! This means that Ork was either diurnal and awake at the time, or nocturnal and asleep, at the time, but we cannot (yet) tell which. Therefore, it is not necessarily true that Ork is the witch doctor, since it could be that he was nocturnal and asleep at the time.

Now, by a rather similar argument, Bork's belief is also correct: If Bork is either diurnal and awake or nocturnal and asleep, *in either case*, his belief is correct, which means he would have to be the witch doctor. Well, this is precisely what Bork believes; so Bork's belief is correct. Since Bork's belief is correct, then either he is diurnal and was awake at the time, or he is nocturnal and was asleep at the time. But in either case he must be the witch doctor.

Since Bork is the witch doctor, then Ork is not. Therefore, Ork could not have been awake at the time and diurnal, for we showed that if he had been, then *he* would have been the witch doctor. So, Ork was asleep at the time, and also nocturnal. Therefore, Bork was also asleep at the time, and since Bork's belief at the time was correct, then Bork must be nocturnal. So the witch doctor is nocturnal.

11 ✦ From the fact that the inhabitant believed that he was diurnal and awake, all that follows is that he was not nocturnal and asleep, and so there are three possibilities:

(1) He was nocturnal and awake (and believed falsely).

(2) He was diurnal and asleep (and believed falsely).

(3) He was diurnal and awake (and believed truly).

Now, suppose I had told my friend whether the native was diurnal or nocturnal; could my friend have then solved the problem? Well, that would depend on what I told him. If I told him that the native was nocturnal, then he would have known that Case 1 above was the only possibility, and so he would have known that the native was awake. On the other hand, if I told him that the native was diurnal, that would have ruled out (1) but would leave open both (2) and (3), and my friend wouldn't have any way of knowing which of these two latter possibilities actually held; so he then could not have solved the problem.

Now, my friend did not ask me whether the native was diurnal or nocturnal; all he asked was whether he could solve the problem *if* I told him whether the native was diurnal or nocturnal. If, in fact, the native were diurnal, then I would have had to answer no to my friend's question (because, as I have shown, if I told him that the native was diurnal, he couldn't solve the problem), but if the native were nocturnal, then I would have had to answer yes to his question (because, as I have shown, if I told him that the native was nocturnal, then my friend could solve the problem). Therefore, since my friend knew that the native was nocturnal and awake, I must have answered yes.

12 ✦ From the fact that she believed that she was nocturnal and asleep, all that follows is that she was not diurnal and awake, and so three possibilities remain:

(1) She was nocturnal and asleep.

(2) She was nocturnal and awake.

(3) She was diurnal and asleep.

If I had answered yes to my first friend's question, he would have known that (3) is the only possibility (by an argument similar to the solution of the last puzzle). But since he didn't solve it, I must have answered no. This, then, rules out (3), so we are left with possibilities (1) and (2).

Now, consider my second friend. If I had answered yes, then he could have figured out that (2) is the only real possibility (because (2) is the only one in which she is awake, whereas (1) and (3) both hold if she is asleep). Since this second friend couldn't solve the problem either, I must have answered him no as well, and this rules out possibility (2). What remains is that possibility (1) is the only valid one—that is, the native was nocturnal and asleep, as she herself correctly believed.

In brief summary, the fact that my first friend couldn't solve the problem rules out (3), and the fact that my second friend couldn't solve it rules out (2). What remains is (1): she was nocturnal and asleep.

Epilogue ◆ I told you at the beginning of the chapter that I *dreamed* there was such an island. If there really were such an island, then I would have dreamed truly; hence if I were one of the inhabitants, I would have to be nocturnal.

◊ 7 ◊

Metapuzzles

The last two puzzles of the last chapter (not counting the epilogue) are examples of a fascinating type of puzzle that I am tempted to call *metapuzzles*—or puzzles about puzzles. We are given a puzzle without sufficient data to solve it, and then we are given that someone else could or could not solve it given certain additional information, but we are not always told just what this additional information is. We may, however, be given partial information about it, which enables the reader to solve the problem. This remarkable genre is unfortunately rather rare in the literature. What follow here are five such puzzles, starting with some very easy ones and progressing to the last, which is the crowning puzzle of this and the preceding chapters.

1 ◆ The Case of John

This case involved a judicial investigation of identical twins. It was known that at least one of them never told the truth, but it was not known which. One of the twins was named John, and he had committed a crime. (John was not necessarily the one who always lied.) The purpose of the investigation was to find out which one was John.

"Are you John?" the judge asked the first twin.

"Yes, I am," was the reply.

"Are you John?" the judge asked the second twin.

The second twin then answered either yes or no, and the judge then knew which one was John.

Was John the first twin or the second?

2 ◆ A Transylvanian Metapuzzle

We learned from Chapter 4 that every Transylvanian is one of four types: (1) a sane human; (2) an insane human; (3) a sane vampire; (4) an insane vampire. Sane humans make only true statements (they are both accurate and honest); insane humans make only false statements (out of delusion, not intention); sane vampires make only false statements (out of dishonesty, not delusion); and insane vampires make only true statements (they believe the statement is false, but lie and say the statement is true).

Three logicians were once discussing their separate trips to Transylvania.

"When I was there," said the first logician, "I met a Transylvanian named Igor. I asked him whether he was a sane human. Igor answered me [yes or no], but I couldn't tell from his answer what he was."

"That's a surprising coincidence," said the second logician. "I met that same Igor on *my* visit. I asked him whether he was a sane vampire and he answered me [yes or no], and I couldn't figure out what he was."

"This is a double coincidence!" exclaimed the third logician. "I also met Igor and asked him whether he was an insane vampire. He answered me [yes or no], but I couldn't deduce what he was either."

Is Igor sane or insane? Is he a human or a vampire?

3 ◆ A Knight-Knave Metapuzzle

My book *What Is the Name of This Book?* contains a host of puzzles about an island on which every inhabitant is either a knight or a knave; knights always tell the truth and knaves always lie. Here is a knight-knave metapuzzle.

A logician once visited this island and came across two inhabitants, A and B. He asked A, "Are both of you knights?" A answered either yes or no. The logician thought for a while, but did not yet have enough information to determine what they were. The logician then asked A, "Are you two of the same type?" (Same type means both knights or both knaves.) A answered either yes or no, and the logician then knew what type each one was.

What type is each?

4 ◆ Knights, Knaves, and Normals

On the island of Knights, Knaves, and Normals, knights always tell the truth, knaves always lie, and those called *normal* can either lie or tell the truth (and sometimes one and sometimes the other).

One day I visited this island and met two inhabitants, A and B. I already knew that one of them was a knight and the other was normal, but I didn't know which was which. I asked A whether B was normal, and he answered me, either yes or no. I then knew which was which.

Which of the two is normal?

5 ◆ Who Is the Spy?

Now we come to a far more intricate metapuzzle!

This case involves a trial of three defendants: A, B, and C. It was known at the outset of the trial that one of the three was a knight (he always told the truth), one a knave (he always lied), and the other was a *spy* who was normal (he sometimes lied and sometimes told the truth). The purpose of the trial was to find the spy.

First, A was asked to make a statement. He said either that C is a knave or that C was the spy, but we are not told which. Then B said either that A is a knight, or that A is a knave, or that A was the spy, but we are not told which. Then C made a statement about B, and he said either that B was a knight, or that B was a knave, or that B was the spy, but we are not told which. The judge then knew who the spy was and convicted him.

This case was described to a logician, who worked on the problem for a while, and then said, "I do not have enough information to know which one is the spy." The logician was then told what A said, and he then figured out who the spy was.

Which one is the spy—A, B, or C?

◆ SOLUTIONS ◆

1 ◆ If the second twin had also answered yes, the judge obviously could not have known which one was John; hence the second one must have answered no. This means that either both twins told the truth or both lied. But they couldn't have both told the truth, because it is given that at least one of them always lies. Therefore, both lied, which means that the second twin is John. (It cannot be decided which of the two always lies.)

2 ◆ The first logician asked Igor whether he was a sane human. If Igor *is* a sane human, he would answer yes; if he is an insane human, he would also answer yes (because, being insane, he would erroneously believe that he is a sane human and then honestly express this belief); if Igor is a sane vampire, he would also answer yes (because, being sane, he knows he isn't a sane human, but would lie and say he was); but if Igor is an insane vampire, then he would answer no (because, being an insane vampire, he believes he is a sane human and lies about what he believes). So an insane vampire will answer no to this question; the other three types will answer yes. Now, if Igor had answered no, then the first logician would have known that Igor was an insane vampire. But the first logician didn't know what Igor was; hence he must have gotten a yes answer. All we can infer from this is that Igor is not an insane vampire.

As to the second logician's question, "Are you a sane vampire?," an insane human would answer yes, and each of the other three types would answer no. (We leave the verification of this to the reader.) Since the second logician couldn't tell from Igor's answer what Igor was, the answer must have been no, which means that Igor is not an insane human.

As to the third logician's question, "Are you an insane vampire?," a sane human would answer no, and each of the other three types would answer yes. Since the third logician couldn't figure out what Igor was, he must have gotten the answer yes, which means that Igor is not a sane human.

Since Igor is neither an insane vampire nor an insane human nor a sane human, he must be a sane vampire.

3 ◆ There are four possible cases:
Case 1: A and B are both knights.
Case 2: A is a knight and B is a knave.
Case 3: A is a knave and B is a knight.
Case 4: A and B are both knaves.
The logician first asked A whether both of them were knights. If Case 1, Case 3, or Case 4 holds, A will answer yes; if Case 2 holds, A will answer no. (We leave the verification of this to the reader.) Since the logician didn't know from A's answer what the natives were, then A must have answered yes. All the logician then knew was that Case 2 was out. Next, the logician asked A whether both were of the same type. In Cases 1 and 3, A would answer yes, and in Cases 2 and 4, A would answer no. (Again, I leave the verification of this to the reader.) So if the logician had gotten the answer yes, all he would have known is that either Case 1 or Case 3 holds, but he wouldn't know which. So he must have gotten the answer no. He then knew that either Case 2 or Case 4 holds, but he had already ruled out Case 2. So he knew that Case 4 must hold. And so A and B are both knaves.

4 ◆ If A had replied yes, then A could have been a knight, or A could have been normal (and lied), and I couldn't have known which. If A had replied no, then A couldn't be a knight (for then B would be normal, and A would have lied); so A would have to be normal. The only way I could have known which was which is that A said no. Hence A is the normal one.

5 ◆ We, of course, assume that the judge was a perfect reasoner and also that the logician to whom the problem was told was a perfect reasoner.
There are two possibilities: either the logician was told

that A said that C was a knave, or he was told that A said that C is the spy. We must examine both possibilities.

Possibility I: A said that C is a knave.

There are now three possible cases for what B said, and we must examine each:

Case 1: B said that A is a knight. Then: (1) if A is a knight, C is a knave (because A said that C is a knave), hence B is the spy; (2) if A is a knave, then B's statement is false, which means that B must be the spy (he's not a knave since A is), hence C is a knight; (3) if A is the spy, then B's statement is false, which means B is the knave, hence C is the knight. Thus we have either:

(1) A knight, B spy, C knave.

(2) A knave, B spy, C knight.

(3) A spy, B knave, C knight.

Now, suppose C said that B is the spy. Then (1) and (3) are ruled out. (If (1), C, a knave, couldn't claim that B is a spy, because B is, and if (3), C, a knight, couldn't claim that B is a spy, because B isn't.) This leaves only (2) open, and the judge would then know that B was the spy.

Suppose C said that B is a knight. Then (1) is the only possibility, and the judge would know this and again convict B.

Suppose C said that B is a knave. Then the judge couldn't have known whether (1) or (3) holds; hence he couldn't have known whether A or B was the spy, so he couldn't have convicted anyone. Therefore, C didn't say that B is a knave. (Of course, we are still working under the assumption for Case 1—that B said that A is a knight.)

So, if Case 1 holds, then B is the only one the judge could have convicted.

Case 2: B said that A is the spy. We leave it to the reader to verify that the following are the only possibilities:

(1) A knight, B spy, C knave.

(2) A knave, B spy, C knight.

(3) A spy, B knight, C knave.

If C said that B is the spy, then either (2) or (3) could hold, and the judge couldn't have found anyone guilty. If C said that B is a knight, then only (1) can hold, and the judge convicted B. If C said that B is a knave, then either (1) or (3) could hold, and the judge couldn't have convicted anyone. Therefore, C must have said that B is a knight, and B was the one convicted.

So, under Case 2, B was again the one convicted.

Case 3: B said that A is a knave. In this case there are four possibilities (as the reader can verify):

(1) A knight, B spy, C knave.

(2) A knave, B spy, C knight.

(3) A knave, B knight, C spy.

(4) A spy, B knave, C knight.

If C said that B is the spy, (2) or (3) could hold, and the judge couldn't have determined which one was guilty. If C said that B is a knight, (1) or (3) could hold, and the judge, again, couldn't have convicted anyone. If C said that B is a knave, (1), (3), or (4) could hold, and once more the judge could not have determined where guilt lay.

Thus Case 3 is ruled out. So we now know that either Case 1 or Case 2 holds, and in both cases, the judge convicted B.

So if Possibility I obtains (if A said that C is a knave), then B must be the spy. Therefore, if the logician had been told that A said that C is a knave, he could solve the problem and know that B was the spy.

Possibility II: Now, suppose the logician had been told that A said that C is the spy. I will show that the logician would then be unable to solve the problem, because there would be a possibility that the judge convicted A and a possibility that the judge convicted B, and the logician couldn't know which.

To prove this, let us assume that A said that C was the spy. Then here is one way the judge could have convicted A: Suppose B said that A is a knight and C said that B is a knave. If A is the spy, B could be a knave (who falsely claimed that A is a knight), and C could be a knight (who truthfully claims that B is a knave). A (the spy) would have falsely claimed that C is the spy. So it really is possible that A, B, and C made these three statements and that A is the spy. Now, if B were the spy, then A would have to be a knave in order to claim that C is the spy, and C would also have to be a knave for claiming that B is a knave, and so this is not possible. If C were the spy, then A would have to be a knight for truthfully claiming that C is a spy, and B would also have to be a knight for truthfully claiming that A is a knight, so this is also not possible. Therefore, A must be the spy (if B said that A is a knight and C said that B is a knave). So it is possible that A was the one convicted.

Here is a way that B could have been convicted: suppose B said that A is a knight and C said that B is the spy. (We continue to assume that A said that C is the spy.) If A is the spy, B is a knave for saying that A is a knight and C is also a knave for saying that B is the spy, so this is not possible. If C is the spy, then A is a knight (since he said C is the spy), and B is also a knight for saying that A is a knight, so this is also not possible. But if B is the spy, there is no contradiction (A could be a knave who said C is the spy; C could be a knight who said B is the spy; and B could have said that A is a knight). So it is possible that A, B, and C did make these three statements, in which case the judge convicted B.

I have now shown that if A said that C was the spy, there is a possibility that the judge convicted A and a possibility that the judge convicted B, and there is no way to tell which. Therefore, if the logician had been told that A said that C was the spy, there is no way the logician could have solved the problem. But we are given that the logician did solve the problem; hence he must have been told that A said that C is a knave. Then (as we have seen), the judge could have convicted only B. So B is the spy.

◆◀◆

PART THREE

THE
MYSTERY
OF THE
MONTE CARLO
LOCK

◆ 8 ◆

The Mystery
of the
Monte Carlo Lock

We last left Inspector Craig seated comfortably aboard a train outward bound from Transylvania, relieved at the thought of returning home. "Enough of these vampires!" he said to himself. "I'll be glad to get back to London, where things are normal!"

Little did Craig realize that another adventure awaited him before his return—an adventure of a very different nature from the two already related, and one that should appeal to those who enjoy combinatorial puzzles. This is what happened:

The inspector decided to stop off in Paris to attend to a few matters, and when he had finished he took a train from Paris to Calais, planning to cross the Channel to Dover. But, just as he got off at Calais, he was met by a French police officer who handed him a wire from Monte Carlo, begging him to come at once to help solve an "important problem."

"Oh, heavens," thought Craig, "I'll never get home at this rate!"

Still, duty was duty, and so Craig completely changed his plans, went to Monte Carlo, and was met at the station by an official named Martinez, who promptly took him to one of the banks.

"The problem is this," explained Martinez. "We have lost the combination to our biggest safe and to blow it open would be prohibitively expensive!"

"How ever did *that* happen?" asked Craig.

"The combination is written on only one card, and one of the employees carelessly left it inside the safe when he locked it!"

"Good heavens!" exclaimed Craig. "No one remembers the combination?"

"Absolutely no one," sighed Martinez. "And the worst of it is that if the wrong combination is used, the lock will be jammed permanently. Then there will be no recourse left but to blow open the safe, which, as I said, just isn't feasible—not only because of the cost of the mechanism but also because some extremely valuable and highly fragile materials are stored in it."

"Now, just a minute!" said Craig, "how can it be that you use a lock mechanism that can be permanently damaged by a wrong combination?"

"I was very much against purchasing the lock," said Martinez, "but I was overruled by the board of directors. They claimed that the mechanism had some uniquely valuable features which more than compensated for the disadvantage of possibly ruining it by using the wrong combination."

"This is really the most ridiculous situation I've ever heard!" said Craig.

"I heartily agree!" cried Martinez. "But what is to be *done?*"

"Frankly, I can't think of anything," replied Craig, "and *I* certainly cannot be of any help, since there are no clues. I'm very much afraid I have made this trip for nothing!"

"Ah, but there are clues!" said Martinez, a little more brightly. "Otherwise I would never have put you to the trouble of coming here."

"Oh?" said Craig.

"Yes," said Martinez. "Some time ago we had a very interesting though rather queer employee, a mathematician particularly interested in combinatorial puzzles. He took a keen interest in combination locks and studied the mechanism of this safe with great care. He pronounced it the most unusual and clever locking mechanism he had ever seen. He was constantly inventing puzzles, with which he amused many of us, and once he wrote a paper listing several properties of the locking mechanism, and asserting that from these properties we could actually *deduce* a combination that would open the safe. He gave this to us as a recreational puzzle, but it was far too difficult for any of us to solve, so we soon forgot it."

"And where is this paper?" asked Craig. "I suppose it is also locked up in the safe with the card bearing the combination?"

"Happily, no," said Martinez, as he produced the manuscript from his desk drawer. "Fortunately, I kept it in here."

Inspector Craig studied the manuscript carefully.

"I can see why none of you solved the puzzle; it appears extremely difficult! Wouldn't it be easier simply to contact the author? Surely he remembers or could reconstruct the combination, couldn't he?"

"He worked here under the name of 'Martin Farkus,' but that was probably an assumed name," replied Martinez. "No efforts to find him have been successful."

"Hm!" replied Craig, "I guess the only alternative is to try and solve this puzzle, but it might take weeks or several months."

"There is one more thing I must tell you," said Martinez. "It is absolutely imperative that the safe be opened by June first; it contains some state documents that *have* to be produced on the morning of June second. If we cannot find the combination by then, we will be forced to blow open the safe regardless of cost. The document itself won't be hurt by the explosion, since it is in a very stout inner safe, as far as possible from the door of the outer safe. And as for the other items—well, this document comes first! But it would be worth quite a sum of money to us not to have to resort to that alternative!"

"I'll see what I can do," said Craig, rising. "I can't promise you anything, though of course I'll do my best."

Now, let me tell you about the contents of Farkus's manuscript. To begin with, the combinations used letters, not numbers. And so by a *combination*, we will mean any string of any of the twenty-six capital letters of the alphabet. It can be of any length and contain any number of letters occurring any number of times; for example, BABXL is a combination; so is XEGGEXY. Also, a letter standing alone counts as a combination (a combination of length 1). Now, certain combinations will open the lock, certain ones will jam the lock, and the remaining combinations have no effect on the mechanism whatever. Those that have no effect on the mechanism are called *neutral*. We shall use the small letters x and y to represent arbitrary combinations, and by xy is meant combination x followed by combination y; for example, if x is the combination GAQ and y is the combination DZBF, then xy is the combination GAQDZBF. By the *reverse* of a combination is meant the combination written backwards; for example, the reverse of the combination BQFR is RFQB. By the *repeat*, xx, of a combination x is meant the combination followed by itself; for example, the repeat of BQFR is BQFRBQFR.

Now, Farkus (or whatever his real name was) referred to certain combinations as being *specially related* to others (or possibly to themselves), but he never defined what he meant by this term. Nevertheless, he listed enough properties of this "special relation" (whatever that might be) to enable a clever person to find a combination that opens the lock! He listed the following five key properties (which he said held for any combinations x and y):

Property Q: For any combination x, the combination QxQ is specially related to x. (For example, QCFRQ is specially related to CFR.)

Property L: If x is specially related to y, then Lx is specially related to Qy. (For example, since QCFRQ is specially related to CFR, then LQCFRQ is specially related to QCFR.)

Property V (the reversal property): If x is specially related to y, then Vx is specially related to the reverse of y. (For example, since QCFRQ is specially related to CFR, then VQCFRQ is specially related to RFC.)

Property R (the repetition property): If x is specially related to y, then Rx is specially related to yy (the repeat of y). (For example, since QCFRQ is specially related to CFR, then RQCFRQ is specially related to CFRCFR. Also—as we saw in the example accompanying Property V—VQCFRQ is specially related to RFC, and hence RVQCFRQ is specially related to RFCRFC.)

Property Sp: If x is specially related to y, then if x jams the lock, y is neutral, and if x is neutral, then y jams the lock. (For example, we have seen that RVQCFRQ is specially related to RFCRFC. Therefore, if RVQCFRQ should jam the lock, then RFCRFC would have no effect on the mechanism, and if LVQCRFQ has no effect on the mechanism, then RFCRFC jams the lock.)

From these five conditions, it is indeed possible to find a combination that opens the lock. (The shortest one I know is of length 10, and there are others.)

Now, the reader is hardly expected to solve this puzzle at this point; there is a whole theory behind this mechanism which will gradually unfold in the course of the next few chapters. This theory is related to some very interesting discoveries in mathematics and logic that will be apparent later on.

As a matter of fact, Craig worked on this puzzle for several days after his interview with Martinez, but was unable to solve it.

"No sense remaining here any longer," thought Craig. "I have no idea how long this will take, and I might just as well work on it at home."

And so Craig went back to London. That the puzzle ever did get solved was due not only to the ingenuity of Craig and two of his friends (whom we shall meet presently), but also to the remarkable concatenation of circumstances about to unfold.

◆ 9 ◆

A Curious
Number Machine

After Craig's return to London, he at first spent a good deal of time on the Monte Carlo lock puzzle. Then, since he was getting nowhere, he decided that it might be best to rest a while from the problem and went to visit an old friend named Norman McCulloch whom he had not seen for years. He and McCulloch had been fellow students at Oxford, and Craig recalled him in those days as a delightful, if somewhat eccentric, chap who was constantly inventing all sorts of curious gadgets. Now, this whole story takes place in the days before modern computers were invented, but McCulloch had put together a crude mechanical computer of a sort.

"I've been having ever so much fun with this device," explained McCulloch. "I've not yet found any practical use for it, but it has some intriguing features."

"What does it do?" asked Craig.

"Well," replied McCulloch, "you put a number into the machine, and after a while a number comes out of the machine."

"The same number or a different one?" asked Craig.

"That depends on what number you put in."

"I see," replied Craig.

"Now," continued McCulloch, "the machine doesn't accept *all* numbers—only some. Those which the machine accepts, I call *acceptable* numbers."

"That sounds like perfectly logical terminology," said Craig, "but I would like to know which numbers are acceptable and which are not. Is there a definite law concerning this? Also, is there a definite law concerning what number comes out once you have decided what acceptable number to put in?"

"No," replied McCulloch, "*deciding* to put the number in is not enough; you have actually to put the number in."

"Oh, well, of course!" said Craig. "I meant to ask whether once the number has been put in, if it is definitely determined what number comes out."

"Of course it is," replied McCulloch. "My machine is not a random device! It operates according to strictly deterministic laws.

"Let me explain the rules," he continued. "To begin with, by a *number* I mean a positive whole number; my present machine doesn't handle negative numbers or fractions. A number N is written in the usual way as a string of the digits 0,1,2,3,4,5,6,7,8,9. However, the only numbers my machine handles are those in which 0 does not occur; for example, numbers like 23 or 5492, but not numbers like 502 or 3250607. Given two numbers N,M—now by NM I *don't* mean N times M! By NM I mean the number obtained by first writing the digits of N in the order in which they occur, and then following it by the digits of M; so, for example, if N is the number 53 and M is the number 728, by NM I mean the number 53728. Or if N is 4 and M is 39, by NM I mean 439."

"What a curious operation on numbers!" exclaimed Craig in surprise.

"I know," replied McCulloch, "but this is the operation the machine understands best. Anyway, let me explain to you the rules of operation. I say that a number X *produces* a number Y, meaning that X is acceptable and that when X is put into the machine, Y is the number that comes out. The first rule is as follows:

"*Rule 1:* For any number X, the number 2X (that is, 2 *followed* by X, not 2 times X!) is acceptable, and 2X produces X.

"For example, 253 produces 53; 27482 produces 7482; 23985 produces 3985, and so forth. In other words, if I put a number 2X into the machine, the machine erases the 2 at the beginning and what is left—the X—comes out."

"That's easy enough to understand," replied Craig. "What are the other rules?"

"There is only one more rule," replied McCulloch, "but first let me tell you this: For any number X, the number X2X plays a particularly prominent role; I call the number X2X the *associate* of the number X. So, for example, the associate of 7 is 727; the associate of 594 is 5942594. Now, here is the other rule:

"*Rule 2:* For any numbers X and Y, if X produces Y, then 3X produces the associate of Y.

"For example, 27 produces 7, by Rule 1; therefore 327 produces the associate of 7, which is 727. Thus 327 produces 727. Again, 2586 produces 586; hence 32586 produces the associate of 586, which is 5862586."

At this point, McCulloch fed the number 32586 into the machine and, after much groaning and squeaking, the number 5862586 finally did come out.

"Machine needs a little oiling," commented McCulloch. "But let's consider another example or two to see if you have fully grasped the rules. Suppose I put in 3327; what will come out? We already know that 327 produces 727; so 3327 produces the associate of 727, which is 7272727. What number does 33327 produce? Well, since 3327 produces 7272727 (as we have just seen), then 33327 must produce the associate of 7272727, which is 727272727272727. As another example, 259 produces 59; 3259 produces 59259; 33259 produces 59259259259; 333259 produces 59259259259259259259259."

"I see," said Craig, "but the only numbers you have mentioned so far which seem to 'produce' anything are numbers beginning with either 2 or 3. What about numbers beginning, say, with 4?"

"Oh, the only numbers accepted by this machine are those beginning with 2 or 3, and not even all of those are acceptable. I am planning one day to build a larger machine which accepts more numbers."

"What numbers beginning with 2 or 3 are not acceptable?" asked Craig.

"Well, 2 alone is not acceptable, since it does not come within the scope of either Rule 1 or Rule 2, but any multidigital number beginning with 2 is acceptable. No number consisting entirely of 3's is acceptable. Also 32 is not acceptable, nor is 332, nor any string of 3's followed by 2. But for any number X, 2X is acceptable; 32X is acceptable; 332X and 3332X are acceptable; and so forth. In short, the only acceptable numbers are 2X, 32X, 332X, 3332X, and any string of 3's followed by 2X. And 2X produces X; 32X produces the associate of X; 332X produces the associate of the associate of X—which it is convenient to call the *double associate* of X; 3332X produces the associate of the associate of the associate of X—this number I call the *triple associate* of X—and so on."

"I fully understand," said Craig, "and now I would like to know just what are the curious features of this machine to which you have alluded?"

"Oh," replied McCulloch, "it leads to all sorts of curious combinatorial puzzles—here, let me show you some!"

1

"To begin with a simple example," said McCulloch, "there is a number N which produces itself; when you put N into the machine, out comes the very same number N. Can you find such a number?"

2

"Very good," said McCulloch, after Craig showed him his solution. "And now for another interesting feature of this machine: There is a number N which produces its own associate—in other words, if you put N into the machine, the number N2N comes out. Can you find such a number?"

Craig found this puzzle more difficult, but he managed to solve it. Can you?

3

"Excellent!" said McCulloch. "But there is one thing I would like to know: how did you go about finding this number? Was it just trial and error, or did you have some systematic plan? Also, is the number you found the only number that produces its own associate, or are there others?"

Craig then explained his method for finding the number N in the last problem, and also answered McCulloch's question as to whether there were other possible solutions. The reader should find Craig's analysis here to be of considerable interest, and it facilitates, moreover, the solutions of several other puzzles of the present chapter.

4

"Apropos of my last question," said McCulloch, "how did you solve the first problem? Is there more than one number that produces itself?"

Craig's answer is given in the solutions.

5

"Next," said McCulloch, "there is a number N which produces 7N (that is, 7 followed by N). Can you find it?"

6

"Now, let's consider another question," said McCulloch. "Is there a number N such that 3N produces the associate of N?"

7

"And is there an N," asked McCulloch, "which produces the associate of 3N?"

8

"A particularly interesting feature of this machine," said McCulloch, "is that for any number A there is some number

Y which produces AY. How do you prove this, and, given a number A, how do you find such a number Y?"

Note: This principle, simple as it is, is more important than McCulloch realized at the time! It will crop up several times in the course of this book. We shall call it *McCulloch's Law.*

9

"Now," continued McCulloch, "given a number A, is there necessarily some Y that produces the associate of AY? For example, is there a number that produces the associate of 56Y, and if so, what number does this?"

10

"Another interesting thing," said McCulloch, "is that there is a number N that produces its own double associate. Can you find it?"

11

"Also," said McCulloch, "given any number A there is a number X that produces the double associate of AX. Can you see how to find such an X, given the number A? For example, can you find an X that produces the double associate of 78X?"

Here are some more problems that McCulloch gave Craig on this day. (Except for the last of them, they are not of theoretical importance, but the reader might have fun playing with them.)

12

Find a number N such that 3N produces 3N.

13

Find a number N such that 3N produces 2N.

14

Find a number N such that 3N produces 32N.

15

Is there an N such that NNN2 and 3N2 produce the same number?

16

Is there an N whose associate produces NN? Is there more than one such N?

17

Is there an N such that NN produces the associate of N?

18

Find an N such that the associate of N produces the double associate of N.

19

Find an N that produces N23.

20 ◆ A Negative Result

"You know," said McCulloch, "for quite some time I have been trying to find a number N that produces the number N2, but so far all my attempts have failed. I wonder whether in fact there is no such number or whether I just haven't been clever enough to find one!"

This problem immediately engaged Craig's attention. He took out a notebook and pencil and started working on it. After a while he said, "Don't lose any more time looking for such a number: it cannot possibly exist!"

How did Craig know this?

◆ SOLUTIONS ◆

1 ◆ One such number is 323. Since 23 produces 3 (by Rule 1), then, by Rule 2, 323 must produce the associate of 3, which is 323—the very same number!

Are there other such numbers? For Craig's answer, see the solution to Problem 4.

2 ◆ The number Craig found was 33233. Now, any number of the form 332X produces the double associate of X, so 33233 produces the double associate of 33—that is, the associate of the associate of 33. Now, the associate of 33 is the original number 33233; hence the double associate of 33 is the associate of 33233. Thus 33233 produces the associate of 33233—that is, it produces its own associate.

How was this number found, and is it the only solution? Craig gives his answers to these questions in the solution to the next problem.

3 ♦ Here is how Craig found a solution to Problem 2 and also settled the question of whether or not there are any other solutions. I shall give his explanation in his own words:

"My problem was to find a number N that produces N2N. This N must be one of the forms 2X, 32X, 332X, 3332X, etc., and I must discover X. Could a number of the form 2X work? Clearly not, since 2X produces X, which is obviously shorter (has fewer digits) than the associate of 2X. So no number of the form 2X could possibly work.

"What about a number of the form 32X? It also produces a number which is too short; it produces the associate of X, which is obviously shorter than the associate of 32X.

"What about a number of the form 332X? Well, it produces the double associate of X, which is X2X2X2X, whereas what is required is to produce the associate of 332X, which is 332X2332X. Now, can X2X2X2X be the same number as 332X2332X? What about the comparative lengths? Well, letting h be the number of digits in X, the number X2X2X2X has $4h + 3$ digits (since there are four X's and three 2's), whereas 332X2332X has $2h + 7$ digits. Can $4h + 3 = 2h + 7$? Yes, if $h = 2$, but for no other h. So lengthwise, a number of the form 332X may be a possibility, but only if h has two digits.

"Are there any other possibilities? What about a number of the form 3332X? It produces the triple associate of X, which is X2X2X2X2X2X2X, whereas what is required is to produce the associate of 3332X, which is 3332X23332X. Could these numbers be the same? Again, letting h be the length of X, the number X2X2X2X2X2X2X2X has $8h + 7$ digits, whereas 3332X23332X has $2h + 9$ digits. The only solution to the equation $8h + 7 = 2h + 9$ is that $h = \frac{1}{3}$, so there is no whole number h that will make $8h + 7 = 7h + 9$; therefore no number of the form 3332X can work.

"What about a number of the form 33332X? It produces the quadruple associate of X, which has a length of $16h + 15$, whereas the associate of X has a length of $2h + 11$. Of course, for any positive integer h, $16h + 15$ is larger than $2h + 11$, so a number of the form 33332X produces something too large.

"If we take a number beginning with five 3's instead of four, the disparity between the lengths of the number it is supposed to produce and the number it actually produces is even greater, and if we take a number beginning with six or more 3's, the disparity is greater yet. Therefore, we are back to 332X as the only possible solution to the problem, so X must be a two-digit number. Thus, the desired N must be of the form 332*ab*, where *a* and *b* are single digits to be determined. Now, 332*ab* produces the double associate of *ab*, which is *ab2ab2ab2ab*. It is *desired* that 332*ab* produce the associate of 332*ab*, which is 332*ab*2332*ab*. Can these two numbers be the same? Let us compare them digit by digit:

$$ab2ab2ab2ab$$
$$332ab2332ab$$

"Comparing the first digits of each number, we see that *a* must be 3. Comparing the second digits, *b* must also be 3. So N = 33233 is a solution, and is the only possible solution."

4 ◆ "To tell you the truth," said Craig, "I solved the first problem by intuition; I didn't find the number 323 by any

systematic method. Also, I have not yet considered whether there is any other number that produces itself.

"But I don't think this should be too difficult to settle: Let's see now, could a number of the form 332X work? It would produce the double associate of X, which is X2X2X2X, which has a length of $4h + 3$, with h being the length of X. But what is required is to produce 332X, which has a length of $h + 3$. Obviously, $4h + 3$ is greater than $h + 3$, if h is a positive number, so 332X produces a number that is too large. What about 3332X, or some number beginning with four or more 3's? No, the disparity would be greater yet; the only possibility is a number of the form 32X (a number of the form 2X is clearly no good; it can't produce 2X, since it produces X). Now, 32X produces X2X, and what is required is that it produce itself, which is 32X. So 32X must be the same as X2X. Letting h be the length of X, 32X has a length of $h + 2$, and X2X has a length of $2h + 1$. So $2h + 1 = h + 2$; this means that h must be 1. So X is a single digit. Now, for what digit a is it the case that $a2a = 32a$? Obviously, a must be 3. Hence 323 is the only solution."

5 ◆ Take N to be 3273. It produces the associate of 73, which is 73273, which is 7N. So 73273 is a solution. (It is, in fact, the only solution, as can be shown by a comparative-lengths argument of the type considered in the last two problems.)

6 ◆ Since 323 produces itself, then 3323 must produce the associate of 323. So, letting N = 323, 3N produces the associate of N. (It is the only solution.)

7 ◆ The solution is 332333. Let us check: Let N be the number 332333. It produces the double associate of 333, which is the associate of 3332333—in other words, the associate of 3N.

8 ✦ This obviously is a straightforward generalization of Problem 5: We saw that for N = 3273, N produces 7N. There is nothing special about 7 that makes this work; for any number A, if we let Y = 32A3, Y produces AY (because it produces the associate of A3, which is A32A3, which is AY). So, for example, if we want a number Y that produces 837Y, we take Y to be 328373.

This fact will subsequently turn out to be of considerable theoretical importance!

9 ✦ The answer is *yes;* take Y to be 332A33. It produces the double associate of A33, which is the associate of A332A33. But A332A33 is AY, so Y produces the associate of AY.

For the particular example suggested by McCulloch—to find a number Y that produces the associate of 56Y—the solution is Y = 3325633.

10 ✦ The solution is 3332333. It produces the triple associate of 333, which is the double associate of the associate of 333. Now, the associate of 333 is 3332333, so 3332333 produces the double associate of 3332333.

The following general pattern should be noted: 323 produces itself; 33233 produces its own associate; 3332333 produces its own double associate. Also, 333323333 produces its own triple associate, 33333233333 produces its own quadruple associate, and so forth (as the reader can check for himself).

11 ✦ The solution is X = 3332A333. It produces the triple associate of A333, which is the double associate of the associate of A333. Now, the associate of A333 is A3332A333, which is AX. So X produces the double associate of AX.

For the particular example, A is 78, so the solution is 333278333.

12 ♦ Obviously, the answer is 23. (We already know that 323 produces 323, so, letting N = 23, 3N produces 3N.)

13 ♦ The answer is 22.

14 ♦ The answer is 232.

15 ♦ Of course: N = 2.

16 ♦ Any string of 2's will work.

17 ♦ Yes, 32 works.

18 ♦ Take N = 33.

19 ♦ Take N = 32323.

20 ♦ As the reader can verify for himself, any number N beginning with two or more 3's will produce a number of greater length than that of N2 (for example, if N is of the form 332X, and h is the length of X, N produces the double associate of X, which has a length of $4h + 3$, whereas N2 has a length of $h + 4$). Also, no N of the form 2X could work, so if there is any N that produces N2, it must be of the form 32X. Now, 32X produces X2X, and what is required is to produce 32X2. If X2X is the same number as 32X2, then, letting h be the length of X, it must be that $2h + 1 = h + 3$, which means $h = 2$. So the only number that could work (if there is one) must be of the form 32ab, where a and b are single digits to

be determined. Now, 32*ab* produces *ab2ab*, and what is required is to produce 32*ab2*. So, can *ab2ab* be the same number as 32*ab2*? Let us compare them digit by digit:

$$ab2ab$$
$$32ab2$$

Comparing the first digits, we get $a = 3$; comparing the third digits, we find $a = 2$—and so the problem is impossible. There is no N that produces N2!

◆ 10 ◆

Craig's Law

A couple of weeks later, Craig paid another visit to McCulloch.

"I heard you have enlarged your machine," said Craig, "and some mutual friends have told me that your new machine does some very interesting things. Is that true?"

"Ah, yes!" replied McCulloch, with an air of pride. "My new machine obeys Rules 1 and 2 of my old machine, and in addition, it has two other rules. But I've just brewed some tea—let's have some before I show you the new rules."

After an excellent tea, complete with delicious hot-buttered crumpets, McCulloch began:

"By the *reverse* of a number, I mean the number written backwards; for example, the reverse of 5934 is 4395. Now, here is the first of the additional rules:

"*Rule 3:* For any numbers X and Y, if X produces Y, then 4X produces the reverse of Y.

"Let me illustrate," said McCulloch. "Pick a number Y at random."

"All right," said Craig, "suppose we take 7695."

"Very good," said McCulloch. "Let's take an X which produces 7695—we'll take 27695—and put 427695 into the machine and see what happens."

McCulloch then put 427695 into the machine and, sure enough, out came 5967—the reverse of 7695.

"Before I show you the next rule," said McCulloch, "let me show you some of the things that can be done with this rule—together, of course, with Rules 1 and 2."

1

"You recall," said McCulloch, "that the number 323 produces itself. Also, with my old machine—which didn't have Rule 3 built into it, only Rules 1 and 2—the number 323 was the *only* number that produced itself. With my present machine, the situation is different. Can you find another number that produces itself? Also, how many such numbers are there?"

It didn't take Craig too long to solve this. Can you do it? (The answer, in Craig's own words, is given in the solutions.)

2

"That was excellent," said McCulloch, after Craig had completed his exposition. "Let me give you another problem: I call a number *symmetric* if it reads the same both forwards and backwards—that is, if it is equal to its own reverse. Numbers like 58385 or 7447, for example, are symmetric. Numbers that are not symmetric I call *nonsymmetric*—numbers like 46733 or 3251. Now, there obviously is a number that produces its own reverse—namely, 323—because 323 both produces itself and is symmetric. With my first machine, which did not have Rule 3, there was no nonsymmetric number that produced its own reverse. But with Rule 3, there *is* one—in fact, several. Can you find one?"

3

"And then," said McCulloch, "there are numbers that produce the associates of their own reverse. Can you find one?"

"And now," said McCulloch, "here is the second new rule:
"*Rule 4:* If X produces Y, then 5X produces YY.
"I refer to YY as the *repeat* of Y."
McCulloch then gave Craig the following problems.

4

Find a number that produces its own repeat.

5

Find a number that produces the reverse of its own repeat.

6

"That's curious," said McCulloch after Craig had solved Problem 5. "I obtained a different solution—also one with seven digits."
There are indeed two seven-digit numbers each of which produces the reverse of its own repeat. Can you find the second of these?

7

"For any number X," said McCulloch, "52X obviously produces the repeat of X. Can you find a number X such that 5X produces the repeat of X?"

Craig thought about this for a bit and suddenly burst out laughing; the solution was so obvious!

8

"And now," said McCulloch, "there is a number that produces the repeat of its associate. Can you find it?"

9

"Also," said McCulloch, "there is a number that produces the associate of its own repeat. Can you find it?"

OPERATION NUMBERS

"You know," said Craig quite suddenly, "I just realized that almost all these problems can be solved by one general principle! Your machine has a very pretty property; once this is realized, it is possible to solve not only the problems you have given me but an infinite host of others!

"For example," continued Craig, "there must be a number that produces the repeat of the reverse of its own associate, and a number that produces the associate of the repeat of its own reverse, and a number that—"

"How extraordinary!" interrupted McCulloch. "I was looking for such numbers but couldn't find them. What are they?"

"You'll be able to find them within seconds, once I tell you this law!"

"What *is* the law?" pleaded McCulloch.

"Indeed," continued Craig, who was greatly enjoying McCulloch's mystification, "I can even give you a number X that produces the repeat of the reverse of the double associate of X, or a number Y that produces the reverse of the double associate of YYYY, or a number Z that—"

"Enough!" cried McCulloch. "Why don't you just tell me what this law is and leave the applications till later?"

"Fair enough!" replied Craig.

At this point, the inspector picked up a pad of paper that was lying on the table, took out a pencil, and sat McCulloch down beside him so that his friend could see what he was writing.

"To begin with," said Craig, "I presume that you are familiar with the notion of an *operation* on numbers; for example, the operation of adding 1 to a number, or multiplying a number by 3, or squaring a number; or, what is more relevant for your machine, taking the *reverse* of a number, or the *repeat* of a number, or the *associate* of a number, or perhaps a more complex operation like taking the reverse of the repeat of the associate of a number. Now, I shall use the letter F to stand for some given arbitrary operation, and for any number X, by F(X)—read 'F of X'—I mean the result of performing the operation F on the number X. This, as of course you know, is standard mathematical practice. So, for example, if F is the reverse operation, F(X) is the reverse of X; if F is the repetition operation, F(X) is the repeat of X, and so forth.

"Now, there are certain numbers—any number, in fact, composed of the digits 3, 4, or 5—which I shall call *operation numbers*, since they determine operations that your machine can perform: Let M be any number composed of the digits 3, 4, or 5, and let F be any operation. I will say that M *determines* the operation F, meaning that for any two numbers X and Y where X produces Y, the number MX must produce F(Y). For example, if X produces Y, then 4X produces the reverse of Y—by Rule 3—and so I say that the number 4 *determines* or *represents* the *reversal* operation; similarly, by Rule 4, the number 5 determines the *repetition* operation. The number 3 determines the *association* operation, that is, the operation of taking the associate of a number. Now, suppose F is the operation which, when applied to any number X, yields the associate of the repeat of X. In other words, F(X) is the associate of the repeat of X. Is there a number M that represents this operation, and if so, what is that number?"

"Obviously 35," answered McCulloch, "because if X produces Y, 5X produces the repeat of Y; hence 35X produces the associate of the repeat of Y. Thus, 35 represents the operation of taking the associate of the repeat of a number."

"Right!" replied Craig. "I have now defined what it means for an operation number M to represent an operation, and this operation I will refer to as *Operation M*. So, for example, Operation 4 is the reversal operation; Operation 5 is the repetition operation; Operation 35 is the operation of taking the associate of the repeat, and so forth. . . .

"Here is a question," he continued. "Is it possible for two different numbers to represent the same operation? That is, can there be operation numbers M and N such that M is different from N, yet operation M is the same as operation N?"

McCulloch thought for a moment. "Oh, of course!" he said. "The numbers 45 and 54 are different, but they determine the same operation, since the reverse of the repeat of a number is the same as the repeat of its reverse."

"Good," replied Craig, "though I was thinking of a different example: To begin with, what operation does 44 represent?"

"Well," said McCulloch, "Operation 44 applied to X gives the reverse of the reverse of X, which is X itself. I don't know what name to give to an operation which, when applied to any number X, simply gives X itself."

"In mathematics, it is commonly called the *identity* operation," remarked Craig, "and so the number 44 determines the identity operation. But so does 4444, or any number composed of an even number of 4's, therefore there are infinitely many different numbers that represent the identity operation. And, more generally, given any operation number M, then M followed or preceded by an even number of 4's (or both) represents the same operation as does M alone."

"I see that," said McCulloch.

"And now," said Craig, "given an operation number M and any number X, I want a convenient notation for the result of applying operation M to the number X; I shall simply write this as 'M(X).' For example, 3(X) is the associate of X; 4(X) is the reverse of X; 5(X) is the repeat of X; 435(X) is the reverse of the associate of the repeat of X. Is this notation clear?"

"Oh, yes," replied McCulloch.

"You won't, I trust, ever confuse the notation M(X) with MX; the former means the result of applying operation M to X; the latter is the number M *followed by* the number X, and these are very different things! For example, 3(5) is not 35, but 525."

"I understand that," said McCulloch, "but can it ever happen—by some sort of coincidence—that M(X) is the same as MX?"

"Good question," replied Craig. "I'll have to think about that!"

"First, let's have another cup of tea," suggested McCulloch.

"Excellent!" replied Craig.

While our two friends are enjoying their tea, I'd like to give you some puzzles about operation numbers; they will afford good practice in the use of the notation M(X), which will play a vital role later on.

10

The answer to McCulloch's last question is yes: There *are* an operation number M and a number X such that M(X) = MX. Can you find them?

11

Is there an operation number M whereby M(M) = M?

12

Find an operation number M and a number X whereby M(X) = XXX.

13

Find an operation number M and a number X whereby M(X) = M + 2.

14

Find M and X such that M(X) is the repeat of MX.

15

Find operation numbers M and N such that M(N) is the repeat of N(M).

16

Find two *distinct* operation numbers M and N such that M(N) = N(M).

17

Can you find two operation numbers M and N such that M(N) = N(M) + 39?

18

What about two operation numbers M and N such that M(N) = N(M) + 492?

19

Find two *distinct* operation numbers M and N such that M(N) = MM and N(M) = NN.

CRAIG'S LAW

"You still haven't told me the principle you claim you have discovered," said McCulloch, after they had finished their tea. "I presume that your talk of operation numbers and operations is leading up to this?"

"Oh, yes," replied Craig, "and I think you are now ready to grasp this law. Do you recall some of the earlier problems you gave me? For example, finding a number X that produced its own repeat. In other words, we wanted a number X that produces 5(X). Or, in finding a number X that produced its own associate, we wanted an X that produces 3(X). Or, again, a number X that produces the reverse of X is a number that produces 4(X). But all these are special cases of one general principle—namely, that for *any* operation number M, there must be an X that produces M(X)! In other words, given any operation F that your machine can perform—that is, any operation F which is determined by some operation number M—there must be an X that produces F(X).

"Moreover," continued Craig, "given an operation number M, we can find an X that produces M(X) by a very simple recipe. Once you know this general recipe, then, for example, you can find an X that produces 543(X), which solves the problem of finding an X that produces the repeat of the reverse of the associate of X, and also you can find an X that produces 354(X), which solves the other problem of finding a number that produces the associate of the repeat of its own reverse. Or, as I told you, I can find a number X that produces the repeat of the reverse of the double associate of X— in other words, an X which produces 5433(X). Without the recipe I have in mind, such problems can be exceedingly difficult, but with it they are child's play!"

"I am all ears," said McCulloch. "What is this remarkable recipe?"

"I am about to tell you," said Craig, "but first let's get one elementary fact absolutely straight—namely, that for any operation number M and for any numbers Y and Z, if Y produces Z, then MY produces M(Z). For example, if Y produces Z, then 3Y produces 3(Z)—the associate of Z; 4Y produces 4(Z); 5Y produces 5(Z); 34Y produces 34(Z). And likewise for *any* operation number M, if Y produces Z, MY produces M(Z). In particular, since 2Z is an example of some Y that produces Z, then it is always the case that M2Z produces M(Z). (For example, 32Z produces 3(Z)—the associate of Z; 42Z produces 4(Z)—and for any operation number M, M2Z produces M(Z).) Indeed, we could have defined M(Z) as the number produced by M2Z."

"I understand all that," said McCulloch.

"Well," replied Craig, "this fact is very easy to forget, so let me repeat it, and let us carefully make a note of it and remember it well!

Fact 1: For any operation number M and any numbers Y and Z, if Y produces Z, then MY produces M(Z). (In particular, M2Z produces M(Z).)

"From this fact," Craig went on, "together with a fact which you discovered about your first machine and which also holds for your present machine, it easily follows that, given any operation number M, there must be some number X that produces M(X)—X produces the result of applying operation M to X. And, given M, such an X can be found by a simple general recipe."

20

Craig has discovered a basic principle that will henceforth be called *Craig's Law*—namely, that for any operation number M, there must be some number X that produces M(X). How do you prove Craig's Law and, given an M, how do you find such an X? For example, what X produces 543 (X)? Or, what X produces the repeat of the reverse of the associate of X? And what X produces the associate of the repeat of the reverse of X—that is, what X produces 354(X)?

"I have a few more problems I'd like you to see," said McCulloch, "but it's getting quite late. Why don't you stay the night? I can show you the problems tomorrow."

It happened that Craig was on vacation at the time, so he gladly accepted McCulloch's invitation.

SOME VARIANTS OF CRAIG'S LAW

Next morning, after a hearty breakfast (McCulloch was an excellent host!), McCulloch gave Craig the following problems:

21

Find a number X that produces 7X7X.

22

Find a number X that produces the reverse of 9X.

23

Find a number X that produces the associate of 89X.

"Very clever!" exclaimed Craig, after he had solved these problems. "None of these three problems can be solved by the law I gave you yesterday."

"That's right!" laughed McCulloch.

"And yet," said Craig, "all three can be solved by a common principle: In the first place, the particular numbers 7, 5, and 89 are quite arbitrary; given *any* number A, there is an X that produces the repeat of AX, and there is an X that produces the reverse of AX, and there is an X that produces the associate of AX. There is also an X that produces the repeat of the reverse of AX, or the reverse of the associate of AX—indeed, given *any* operation number M, and given any number A, there must be an X that produces M(AX)—that is, the number obtained by applying operation M to the number AX."

24

Craig, of course, was right: given any operation number M and any number A, there must be an X that produces M(AX). Let us call this principle *Craig's Second Law*. How do you prove this law, and, given an operation number M and a number A, how, explicitly, do you find an X that produces M(AX)?

25

"I just thought of another question," said McCulloch. "For any number X, let $\overleftarrow{X}$ represent the reverse of X. Can you find a number X that produces $\overleftarrow{X}$67? (That is, is there an X that produces the reverse of X followed by 67?) In general, is it true that for any number A there is an X that produces $\overleftarrow{X}$A?"

26

"Another question has occurred to me," said McCulloch. "Is there a number X that produces the *repeat* of $\overleftarrow{X}$67? More generally, is it true that for any A there is some X that produces the repeat of $\overleftarrow{X}$A? Still more generally, is it true that for any A and any operation number M there must be some X that produces M($\overleftarrow{X}$A)?"

Discussion: Craig's Law holds not only for McCulloch's second machine but also for his first one—and, indeed, for any possible machine that obeys Rules 1 and 2. That is, however we extend McCulloch's first machine by adding new rules, the resulting mechanism is still subject to Craig's Law (in fact, to both of Craig's laws).

Craig's first law is related to a famous result in the theory of computable functions known as the *Recursion Theorem* (or sometimes as the *Fixed-Point Theorem*). McCulloch's Rules 1 and 2 are about the most economical ones I have ever seen achieve this result. They have another surprising property (related to another famous result in the theory of computable functions known as the *Double Recursion Theorem*), which will be explained in the next chapter. All this is relevant to the subjects of self-reproducing machines and cloning.

◆ SOLUTIONS ◆

1 ◆ "With your present machine, there are *infinitely* many different numbers that will produce themselves," said Craig. "Right!" said McCulloch. "How do you prove this?"

"Well," replied Craig, "let me call a number S an A-number if it has the property that for any numbers X and Y where X produces Y, SX produces the associate of Y. Now, before you added this new rule, 3 was the only A-number. But with your present machine, there are infinitely many A-numbers, and for *any* A-number S, the number S2S *must* produce itself, since S2S produces the associate of S, which is S2S."

"How do you know there is an infinite amount of A-numbers?" asked McCulloch.

"To begin with," replied Craig, "do you grant that for any numbers X and Y, if X produces Y then 44X will also produce Y?"

"Clever observation!" replied McCulloch. "Of course you are right: if X produces Y, then 4X produces the reverse of Y; hence 44X must produce the reverse of the reverse of Y, which is Y itself."

"Good," said Craig, "and so if X produces Y, 44X will also produce Y, and hence 344X will produce the associate of Y. Therefore, 344 is also an A-number. And since 344 is an A-number, then 3442344 must produce itself!"

"Very good!" said McCulloch. "So now we have two numbers—323 and 3442344—which produce themselves. How does this give us an infinite supply of such numbers?"

"Obviously," said Craig, "if S is an A-number, so is S44, because for any numbers X and Y, if X produces Y, then 44X also produces Y, and so S44X produces the associate of Y, since S is an A-number. So 3 is an A-number; hence so is 344; hence also 34444, and, in general, 3 followed by any *even* number of 4's is an A-number. So 323 produces itself; so does 3442344; so does 34444234444, and so forth. And thus we have infinitely many solutions.

"Incidentally," added Craig, "these are not the *only* solutions; the numbers 443 and 44443 are also A-numbers—indeed, any even number of 4's followed by 3 followed by an even number of 4's, such as 4434444 is an A-number, and so for every such number S, S2S produces itself."

2 ♦ 43243 is one solution: Since 243 produces 43, then 3243 produces the associate of 43. Therefore, 43243 must produce the reverse of the associate of 43—in other words, the reverse of 43243 (since 43243 is the associate of 43). So 43243 produces its own reverse.

At this point the reader may well be wondering how the number 43243 was found. Was it by a comparative-lengths argument? No, comparative-lengths arguments are quite unwieldy for proving things about this present machine. The solution was found by Craig's Law, as we shall see later in this chapter.

3 ♦ One solution is 3432343. We leave it to the reader to calculate the number produced by 3432343, and he will see that it is indeed the associate of the reverse of 3432343. (This solution was also found by using Craig's Law.)

4 ♦ 53253 works. (Craig's Law is again responsible for the answer.)

5 ♦ 4532453 is one solution.

6 ♦ 5432543 is another solution.

7 ♦ Obvious, that is, once we know that some number produces itself. If X produces X, then of course 5X produces the repeat of X. So, for example, 5323 produces the repeat of 323.

8 ♦ 5332533 is a solution. (Craig's Law again.)

9 ♦ 3532353 is a solution; it was also found by Craig's Law. (I hope I am working up the reader's appetite to learn Craig's Law!)

10 ♦ 5 (5) = 55. (Because 5 (5) is the repeat of 5.) So we take 5 for M and also 5 for X. (I never said that M and X must be different!)

11 ♦ 4 (4) = 4. (Since 4 (4) is the reverse of 4, which is 4.) And so M = 4 is one solution. (Actually, any string of 4's would work.)

12 ♦ Try M = 3, and X = 2. (3 (2) = 222.)

13 ♦ 4 (6) = 6, and 6 = 4 + 2, so 4 (6) = 4 + 2. So M = 4 and X = 2.

14 ♦ M = 55, X = 55 is a solution.

15 ♦ M = 4, N = 44 is a solution.

16 ♦ M = 5, N = 55 is a solution.

17 ♦ M = 5, N = 4 is a solution.

18 ♦ M = 3, N = 5 is a solution.

19 ♦ M = 54, N = 45 is a solution.

20 ◆ Let M be any operation number. We know (Fact 1) that for any numbers Y and Z, if Y produces Z, then MY produces M(Z). Therefore (taking MY for Z), if Y produces MY, then MY must produce M(MY). Thus, taking X for MY, the number X will produce M(X)! So the problem boils down to finding some Y that produces MY. But this problem was solved in the last chapter (by McCulloch's Law)—namely, take 32M3 for Y! And so for X, we take M32M3, and X will produce M(X).

Let us double-check: Let X = M32M3. Since 2M3 produces M3, then 32M3 produces M32M3 (by Rule 2), and hence M32M3 produces M(M32M3); thus X produces M(X), where X is M32M3.

To consider some applications: To find an X that produces the repeat of X, we take 5 for M, and so the solution (or rather one solution) is 53253. To find an X that produces its own reverse, we take 4 for M, and X is then 43243. To find an X that produces the associate of the reverse of X, we take 34 for M, and one solution is 3432343.

For McCulloch's first problem—finding an X that produces the repeat of the reverse of X's associate—we take 543 for M (5 for repeat, 4 for reverse, and 3 for associate), and the solution is 543325433. (The reader can verify directly that 543325433 produces the repeat of the reverse of the associate of 543325433.) For McCulloch's second problem—finding an X that produces the associate of the repeat of the reverse of X—we take 354 for M and get the solution 354323543.

Craig's Law is really marvelous!

21, 22, 23, 24 ◆ Problems 21, 22, and 23 are all special cases of Problem 24; so let us first do Problem 24.

We are given an operation number M and an arbitrary number A, and we wish to find an X that produces M(AX).

The trick now is to find some Y that does not produce MY but that does produce AMY: Let's take 32AM3 for Y. Since Y produces AMY, then, by Fact 1, MY must produce M(AMY). Thus, with MY taken for X, X produces M(AX). Since we took 32AM3 for Y, our X is then M32AM3. And so M32AM3 is our desired solution.

To apply this to Problem 21, we first notice that 7X7X is simply the repeat of 7X, and so we want an X that produces the repeat of 7X—the repeat of AX, with A being 7. So A is 7, and we obviously take 5 for M (since 5 represents the repetition operation), and so the solution is 532753. (The reader can verify directly that 532753 does indeed produce the repeat of 7532753.) For Problem 22, A is 9, and we take 4 for M, and the solution is 432943. For Problem 23, A is 89, and we take 3 for M, so the solution is 3328933.

$\underleftarrow{25}$ ◆ Yes, for any $\underleftarrow{\text{Number}}$ A there is an X that produces $\overleftarrow{X}A$—namely, $432\overleftarrow{A}43$. (For this particular problem in which A is 67, $\overleftarrow{A}$ is 76, and so the solution is 4327643.)

$\underleftarrow{26}$ ◆ For the most general case, the $\underleftarrow{\text{trick}}$ is to realize that $\overleftarrow{X}A$ is the reverse of $\overleftarrow{A}X$, and so $M(\overleftarrow{X}A) = M4(\overleftarrow{A}X)$. By Craig's $\underleftarrow{\text{Second}}$ Law, an X that produces $M4(\overleftarrow{A}X)$ is $M432\overleftarrow{A}M43$, so this is a solution. In particular, taking 5 for M and 67 for A, an X that produces the repeat of $\overleftarrow{X}67$ is 543276543 (as the reader can verify directly).

◊ 11 ◊

Fergusson's Laws

And now we come to a further interesting development concerning McCulloch's machines. About two weeks after the last episode, McCulloch received the following letter from Craig:

My dear McCulloch:

I am greatly intrigued by your number machines and so is my friend Malcolm Fergusson. Do you by any chance know Fergusson? He is actively engaged in research in pure logic and has himself constructed several logic machines. His interests, however, extend far and wide; for example, he is very interested in that variety of chess problems known as *retrograde analysis*. He also takes a keen interest in pure combinatory problems—the kind your machines so ably provide. I visited him last week and showed him all your problems, and he was most intrigued. I met him again three days later, and he made some remark to the effect that he suspected that both of your machines have some interesting additional properties which even the inventor did not realize! He was a bit vague about all this and said that he wanted more time to think the matter over.

Fergusson is coming to dine with me next Friday evening. Why don't you join us? I'm sure you will have much in common, and it might be very interesting to find out what he has in mind concerning your machines.

Hoping to see you then, I remain

Sincerely yours,

L. Craig

McCulloch promptly replied:

Dear Craig:

No, I have not met Malcolm Fergusson, but I have heard a good deal about him through mutual friends. Wasn't he a student of the eminent logician Gottlob Frege? I understand he is working on some ideas that are basic to the entire foundation of mathematics, and I certainly welcome this opportunity to meet him. Needless to say, I am very curious as to what he has in mind concerning my machines. I thank you for your invitation, which I happily accept.

Sincerely,

N. McCulloch

◊   ◊   ◊

The two guests arrived. After an excellent dinner (prepared by Craig's landlady, Mrs. Hoffman), the mathematical conversation began.

"I understand that you have constructed some logic machines," said McCulloch. "I would like to know more about them. Can you explain them to me?"

"Ah, that's a long story," replied Fergusson, "and I still haven't solved a basic question concerning their operation. Why don't you and Craig visit my workshop sometime? Then I can tell you the whole story. This evening, however, I would prefer to talk about *your* machines. As I told Craig a few days ago, they have certain properties of which I suspect that even you are unaware."

"What are these properties?" asked McCulloch.

1

"Well," replied Fergusson, "let's start with a concrete example employing your second machine: There are numbers X and Y such that X produces the reverse of Y and Y produces the repeat of X. Can you find them?"

Craig and McCulloch were enormously intrigued by this problem, and immediately set to work trying to solve it. Neither one succeeded. The problem is of course solvable, and the ambitious reader might care to try his hand at it. There is a basic underlying principle involved (which will be explained in this chapter), and once the reader knows it, he will be amused at how simple the matter really is.

2

"I am totally mystified," said Craig, after Fergusson showed them the solution. "I see that your solution works, but how did you ever find it? Did you just stumble on these numbers X and Y by accident, or did you have some rational plan for finding them? To me, it seems like a conjuring trick!"

"Yes," said McCulloch, "it's like pulling a rabbit out of a hat!"

"Ah, yes," laughed Fergusson, who was thoroughly enjoying the mystification, "only it seems I pulled *two* rabbits out of a hat, each of which had a curious effect on the other."

"That's certainly true!" replied Craig. "Only I would like to know how you knew which rabbits to pull!"

"Good question, good question!" replied Fergusson, more jubilant than ever. "Here—let's try another: Find two numbers X and Y such that X produces the repeat of Y and Y produces the reverse of the associate of X."

"Oh, no!" cried McCulloch.

"Just a moment," said Craig. "I think I'm beginning to get an idea: Do you mean to tell us, Fergusson, that for any two operations that the machine can perform—given any two operation numbers M and N—there must exist numbers X and Y such that X produces M(Y) and Y produces N(X)?"

"Precisely!" exclaimed Fergusson, "and so, for example, we can find numbers X and Y such that X produces the double associate of Y and Y produces the repeat of the reverse of X—or any other combination you can name."

"Now, that's remarkable!" cried McCulloch. "These last few days I have been trying to construct a machine with just this property; I had no idea that I already had one!"

"You most assuredly do," rejoined Fergusson.

"How do you prove this?" asked McCulloch.

"Well, let me build up to the proof gradually," replied Fergusson. "The heart of the matter really lies in your Rules 1 and 2. So let me first make some observations about your first machine—the one using just those rules. We'll start with a simple problem: Using just Rules 1 and 2, can you find two *distinct* numbers X and Y such that X produces Y and Y produces X?"

Both Craig and McCulloch promptly set to work on this problem.

"Oh, of course!" said Craig, with a chuckle. "It obviously follows from something McCulloch showed me some weeks ago."

Can you find such an X and Y?

3

"And now," said Fergusson, "for any number A, there are numbers X and Y such that X produces Y and Y produces AX. Given an A, can you see how to find such an X and Y? For example, can you find numbers X and Y such that X produces Y and Y produces 7X?"

"Are we still working with just Rules 1 and 2, or can we use Rules 3 and 4?" asked Craig.

"You only need Rules 1 and 2," replied Fergusson.

Craig and McCulloch went to work on the problem.

"I've got a solution!" said Craig.

4

"That's interesting," said McCulloch, after Craig showed his solution. "I found a different solution!"

There is indeed a second solution. Can you find it?

5

"And now," said Fergusson, "we come to a really vital property: From just Rules 1 and 2, it follows that for any two numbers A and B, there exist numbers X and Y such that X produces AY and Y produces BX. For example, there exist numbers X and Y such that X produces 7Y and Y produces 8X. Can you find them?"

6

"It easily follows," said Fergusson, "from the last problem— or perhaps even more simply from Craig's Second Law—that for any operation numbers M and N there must exist X and Y such that X produces M(Y) and Y produces N(X). This holds not only for your present machine but for *any* machine whose rules include at least Rules 1 and 2. With your present machine, for example, there are numbers X and Y such that X produces the reverse of Y and Y produces the associate of X. Can you find them?"

7

"That's extremely interesting," said McCulloch to Fergusson after he and Craig had solved the last problem, "and now the following question occurs to me: Does my machine obey a 'double' analogue of Craig's Second Law? That is, given two operation numbers M and N and two numbers A and B, do there necessarily exist numbers X and Y such that X produces M(AY) and Y produces N(BX)?"

"Oh, yes," replied Fergusson. "For example, there are numbers X and Y such that X produces the repeat of 7Y and Y produces the reverse of 89X."

Can you find such numbers?

8

"I've thought of another question," said Craig. "Given an operation number M and a number B, is there necessarily an X and a Y such that X produces M(Y) and Y produces BX? For example, are there numbers X and Y such that X produces the associate of Y and Y produces 78X?"

Are there?

9

"As a matter of fact," said Fergusson, "many other combinations are possible. Given any operation numbers M and N and any numbers A and B, you can find numbers X and Y that fulfil any of the following conditions:

(a) X produces M(AY) and Y produces N(X).

(b) X produces M(AY) and Y produces BX.

(c) X produces M(Y) and Y produces X.

(d) X produces M(AY) and Y produces X.

How do you prove these facts?"

10 ✦ Triplicates and Beyond

"Well, I imagine we have combed through just about all the possibilities," said Craig.

"Not really," replied Fergusson. "What I have shown you so far is only the beginning. Did you know, for example, that there are numbers X, Y, and Z such that X produces the reverse of Y, Y produces the repeat of Z, and Z produces the associate of X?"

"Oh, no!" exclaimed McCulloch.

"Oh, yes," rejoined Fergusson. "Given any three operation numbers M, N, and P, there must be numbers X, Y, and Z such that X produces M(Y), Y produces N(Z), and Z produces P(X)."

Can the reader see how to prove this? In particular, what numbers X, Y, and Z are such that X produces the reverse of Y, Y produces the repeat of Z, and Z produces the associate of X?

"Of course," said Fergusson, after Craig and McCulloch had solved the problem. "All sorts of variants of this 'triple' law are possible. For example, given any three operation numbers M, N, and P and any three numbers A, B, and C, there are numbers X, Y, and Z such that X produces M(AY), Y produces N(BZ), and Z produces P(CX). This also holds if you leave out any one or two of the numbers A, B, and C. Also, we can find numbers X, Y, and Z such that X produces AY, Y produces M(Z), and Z produces N(BX)—all sorts of variants are possible. But these you can work out at your leisure.

"Also," he continued, "the same idea works with four or more operation numbers. For example, we could find numbers X, Y, Z, and W such that X produces 78Y, Y produces the repeat of Z, Z produces the reverse of W, and W produces the associate of 62X. The possibilities are really endless. It all stems from the surprising power inherent in Rules 1 and 2."

◆ SOLUTIONS ◆

1 ◆ One solution is to take X = 4325243, Y = 524325243. Since 25243 produces 5243, then 325243 produces the associ-

ate of 5243, which is 524325243, which is Y. Since 325243 produces Y, then 4325243 produces the reverse of Y, but 4325243 is X. Thus X produces the reverse of Y. Also, Y obviously produces the repeat of X (because Y is 52X, and since 2X produces X, 52X produces the repeat of X). Thus X produces the reverse of Y and Y produces the repeat of X.

2 ◆ Craig recalled McCulloch's Law: that for any number A there is some number X (namely, 32A3) that produces AX. In particular, if we take 2 for A, there is a number X (namely, 3223) that produces 2X. And, of course, 2X in turn produces X. So 3223 and 23223 are one pair of numbers that works; 3223 produces 23223 and 23223 produces 3223.

3 ◆ Craig solved the problem in the following manner: He reasoned that all that was necessary was to find some X that produces 27X. Then, if we let Y = 27X, X produces Y and Y produces 7X. Also, he found that there *is* an X that produces 27X—namely, 32273. And so Craig's solution was X = 32273; Y = 2732273.

Of course, this works not only for the particular number 7 but for any number A: If we let X = 322A3 and Y = 2A322A3, X produces Y and Y produces AX.

4 ◆ McCulloch, on the other hand, went about the problem in the following way: He reasoned that all that was necessary was to find some Y that produces 72Y. Then, if we let X be 2Y, X produces Y and Y produces 7X. We know how to find such a Y: Take Y = 32723. So McCulloch's solution was X = 232723; Y = 32723.

5 ◆ All that is necessary is to find an X that produces A2BX. Then, if we let Y = 2BX, X produces AY and Y produces BX.

An X that produces A2BX is 32A2B3. And so a solution is X = 32A2B3, Y = 2B32A2B3. (For the special case A = 7, B = 8, the solution is X = 327283, Y = 28327283.)

6 ✦ Let us first solve this problem using Craig's Second Law, which, we recall, says that for any operation number M and any number A, there is a number X (namely, M32AM3) that produces M(AX). Now, take any two operation numbers M and N. Then by Craig's Second Law (taking N2 for A), there is a number X (namely, M32N2M3) that produces M(N2X). And, of course, N2X produces N(X). So, if we let Y be N2X, X produces M(Y) and Y produces N(X). Thus, a solution is X = M32N2M3 and Y = N2M32N2M3. (For the particular problem suggested by Fergusson, we take 4 for M and 3 for N, and the solution is X = 4323243, Y = 324323243. The reader can check directly that X produces the reverse of Y and Y produces the associate of X—the second half is particularly obvious).

We could have also gone about the problem in the following way: By the solution to Problem 5, we know that there are numbers Z and W such that Z produces NW and W produces MZ (namely, Z = 32N2M3, W = 2M32N2M3). Then, by Fact 1 of the last chapter, MZ produces M(NW) and NW produces N(MZ); so if we let X be MZ and Y be NW, X produces M(Y) and Y produces N(X). We thus get the solution X = M32N2M3, Y = N2M32N2M3.

7 ✦ We now need an X that produces M(AN2BX); such an X is M32AN2BM3, by Craig's Second Law. Then take N2BX for Y. Then X produces M(AY), and Y (which is N2BX) obviously produces N(BX). So the general solution (or at least one such) is X = M32AN2BM3, Y = N2BM32AN2BM3. For the specific problem given here, we obviously take 5 for M, 4 for N, 7 for A, 89 for B.

8 ◆ By Craig's Second Law, there is an X that produces M(2BX)—namely, X = M322BM3. Then let Y = 2BX. So X produces M(Y) and Y produces BX. For the specific problem here, we take 3 for M and 78 for B, getting the solution X = 33227833, Y = 27833227833.

9 ◆ (a) Take an X that produces M(AN2X) and take Y to be N2X. (We can take X to be M32AN23; Y = N2M32AN23.) Then X produces M(AY) and Y produces N(X).

(b) Now take an X that produces M(A2BX) and take Y to be 2BX. (So now a solution is X = M32A2B3; Y = 2BM32A2B3.)

(c) If X produces M(Y), and Y = 2X, we have a solution, so take X = M322M3; Y = 2M322M3.

(d) If X produces M(AY) and Y = 2X, we have a solution, so take X = M32A2M3 and Y = 2M32A2M3.

10 ◆ By Craig's Second Law, there is an X that produces M(N2P2X)—namely, X = M32N2P2M3. Let Y = N2P2X, so X produces M(Y). Let Z = P2X, so Y = N2Z; hence Y produces N(Z). And Z produces P(X).

And so the solution is explicitly X = M32N2P2M3, Y = N2P2M32N2P2M3, Z = P2M32N2P2M3.

For the particular problem, the solution is X = 432523243, Y = 52324232523243 and Z = 32432523243.

The reader can directly compute that X produces the reverse of Y, Y produces the repeat of Z, and Z produces the associate of X.

Incidentally, given any three numbers A, B, and C, we can find numbers U, V, and W such that U produces AV, V produces BW, and W produces CU: Just take a U that produces A2B2CU (if we use the recipe of Craig's Second Law, U = 32A2B2C3). Then let V = 2B2CU and W = 2CU. Then U produces AV, V produces BW, and W produces CU. If now

A, B, and C are operation numbers, take X = AV, Y = BW, and Z = CU, and X produces A(Y), Y produces B(Z), and Z produces C(X), and so we have an alternative method of solving the problem.

◆ 12 ◆

Interlude:
Let's Generalize!

Two days after the last episode, Craig was suddenly and quite unexpectedly sent by Scotland Yard over to Norway on a case which, though interesting, need not concern us. While he is gone, I will take the opportunity to offer you something of my own thoughts about McCulloch's number machines. The reader who is very anxious to find the solution to the Monte Carlo lock puzzle may defer this chapter till later if he wishes.

Mathematicians are very fond of generalizing! It is typical for one mathematician X to prove a theorem, and six months after the theorem is published, for mathematician Y to come along and say to himself, "Aha, a very nice theorem X has proved, but *I* can prove something even more general!" So he publishes a paper titled "A Generalization of X's Theorem." Or Y might perhaps be a little more foxy and do the following: he first *privately* generalizes X's theorem, and then he obtains a special case of his own generalization, and this special case *appears* so different from X's original theorem that Y is able to publish it as a new theorem. Then, of course, another mathematician, Z, comes along who is haunted by the feeling that *somewhere* there lies *something* of an important nature common to both X's theorem and Y's theorem, and after much labor, he finds a common principle. Z then publishes a paper in which he states and proves this new general principle, and adds: "Both X's theorem and Y's theorem can be obtained as special cases of my theorem by the following arguments. . . ."

Well, I am no exception, and so I wish first to point out some features of McCulloch's machines that I doubt either McCulloch, Craig, or Fergusson realized, and then I would like to make a few generalizations.

The first thing that struck me when I reviewed the discussion of McCulloch's second machine was that once Rule 4 (the repetition rule) is introduced, we no longer need Rule 2 (the associate rule) to obtain laws like Craig's and Fergusson's! Indeed, consider a machine which uses only Rules 1 and 4: For such a machine we can find a number X that produces itself; we can find one that produces its own repeat; given any A, we can find a number X that produces AX; we can find an X that produces the repeat of AX or the repeat of the repeat of AX. Also, still supposing Rule 2 has been deleted from McCulloch's machine, we can find an X that produces its own reverse or an X that produces the repeat of its reverse or an X that produces the reverse of AX or an X that produces the repeat of the reverse of AX. Also, suppose we consider a machine that obeys McCulloch's Rules 1, 2, and 4 (leaving out Rule 3, the reversal rule). There are now two different ways to construct a number that produces its own associate; there are two ways to construct a number that produces its own repeat; two ways to construct a number that produces the associate of its repeat or the repeat of its associate.

Finally, given *any* machine satisfying at least Rule 1 and

Rule 4, Craig's laws and Fergusson's laws all hold. And so we could have given alternative solutions to most of the problems of the last two chapters, using Rule 4 instead of Rule 2. (Can the reader see how all this can be done? If not, it will all be explained below.)

I could say much more, but to make a long business short, I will summarize my main observations in the form of three facts:

Fact 1: Just as any machine obeying Rules 1 and 2 also obeys McCulloch's Law (that for any A there is some X which produces AX), so does any machine obeying Rules 1 and 4.

Fact 2: Any machine obeying McCulloch's Law also obeys Craig's two laws.

Fact 3: Any machine obeying *both* Craig's Second Law *and* Rule 1 must also obey all of Fergusson's laws.

Can the reader see how to prove all this?

◆ SOLUTIONS ◆

Let us first consider any machine obeying Rules 1 and 4: For any X, 52X produces XX; hence if we take 52 for X, we see that 5252 produces 5252. So we have a number that produces itself. Also, 552552 produces its own repeat. Also, for any A, to find an X that produces AX, take X to be 52A52 (it produces the repeat of A52, which is A52A52, which is AX). This proves Fact 1. (If we want an X that produces the repeat of AX, take 552A552 for X.)

Now, let us consider a machine obeying McCulloch's Rules 1, 3, and 4. A number that produces its own reverse is 452452 (it produces the reverse of the repeat of 452; in other words, the reverse of 452452). (Compare this with the former solution 43243.) A number that produces the repeat of its own reverse is 54525452. (Compare with the former solution 5432543.)

Now, consider a machine obeying Rules 1, 2, and 4. We know that 33233 produces its own associate, but so does 352352. As for an X that produces its own repeat, we already have the two solutions 35235 and 552552. As for an X that produces the associate of its repeat, one solution is 3532353; another is 35523552. As for a number that produces the repeat of its associate, one solution is 5332533, and another is 53525352.

Now, consider an arbitrary machine obeying at least Rule 1 and Rule 4 of McCulloch's machines. Given an operation number M, an X that produces M(X) is M52M52. (Compare this with the former solution M32M3, using Rule 2 instead of Rule 4.) And given an operation number M and a number A, an X that produces M(AX) is M52AM52. (Compare this with the former solution M32AM3.) This shows that from Rules 1 and 4 we can get both of Craig's laws. However, I have stated (Fact 2) the more general proposition that McCulloch's Law alone is enough to yield Craig's laws; this can be proved in the manner of Chapter 10—namely, given an operation number M, there is some Y that produces MY, and hence MY produces M(MY); hence X produces M(X), where X = MY. And for any A, if there is some Y that produes AMY, then MY produces M(AMY), and so X produces M(AX) for X = MY.

As for Fact 3, it can be proved just as in the last chapter. (For example, given operation numbers M and N, if Craig's Second Law holds, there is some X that produces M(N2X), and if we take N2X for Y, X produces M(Y) and Y produces N(X).)

◇ 13 ◇

The Key

Craig's affair in Norway took less time than expected, and he returned home exactly three weeks from the day he departed. When he got to his house, he found a note from McCulloch:

Dear Craig:

If, by any chance, you get back by Friday, May 12, I would very much like to have you come for dinner. I have invited Fergusson.

Best regards,

Norman McCulloch

"Excellent!" said Craig to himself. "I returned just in time!"

When Craig arrived at McCulloch's, Fergusson had already been there some fifteen minutes.

"Well, well, welcome back!" said McCulloch.

"While you were gone," said Fergusson, "McCulloch invented a new number machine!"

"Oh?" replied Craig.

"I didn't invent it all by myself," said McCulloch. "Fergusson was partly responsible. But this machine is extremely interesting; it has the following four rules:

M-I: For any number X, 2X2 produces X.

M-II: If X produces Y, then 6X produces 2Y.

M-III: If X produces Y, then 4X produces Y̅ (as with the last machine).

M-IV: If X produces Y, then 5X produces YY (as with the last machine).

"This machine," said McCulloch, "has all the pretty properties of my last machine—it obeys your two laws and also Fergusson's double analogues."

Craig studied these rules for a while with unusual intensity.

"I can't even get off the ground," he said at last. "I can't even find a number that produces itself. Are there any?"

"Oh, yes," replied McCulloch. "Though they're much more difficult to find than they were with my last machine. In fact, I couldn't solve this problem, although Fergusson did. The shortest number we found that produces itself has ten digits."

Craig again became absorbed in thought. "Surely, the first two rules are not sufficient to yield such a number, are they?"

"Certainly not!" replied McCulloch. "One needs all four rules to get such a number."

"Remarkable!" said Craig, who then went off once more into a deep study.

"Good gracious!" he suddenly exclaimed, virtually leaping out of his chair. "Why, this solves the lock puzzle!"

"What ever are you talking about?" asked Fergusson.

"Oh, I'm sorry!" said Craig, who then told them of the entire Monte Carlo affair.

"I trust you will keep this confidential," concluded Craig, "and now, McCulloch, if you will show me a number that produces itself, I can then immediately find a combination that will open the lock."

So there are three puzzles for the reader:

(1) What number X produces itself in this latest machine?

(2) What combination will open the lock?

(3) How are the first two questions related?

EPILOGUE

Early the next morning, Craig dispatched a trusted messenger to deliver the combination to Martinez in Monte Carlo. The messenger arrived in time, and the safe was opened without incident.

True to Martinez's word, the board of directors sent Craig a handsome reward, which Craig insisted on sharing with McCulloch and Fergusson. To celebrate, the three friends spent a delightful evening at the Lion's Inn.

"Ah, yes," said Craig, after a glass of fine sherry, "this has been as interesting a case as has ever come my way! And isn't it remarkable that these number machines—invented purely out of intellectual curiosity—should have turned out to have such an unexpected practical application?"

♦ SOLUTIONS ♦

Let me first say a little more about the Monte Carlo lock puzzle.

In Farkus's last condition, nothing was said that required y to be a different combination from x. And so, taking x and y

to be the same, the condition reads: "If x is specially related to x, then if x jams the lock, x is neutral, and if x is neutral, then x jams the lock." Now, it is impossible that x can both jam the lock and be neutral; hence if x is specially related to x, then x can neither jam the lock nor be neutral; hence it must open the lock! So, if we can find a combination x that is specially related to itself, then such an x will open the lock.

Craig, of course, realized this before he came back to London. But how do you find a combination x that is specially related to itself? This is the problem Craig could not solve before he had the good fortune of seeing McCulloch's third machine.

As it turns out, the problem of finding a combination that, on the basis of Farkus's conditions, can be shown to be specially related to itself, is virtually identical with the problem of finding a number that produces itself in McCulloch's latest machine. The only essential difference is that the combinations are strings of letters, whereas the number machines work with strings of digits, but we can easily transform either problem into the other by the following simple device:

To begin with, the only combinations we need consider are those using the letters Q,L,V,R (these are obviously the only letters that play a significant role). Now suppose, instead of using these letters, we had used the respective digits 2,6,4,5 (that is, 2 for Q, 6 for L, 4 for V, 5 for R). To make this easier to remember:

$$\begin{array}{cccc} Q & L & V & R \\ 2 & 6 & 4 & 5 \end{array}$$

Now, let us see what Farkus's first four conditions look like when written in number notation rather than letter notation. (1) For any number X, 2X2 is specially related to X.

(2) If X is specially related to Y, then 6X is specially related to 2Y.

(3) If $\overleftarrow{X}$ is specially related to Y, then 4X is specially related to $\overleftarrow{Y}$.

(4) If X is specially related to Y, then 5X is specially related to YY.

We at once see that these are exactly the conditions of the present number machine, except that the phrase *specially related to* is used instead of *produces*. (I could have used the term *produces* instead of *specially related to* when I presented the conditions in Chapter 8, but I did not want to give the reader too much of a hint!) And so we see how either problem can be transformed into the other.

Let me state this again, and this time more precisely: For any combination x of the letters Q,L,V,R let $\bar{x}$ be the number obtained by replacing Q by 2, L by 6, V by 4, and R by 3. For example, if x is the combination VQRLQ, then $\bar{x}$ is the number 42562. Let us call $\bar{x}$ the *code number* of x. (Incidentally, the idea of assigning numbers to expressions originated with the logician Kurt Gödel and is technically known as *Gödel numbering*. It is of great importance, as we will see in Part IV.)

Now we can precisely state the main point of the last paragraph thus: For any combination x and y of the four letters Q,L,V,R, if $\bar{x}$ can be shown to produce $\bar{y}$ on the basis of conditions M-I through M-IV of McCulloch's latest machine, then x can be shown to be specially related to y on the basis of Farkus's first four conditions—and conversely.

So, if we can find a number that must produce itself in the newest number machine, then it must be the code number of a combination that is specially related to itself, and this combination will open the lock.

Now, how do we find a number N that produces itself in

this present machine? We first look for a number H such that for any numbers X and Y, if X produces Y, then HX produces Y2Y2. If we can find such an H, then for any number Y, H2Y2 will produce Y2Y2 (because 2Y2 produces Y, by M-I), and hence H2H2 will produce H2H2, and we will have found our desired N. But how do we find such an H?

The problem boils down to this: Starting with a given number Y, how can we wind up with Y2Y2 by successively applying operations that the present machine can perform? Well, we can get Y2Y2 from Y this way: First reverse Y, getting $\overleftarrow{Y}$; then put 2 to the left of $\overleftarrow{Y}$; getting $2\overleftarrow{Y}$; then reverse $2\overleftarrow{Y}$, getting Y2; then repeat Y2, getting Y2Y2. These operations are respectively represented by the operation numbers 4, 6, 4, and 5, and so we take H to be 5464.

Let us check that this H really works: Suppose X produces Y; we are to check that 5464X produces Y2Y2. Well, since X produces Y, 4X produces $\overleftarrow{Y}$ (by M-III); hence 64X produces $2\overleftarrow{Y}$ (by M-II); hence 464X produces Y2 (by M-III); hence 5464X produces Y2Y2 (by M-IV). So if X produces Y, then HX does indeed produce Y2Y2.

Now that we have found our H, we accordingly take N to be H2H2, so the number 5464254642 produces itself (as the reader can verify directly).

Now that we know that 5464254642 produces itself, we know that it must be the code number of a combination that opens the lock. This combination is RVLVQRVLVQ.

Of course, the Monte Carlo lock problem can be solved directly, rather than by translating it into a number-machine problem, but I did the latter because, for one thing, it happened historically that this is the way Craig found the solution. For another thing, I felt it would be of interest for the reader to see an example of how two mathematical problems can have different contents but the same abstract form.

To verify directly that RVLVQRVLVQ is specially related to itself (and hence opens the lock), we reason as follows: QRVLVQ is specially related to RVLV (by Property Q); hence VQRVLVQ is specially related to the reverse of RVLV (by Property V), which is VLVR. Therefore, LVQRVLVQ is specially related to QVLVR (by Property L), and hence VLVQRVLVQ is specially related to the reverse of QVLVR, which is RVLVQ. Hence (by Property R), RVLVQRVLVQ is specially related to the repeat of RVLVQ, which is RVLVQRVLVQ. And so RVLVQRVLVQ is specially related to itself.

◆◆◆

PART FOUR

SOLVABLE OR UNSOLVABLE?

◆ 14 ◆

Fergusson's Logic Machine

Some months after the celebrated solution of the Monte Carlo lock mystery, Craig and McCulloch paid a visit to Fergusson to learn about his logic machine. It did not take long for the conversation to turn to the nature of provability.

"I must tell you an interesting and revealing incident," said Fergusson. "A student was asked on a geometry examination to prove the Pythagorean theorem. He handed in his paper, and the Mathematics-Master returned it with a grade of zero and the comment, 'This is no proof!' Later, the lad went to the Mathematics-Master and said, 'Sir, how can you say that what I handed you is not a proof? You have never once in this course defined what a proof is! You have been admirably precise in your definitions of such things as triangles, squares, circles, parallelity, perpendicularity, and other geometric notions, but never once have you defined exactly what you mean by the word 'proof.' How, then, can you so assuredly assert that what I have handed you is not a proof? How would you *prove* that it is not a proof?' "

"Brilliant!" exclaimed Craig, clapping his hands. "That boy will go far. How did the Master respond?"

"Oh," replied Fergusson, "unfortunately the Master was a dry pedantic sort with no sense of humor and no imagination.

He took off additional marks on the grounds that the boy was being impertinent."

"How unfortunate!" exclaimed Craig in indignation. "Had I been the Master, I would have given the boy highest honors for such a keen observation!"

"Of course," replied Fergusson. "So would I. But you know how it is with unfortunately too many teachers; they have no creative ability of their own and feel threatened by students who can think for themselves."

"I must admit," said McCulloch, "that if I had been in the Master's place, I also could not have answered the boy's question. Of course, I would have complimented him for raising the question, but I don't see how I could have answered it. Just what is a proof, anyhow? I somehow seem to recognize a correct proof when I see one, and I can usually spot an invalid argument when I come across one; still, if asked for a *definition* of a proof, I would be sorely pressed!"

"That's the situation with almost all working mathematicians," replied Fergusson. "More than ninety-nine percent of them can recognize a correct proof or spot an invalidity in an incorrect proof, even though they cannot define what they mean by a proof. One task we logicians are interested in is that of analyzing the notion of 'proof'—to make it as rigorous as any other notion in mathematics."

"If most mathematicians already know what a proof is, even though they can't define one," said Craig, "why is it so important that the notion be defined?"

"There are several reasons," replied Fergusson. "Although even if there were none, I would like to know the definition for its own sake. It has frequently happened in the history of mathematics that certain basic notions—for example, continuity—were intuitively apprehended long before they were rigorously defined. Once defined, however, the notion acquires a new dimension; facts about it can be established that would be exceedingly difficult, if not impossible, to discover without a firm criterion of when the notion does or does not apply. The notion of 'proof' is no exception; it has sometimes happened that a proof utilizes a new principle—such as the Axiom of Choice—and that controversies arise as to whether the principle is legitimate. A precise definition of 'proof' pinpoints just what mathematical principles are or are not being used.

"For another thing, it becomes particularly critical to have a precise notion of 'proof' when one wishes to establish that a given mathematical statement is *not* provable from a given set of axioms. The situation is analogous to ruler-and-compass constructions in Euclidean geometry: to show that a certain construction, such as trisecting an angle, squaring a circle, or constructing a cube with twice the volume of a given cube, is *not* possible involves a more critical characterization of the notion of 'construction' than does a positive result in the form that such-and-such a construction *is* possible with ruler and compass. And so it is with provability: to show that a given statement is *not* provable from a given set of axioms requires a more critical characterization of the notion of *proof* than a positive result in the form that a given statement *is* provable from the axiom."

A GÖDELIAN PUZZLE

"Now," continued Fergusson, "given an axiom system, a proof in the system consists of a finite sequence of sentences constructed according to very precise rules. It is a simple

matter to decide purely mechanically whether a given sequence of sentences is or is not a proof in the system; indeed,
it is a simple matter to construct a machine that does this. It
is an altogether different matter to construct a machine that
will decide which sentences of an axiom system are provable
and which ones are not. Whether or not this can be done
may, I suspect, depend on the axiom system. . . .

"My current interest is in mechanical theorem-proving—
that is, in machines that prove various mathematical truths.
Here is my latest one," Fergusson said, pointing proudly to
an extremely odd-looking contraption.

Craig and McCulloch stood several minutes before the
machine trying to figure out its functions.

"Just what does it do?" Craig finally asked.

"It proves various facts about the positive whole numbers," replied Fergusson. "I am working in a language that
contains names of various sets of numbers—specifically, positive integers. There are infinitely many sets of numbers
nameable in this language. For example, we have a name for
the set of even numbers, one for the set of odd numbers, one
for the set of prime numbers, one for the set of all numbers
divisible by 3—just about every set that number-theorists are
interested in has a name in the language. Now, although
there are infinitely many nameable sets, there are no more
nameable sets than there are positive integers. And to each
positive integer n is associated a certain nameable set A_n. We
can thus think of all the nameable sets arranged in an infinite
sequence $A_1, A_2, \ldots, A_n. \ldots$ (If you like, you can think of a
book with infinitely many pages, and for each positive integer n, the nth page contains a description of a set of positive integers. Then think of the set A_n as the set described on
page n of the book.)

"I employ the mathematical symbol 'ϵ,' which represents the English phrase 'belongs to' or 'is a member of,' and for every number x and every number y, we have the sentence $x \in A_y$, which is read 'x belongs to the set A_y.' This is the only type of sentence my machine investigates; the function of the machine is to try and discover what numbers belong to what nameable sets.

"Now, each sentence $x \in A_y$ has a *code* number—namely, a number which, when written in the usual base 10 notation, consists of a string of 1's of length x followed by a string of 0's of length y. For example, the code number of the sentence $3 \in A_2$ is 11100; the code number of $1 \in A_5$ is 100000. For any x and y, by $x*y$ I mean the code number of the sentence $x \in A_y$; thus, $x*y$ consists of a string of 1's of length x followed by a string of 0's of length y.

"The machine operates in the following manner," continued Fergusson. "Whenever it discovers that a number x belongs to a set A_y, it then prints out the number $x*y$—the code number of the sentence $x \in A_y$. If the machine prints $x*y$, then I say that the machine has *proved* the sentence $x \in A_y$. And I say that the sentence $x \in A_y$ is *provable* (by the machine) if the machine is capable of printing out the number $x*y$.

"Now, I know that my machine is always accurate in the sense that every sentence provable by the machine is true."

"Just a moment," interrupted Craig, "what do you mean by *true*? How does *true* differ from *provable*?"

"Oh," replied Fergusson, "the two concepts are entirely different: I call a sentence $x \in A_y$ *true* if x is really a member of the set A_y. That is entirely different from saying that the machine is capable of printing out the number $x*y$. If the latter holds, then I say that the sentence $x \in A_y$ is *provable*—that is, by the machine."

"Oh, now I understand," said Craig. "In other words, when

you say that your machine is accurate—that every sentence provable by the machine is a true sentence—what you mean. is that the machine never prints out a number $x*y$ unless x is really a member of the set A_y. Is that correct?"

"Exactly!" replied Fergusson.

"Tell me," said Craig, "how do you know that your machine is always accurate?"

"To answer that," replied Fergusson, "I must tell you all the details of the machine. The machine operates on the basis of certain axioms about the positive integer; these axioms have been programmed into the machine in the form of certain instructions. The axioms are all well-known mathematical truths. The machine cannot prove any statement that is not a logical consequence of the axioms. Since the axioms are all true, and any logical consequence of true statements must be true, then the machine is incapable of proving a false sentence. I can tell you the axioms if you like, and then you can see for yourselves that the machine can prove only true sentences."

"Before you do that," said McCulloch, "I would like to ask another question. Suppose I am willing temporarily to take your word that every sentence provable by the machine is true. What about the converse? Is every true sentence of the form $x \in A_y$ provable by the machine? In other words, is the machine capable of proving *all* true sentences of the form $x \in A_y$, or only some?"

"A most important question," replied Fergusson, "but, alas, I don't know the answer! That is precisely the basic problem I have been unable to solve! I have been working on it on and off for months but have gotten nowhere. I know for sure that the machine can prove every statement $x \in A_y$ that is a logical consequence of the axioms, but I don't know whether I have programmed in enough axioms. The axioms in question represent just about the sum total of what mathematicians know about the system of positive integers; still, there may not be enough to settle completely which numbers x belong to which nameable sets A_y. So far, every sentence $x \in A_y$ that I have examined and found to be true on purely mathematical grounds I have found to be a logical consequence of the axioms, and so the machine is capable of proving it. But just because I have not yet been able to find a true sentence that the machine cannot prove doesn't mean that there isn't one; it might be that I just haven't found it. Or, then again, it may be that the machine *can* prove all true sentences; but I have not yet been able to prove this fact. I just don't know!"

To make a long story short, at this point Fergusson told Craig and McCulloch all the axioms used by the machine, as well as the purely logical rules that enabled it to prove new sentences from old ones. Once Craig and McCulloch knew these details of the machine's operation, they could see immediately that it was indeed accurate—that it did prove only true sentences. But this still left unsolved the problem of whether the machine could prove all true sentences or only some. The three met together several times during the next few months and slowly but surely closed in on the problem, until they finally solved it.

I will not burden the reader with all the details, but will mention only those that are relevant to the solution of the problem. The turning point in the investigation came when the three men worked out three key properties of the machine; these properties sufficed to settle the question. It was, I believe, Craig and McCulloch who first brought the three properties to light, but it was Fergusson who applied the finishing touches. I will tell you what these properties are in a moment; but first, a little preliminary notation.

For any set A of positive integers, by its *complement* Ā is meant the set of all positive integers that are not in A. (For example, if A is the set of even numbers, then its complement Ā is the set of odd numbers; if A is the set of numbers divisible by 5, then its complement Ā is the set of numbers that are not divisible by 5.)

For any set A of positive integers, by A* we shall mean the set of all positive integers x such that $x*x$ is a member of A. Thus, for any number x, to say that x lies in A* is equivalent to saying that $x*x$ lies in A.

Now, here are the three key properties that Craig and McCulloch discovered about the machine:

Property 1: The set A_8 is the set of all numbers that the machine is capable of printing.

Property 2: For each positive integer n, $A_{3\cdot n}$ is the complement of A_n. (By 3·n we mean 3 times n.)

Property 3: For every positive integer n, the set $A_{3\cdot n+1}$ is the set A_n* (the set of all numbers x such that $x*x$ belong to A_n).

1

From Properties 1, 2, and 3, it can be rigorously deduced that Fergusson's machine is *not* able to prove all true sentences! The problem for the reader is to find a sentence that is true but not provable by the machine. That is, we are to find numbers n and m (either the same or different) such that n is in fact a member of the set A_m, yet the code number $n*m$ of the sentence $n \in A_m$ cannot possibly be printed by the machine.

2

In the solution given for Problem 1, the numbers n and m were both less than 100. There is another such solution in which n and m are both less than 100 (and again, m might be the same as n or different; I'm not telling which). Can the reader find it?

3

Without any restriction on the sizes of n and m, how many solutions are there? That is, how many sentences are there which are true but not provable by Fergusson's machine?

EPILOGUE

Fergusson did not easily give up his aspiration of constructing a machine that could prove all arithmetic truths without proving any falsehoods, and he constructed many, many more logic machines.* But for each machine he constructed, either he or Craig or McCulloch discovered a true sentence that the machine could not prove. And so he finally gave up the attempt to construct a purely mechanical device that was both accurate and could prove all true arithmetic sentences.

That Fergusson's heroic attempt failed was not due to any lack of ingenuity on his part. We must remember that he lived several decades before the discoveries of such logicians as Gödel, Tarski, Kleene, Turing, Post, Church, and others, to

---

* Some of them were quite interesting, and I hope to tell you about them in another book.

whose work we will soon turn. Had he lived to see what these men produced, he would have realized that his failure stemmed exclusively from the fact that what he was attempting was inherently impossible! And so, with a salute to Fergusson, and his colleagues Craig and McCulloch, we shall jump ahead three or four decades and take a look at the critical year 1931.

◆ SOLUTIONS ◆

1 ◆ One solution is that the sentence $75 \in A_{75}$ is true but not provable by the machine. Here is the reason why.

Suppose the sentence $75 \in A_{75}$ were false. Then 75 doesn't belong to the set A_{75}. Hence 75 must belong to A_{25} (by Property 2, which makes A_{75} the complement of A_{25}). This implies (by Property 3) that $75*75$ belongs to A_8, since $25 = 3.8 + 1$; and hence that $75*75$ can be printed by the machine; in other words, that $75 \in A_{75}$ is provable by the machine. Thus, if the sentence $75 \in A_{75}$ were false, it would be provable by the machine. But we are given that the machine is accurate and never proves false sentences. Therefore, the sentence $75 \in A_{75}$ cannot be false; it must be true.

Since the sentence $75 \in A_{75}$ is true, then 75 does belong to the set A_{75}. Hence 75 cannot belong to the set A_{25} (by Property 2), and hence the number $75*75$ cannot belong to A_8, because if $75*75$ did belong to A_8, then, by Property 3, 75 would belong to A_{25}. Since $75*75$ doesn't belong to A_8, then the sentences $75 \in A_{75}$ is not provable by the machine. And so the sentence $75 \in A_{75}$ is true but not provable by the machine.

2 ◆ Before giving other solutions, let us observe the following general fact: The key set K is the set of all numbers x such that the sentence $x \in A_x$ is not provable by the machine—or what is the same thing, the set of all numbers x such that $x*x$ cannot be printed by the machine. Now, A_{75} is this set K, because to say that x belongs to A_{75} is equivalent to saying that x does not belong to A_{25}, which in turn is equivalent to saying that $x*x$ does not belong to A_8, which is the set of all numbers that the machine *can* print. So A_{75} = K. But also A_{73} = K, because to say that a number x belongs to A_{73} is equivalent to saying that $x*x$ belongs to A_{24} (by Property 3, since $73 = 3 \cdot 24 + 1$), which in turn is equivalent to saying that $x*x$ does not belong to A_8 (by Property 2). Thus, A_{73} is the set of all numbers x such that $x*x$ does not belong to A_8—or, what is the same thing, such that $x \in A_x$ is not provable by the machine. Thus, A_{73} is the same set as A_{75}, since both are the same as the set K. Moreover, given *any* number n such that A_n = K, the sentence $n \in A_n$ must be true but not provable by the machine—this by essentially the same argument as for the special case $n = 75$ (an argument we give in a still more general form in the next chapter). And so $73 \in A_{73}$ is another example of a true sentence whose code number the machine cannot print.

3 • For any n, the set $A_{9 \cdot n}$ must be the same as the set A_n, because $A_{9 \cdot n}$ is the complement of $A_{3 \cdot n}$, and $A_{3 \cdot n}$ is the complement of A_n; hence $A_{9 \cdot n}$ is the same set as A_n. And so A_{675} is the same as the set A_{75}, and so $675 \in A_{675}$ is another solution. Also $2175 \in A_{2175}$ is a solution. Indeed, there are infinitely many true sentences that Fergusson's machine cannot prove: for any n that is 75 times some multiple of 9, or 73 times some multiple of 9, the sentence $n \in A_n$ is true but not provable by the machine.

◆ 15 ◆

Provability and Truth

The year 1931 was indeed a great landmark in the history of mathematical logic; this was the year in which Kurt Gödel published his famous Incompleteness Theorem. Gödel begins his epoch-making paper* as follows:

> The development of mathematics in the direction of greater precision has led to large areas of it being formalized, so that proofs can be carried out according to a few mechanical rules. The most comprehensive formal systems to date are, on the one hand, the *Principia Mathematica* of Whitehead and Russell and, on the other, the Zermelo-Fraenkel system of axiomatic set theory. Both systems are so extensive that all methods of proof used in mathematics today can be formalized in them; i.e., can be reduced to a few axioms and rules of inference. It would seem reasonable, therefore, to surmise that these axioms and rules of inference are sufficient to decide *all* mathematical questions which can be

---

* "Über formal unentscheidbare Sätze der *Principia Mathematica* und verwandter Systeme I" ("On Formally Undecidable Propositions of *Principia Mathematica* and Related Systems"), *Monatshefte für Mathematik und Physik* 38, 173–198.

formulated in the system concerned. In what follows it will be shown that this is not the case, but rather that, in both of the cited systems, there exist relatively simple problems of the theory of ordinary whole numbers which cannot be decided on the basis of the axioms.†

Gödel then goes on to explain that the situation does not depend on the special nature of the two systems under consideration, but holds for an extensive variety of mathematical systems.

Just what is this "extensive variety" of mathematical systems? Various interpretations have been given, and Gödel's theorem has accordingly been generalized in several ways. Curiously enough, one of the ways that is most direct and most easily accessible to the general reader is also the way that appears to be the least well known. What makes this even more curious is that the way in question is the very one indicated by Gödel himself in the introductory section of his original paper! To which we shall now turn.

Let us consider an axiom system with the following properties: First of all, we have names for various sets of (positive whole) numbers, and we have all these nameable sets arranged in an infinite sequence $A_1, A_2, \ldots, A_n, \ldots$ (just as in Fergusson's system of the last chapter). We shall call a number n an *index* of a nameable set A if $A = A_n$. (Thus, for example, if the sets $A_2, A_7,$ and A_{13} all happen to be the same, then 2, 7, and 13 are all indices of this set.) As with Fergusson's system, we have associated with every number x and every number y a certain sentence—written $x \in A_y$—which is called *true* if x belongs to A_y and *false* if x doesn't belong to A_y. We no longer assume, however, that the sentences $x \in A_y$ are the only sentences of the system; there may be others. But

† Composite translation.

181

every other such sentence is classified as either a true sentence or a false one.

Every sentence of the system is assigned a code number, which we will now call its *Gödel number*, and we will let $x*y$ be the Gödel number of the sentence x ϵ A_y. (We no longer need assume that $x*y$ consists of a string of 1's of length x followed by a string of o's of length y; this is nothing at all like the code numbering that Gödel actually used. There are many different code numberings that work, and which one works most smoothly depends on the particular system under consideration. Anyway, for the general theorem we are about to prove, nothing about the particular Gödel numbering need be assumed.)

Certain sentences are taken as *axioms* of the system, and certain rules are provided that enable one to prove various sentences from the axioms. There is, thus, a well-defined property of a sentence being *provable* in the system. It is assumed that the system is *correct*, in the sense that every sentence provable in the system is true; hence, in particular, that whenever a sentence $x \epsilon A_y$ is provable in the system, then x really is a member of the set A_y.

We let P be the set of Gödel numbers of all the sentences provable in the system. For any set A of numbers, we again let $\bar{A}$ be the complement of A (the set of all numbers not in A) and we let A^* be the set of all numbers x such that $x*x$ belongs to A. We are now interested in systems in which the following conditions, G1, G2, and G3, hold:

G1: The set P is nameable in the system. Stated otherwise, there is at least one number p such that A_p is the set of Gödel numbers of the provable sentences. (For Fergusson's system, 8 was such a number p.)

G2: The complement of any set nameable in the system is also nameable in the system. Stated otherwise, for any number x there is some number x' such that $A_{x'}$ is the complement of A_x. (For Fergusson's system, $3 \cdot x$ was such a number x'.)

G3: For any nameable set A, the set A^* is also nameable in the system. Stated otherwise, for any number x there is some number x^* such that A_{x^*} is the set of all numbers n such that $n*n$ lies in A_x. (For Fergusson's system, $3 \cdot x + 1$ was such a number x^*.)

The conditions F1, F2, and F3 characterizing Fergusson's machine are obviously nothing more than special cases of conditions G1, G2, and G3. These latter general conditions are of considerable importance, because they do hold for a wide variety of mathematical systems, including the two systems treated in Gödel's paper. That is, it is possible to arrange all the nameable sets in an infinite sequence A_1, A_2, ..., A_n, ... and to exhibit a particular Gödel numbering of the sentences such that the conditions G1, G2, and G3 do hold. Therefore, anything provable about systems satisfying the conditions G1, G2, and G3 will apply to many important systems.

We can now state and prove the following abstract form of Gödel's theorem.

Theorem G: Given any correct system satisfying conditions G1, G2, and G3, there must be a sentence that is true but not provable in the system.

The proof of Theorem G is a straightforward generalization of the proof that the reader already knows for Fergusson's system: We let K be the set of all numbers x such that $x*x$ is not in the set P. Since P is nameable (by G1), so is its complement $\bar{P}$ (by G_2), and hence so is the set $\bar{P}^*$ (by G_3); but $\bar{P}^*$ is the set K (because $\bar{P}^*$ is the set of all numbers x such that $x*x$ lies in $\bar{P}$, or, what is the same thing, the set of all x such that $x*x$ doesn't lie in P). And so the set K is nameable in the system, which means that $K = A_k$ for at least one number

k. (For Fergusson's system, 73 was one such number k, and so was 75.) Thus, for any number x, the truth of the sentence $x \in A_k$ is tantamount to the assertion that $x*x$ is not in P, which is tantamount to the fact that the sentence $x \in A_x$ is not provable (in the system). In particular, if we take k for x, the truth of the sentence $k \in A_k$ is tantamount to its nonprovability in the system, which means that it is either true and not provable in the system or false but provable in the system. The latter possibility is out, since we are given that the system is correct; hence it must be that the form holds—the sentence is true but not provable in the system.

Discussion: In *What Is the Name of This Book?* I considered the analogous situation of an island on which every inhabitant is either a *knight* who always tells the truth or a *knave* who always lies. Certain knights were called *established* knights and certain knaves were called *established* knaves. (The knights correspond to *true* sentences, and the established knights correspond to sentences that are not only true but *provable*.) Now, it is impossible for any inhabitant of the island to say, "I am not a knight," because a knight would never lie and claim he wasn't a knight, and a knave would never truthfully admit to not being a knight. Therefore, no inhabitant of the island can claim that he is not a knight. However, it *is* possible for an inhabitant to say, "I am not an established knight." If he says that, no contradiction arises, but something interesting follows—namely, that the speaker must *in fact* be a knight but not an established knight. For a knave would never make the truthful claim that he is not an established knight (for in truth he isn't), and so the speaker must be a knight. Since he is a knight, his statement must be true; so he is a knight but, as he says, not an established knight—just as the sentence $k \in A_k$, which asserts its own nonprovability in the system, must be true but not provable in the system.

GÖDEL SENTENCES AND TARSKI'S THEOREM

Let us now consider a system satisfying at least conditions G_2, G_3 (for the time being, condition G_1 is not relevant). We have defined P to be the set of Gödel numbers of the provable sentences of the system; let us now define T to be the set of Gödel numbers of all the *true* sentences of the system. In the year 1933, the logician Alfred Tarski raised and answered the following question: Is the set T nameable in the system, or not? This question can be answered purely on the basis of conditions G_2 and G_3. I will give the answer shortly, but first let's turn to a still more basic question of systems that satisfy at least the condition G_3.

Given any sentence X and any set A of positive whole numbers, we shall call X a *Gödel sentence* for A if either X is true and its Gödel number lies in A, or X is false and its Gödel number lies outside A. (Such a sentence can be thought of as asserting that its own Gödel number lies in A; if the sentence is true, then its Gödel number really is in A; if the sentence is false, then its Gödel number is not in A.) Now, we shall call a system *Gödelian* if for every set A nameable in the system there is at least one Gödel sentence for A.

The following fact is basic:

Theorem C: If a system satisfies condition G_3, then it is Gödelian.

1

Prove Theorem C.

2

To take a special case, consider Fergusson's system. Find a Gödel sentence for the set A_{100}.

3

Suppose a system is Gödelian (without necessarily satisfying condition G3). If the system is correct and satisfies conditions G1 and G2, does it necessarily contain a sentence that is true but not provable in the system?

4

Let T be the set of Gödel numbers of the true sentences. Is there a Gödel sentence for T? Is there a Gödel sentence for $\bar{T}$, the complement of T?

Now we are in a good position to give the answer to Tarski's question. The following is an abstract version of Tarski's theorem.

Theorem T: Given any system satisfying conditions G2 and G3, the set T of Gödel numbers of the true sentence is *not* nameable in the system.

Note: The word *definable* is sometimes used in place of *nameable*, and Theorem T is sometimes paraphrased as follows: For sufficiently rich systems, truth within the system is not definable within the system.

5

Prove Theorem T.

6

It is instructive to note that once Theorem T has been proved, one can immediately obtain Theorem G as a corollary. Can the reader see how?

A DUAL FORM
OF GÖDEL'S ARGUMENT

The various systems that have been proved incomplete by Gödel's argument also have the property that associated with each sentence X is a sentence X' called the *negation* of X, which is true if and only if X is false. A sentence X is called *disprovable* or *refutable* in the system if its negation X' is provable in the system. Assuming the system to be correct, no false sentence is provable in the system and no true sentence is refutable in the system.

We have seen that conditions G1, G2, G3 imply the existence of a Gödel sentence G for the set $\bar{P}$, and that such a sentence G is true but not provable in the system (assuming the system is correct). Since G is true, it can't be refutable in the system either (again by the assumption of correctness). So the sentence G is neither provable nor refutable in the system. (Such a sentence is called *undecidable* in the system.)

In a 1960 monograph, "Theory of Formal Systems," I considered a "dual" form of Gödel's argument: Instead of a sentence that asserts its own nonprovability, what about constructing a sentence that asserts its own refutability? More precisely, let R be the set of Gödel numbers of the refutable sentences. Suppose X is a Gödel sentence for R; what is the status of X? This idea is carried out in the next problem.

7

Let us now consider a correct system that satisfies condition G_3, but instead of assuming conditions G_1, G_2, we assume the following single condition:

G_1': The set R is nameable in the system.

(Thus we assume that the system is correct and satisfies conditions G_1' and G_3.)

(a) Prove that there is a sentence which is neither provable nor refutable in the system.

(b) To take a special case, suppose we are given that A_{10} is the set R and that for any number n, $A_{5 \cdot n}$ is the set of all x such that $x*x$ is in A_n (this is a special case of G_3). The problem now is actually to find a sentence that is neither provable nor refutable in the system, and to determine whether the sentence is true or false.

Remarks: (1) Gödel's method of obtaining an undecidable sentence boils down to constructing a Gödel sentence for $\bar{P}$, the complement of P; such a sentence (which can be thought of as asserting its own nonprovability) must be true but not provable in the system. The "dual" method boils down to constructing a Gödel sentence for the set R rather than for the set $\bar{P}$; such a sentence (which can be thought of as asserting its own refutability) must be false but not refutable. (Since it is false, it is not provable either, hence is undecidable in the system.) I should remark that the systems treated in Gödel's original paper satisfy all four conditions, G1, G2, G3, and G1′, so either method can be used for constructing undecidable sentences.

(2) Just as a sentence that asserts its nonprovability is like a native of a knight-knave island who claims that he is not an established knight, so a sentence that asserts its own refutability is like a native of the island who claims that he is an established *knave*; such a native is indeed a knave, but not an established one. (I leave the proof of this to the reader.)

♦ SOLUTIONS ♦

1 ♦ Suppose the system does satisfy condition G3. Let S be any set nameable in the system. Then, by G3, the set S^* is nameable in the system. So there is some number b such that $A_b = S^*$. Now, a number x belongs to S^* just in case $x*x$ belongs to S. So a number x belongs to A_b just in case $x*x$ belongs to S. In particular, taking b for x, the number b belongs to A_b just in case $b*b$ belongs to S. Also, b belongs to A_b if and only if the sentence $b \in A_b$ is true. So $b \in A_b$ is true if and only if $b*b$ belongs to S. Also, $b*b$ is the Gödel number of the sentence $b \in A_b$. And so we see that $b \in A_b$ is true if and only if its Gödel number belongs to S. So if $b \in A_b$ is true, its Gödel number belongs to S; if $b \in A_b$ is false, its Gödel number does not belong to S. Thus, the sentence $b \in A_b$ is a Gödel sentence for S.

2 ♦ In Fergusson's system, given any number n, $A_{3 \cdot n+1}$ is the set A_n^*. And so A_{301} is the set A_{100}^*. And so we use the result of the last problem and take 301 for b. Thus, $301 \in A_{301}$ is a Gödel sentence for the set A_{100}. More generally, for *any* num-

ber n, if we let $b = 3 \cdot n + 1$, the sentence $b \in A_b$ is a Gödel sentence for A_n in Fergusson's system.

3 ♦ Yes, it does: Suppose the system is Gödelian and conditions G1 and G2 both hold, and suppose also that the system is correct. By G1 the set P is nameable; hence, by G2, $\bar{P}$, the complement of P, is nameable. Then, since the system is Gödelian, there is a Gödel sentence X for $\bar{P}$. This means that X is true if and only if X's Gödel number is in $\bar{P}$. But to say that X's Gödel number is in $\bar{P}$ is to say that it is not in P, which is the same thing as saying that X is not provable. Thus, a Gödel sentence for $\bar{P}$ is nothing more nor less than a sentence that is true if and only if it is not provable in the system, and (as we have seen) such a sentence must be true but not provable in the system (assuming the system is correct).

Indeed, the essence of Gödel's argument is the construction of a Gödel sentence for the set $\bar{P}$.

4 ♦ Obviously, every sentence X is a Gödel sentence for T, because if X is true its Gödel number is in T, and if X is false its Gödel number is not in T. Therefore, *no* sentence can be a Gödel sentence for $\bar{T}$, because it cannot be that either X is true and its Gödel number is in $\bar{T}$, or that X is false and its Gödel number is not in $\bar{T}$.

It might be instructive for the reader to observe that for *any* number set A and for any sentence X, X is either a Gödel sentence for A or X is a Gödel sentence for $\bar{A}$, but never both.

5 ♦ Let us first consider any system satisfying condition G3. By Problem 1, given any set nameable in the system, there is a Gödel sentence for it. Also, by the last problem, there is no Gödel sentence for the set $\bar{T}$. Therefore, if the system satisfies

G3, the set $\bar{T}$ is not nameable in the system. If the system also satisfies condition G2, then T is not nameable in the system either—because if it were, then, by G2, so would its complement $\bar{T}$ be nameable, which it isn't. This proves that in a system satisfying G2 and G3, the set T is not nameable in the system.

In summary: (a) If G3 holds, then $\bar{T}$ is not nameable; (b) if G2 and G3 both hold, then neither T nor $\bar{T}$ is nameable in the system.

6 ◆ If we have first proved Theorem T, we can obtain Theorem G as follows:

Suppose we have a correct system satisfying conditions G1, G2, G3. From G2 and G3, using Theorem T, we see that T is not nameable in the system. But, by G1, P *is* nameable in the system. Since P is nameable and T is not, then P and T must be different sets. However, every number in P is also in T, since we are given that the system is correct in that every provable sentence is true. Therefore, since T is not the same as the set P, there must be at least one number n in T that is not in P. Since n is in T, it must be the Gödel number of a sentence X which is true. But since n is not in P, then X is not provable in the system. Thus, X is true but not provable in the system. Thus Theorem G holds.

7 ◆ We are given conditions G1′ and G3.

(a) By G1′, the set R is nameable in the system. Then, by condition G3, the set R* is nameable in the system. Hence, there is some number h such that $A_h = R^*$. Now, by the definition of R*, a number x is in R* if and only if $x*x$ is in R. Therefore, for any x, x belongs to A_h if and only if $x*x$ belongs to R. In particular, if we take h for x, h belongs to A_h if and only if $h*h$ belongs to R. Now, h belongs to A_h if and only if the sentence $h \in A_h$ is true. Also, since $h * h$ is the Gödel number of the sentence $h \in A_h$, then $h * h$ belongs to R if and only if the sentence $h \in A_h$ is refutable. Therefore, the sentence $h \in A_h$ is true if and only if it is refutable. This means that the sentence is either true and refutable or false and not refutable. It cannot be true and refutable, since we are given that the machine is correct; hence it must be false but not refutable. Since the sentence is false, it cannot be provable either (again, because the system is correct). Therefore, the sentence $h \in A_h$ is neither provable nor refutable (and, also, it is false).

(b) We are now given that A_{10} is R, and also that for any n, $A_{5 \cdot n}$ is the set $A_n{}^*$. Therefore, A_{50} is the set R*. And so, by Solution (a), taking 50 for h, the sentence $50 \in A_{50}$ is neither provable nor refutable. Also, the sentence is false.

◆ 16 ◆

Machines That Talk About Themselves

We shall now consider Gödel's argument from a slightly different perspective, which puts the central idea in a remarkably clear light.

We shall take the four symbols P,N,A, – and consider all possible combinations of these symbols. By an *expression* we mean any combination of the symbols. For example, P – – NA – P is an expression; so is – PN – – A – P – . Certain expressions will be assigned a meaning, and these expressions will be called *sentences*.

Suppose we have a machine that can print out some expressions but not others. We call an expression *printable* if the machine can print it. We assume that any expression that the machine can print will be printed sooner or later. Given any expression X, if we wish to express the proposition that X is printable, we write P – X. So, for example, P – ANN says that ANN is printable (this may be true or false, but that's what it says!). If we want to say that X is *not* printable, we write NP – X. (The symbol N is the abbreviation of the word *not*, just as the symbol P represents the word *printable*. And so NP – X is to be read, crudely, as "Not printable X," or, in better English, "X is not printable.")

By the *associate* of an expression X we mean the expression X – X. We use the symbol A to stand for "the associate of," and so, for any given X, if we wish to state that the associate of X is printable we write PA – X (read "printable the associate of X," or in better English, "the associate of X is printable"). If we wish to say that the associate of X is *not* printable, we write NPA – X (read "not printable the associate of X," or, in better English, "the associate of X is not printable").

Now, the reader may well wonder why we use the dash as a symbol: why don't we simply use PX rather than P – X to express the proposition that X is printable? The reason is that omission of the dash would create a contextual ambiguity. What, for example, would PAN mean? Would it mean that the associate of N is printable or that the expression AN is printable? With the use of the dash, no such ambiguity arises. If we want to say that the associate of N is printable, we write down PA – N; whereas, if we want to say that AN is printable, we write down P – AN. Again, suppose we want to say that – X is printable; do we write P – X? No, that would state that X is printable. To say that – X is printable, we must write P – – X.

Perhaps some more examples might help: P – – says that – is printable; PA – – says that – – – (the associate of –) is printable; P – – – – also says that – – – is printable; NPA – – P – A says that the associate of – P – A is not printable; in other words, that – P – A – – P – A is not printable. NP – – P – A – – P – A says the same thing.

We now define a *sentence* as any expression of one of the four forms P – X, NP – X, PA – X, and NPA – X, where X is any expression whatever. We call P – X *true* if X is printable, and *false* if X is not printable. We call NP – X true if X is *not* printable and false if X *is* printable. We call PA – X true if the associate of X is printable, and false if the associate of X is not printable. Finally, we call NA – X true if the associate of X is not printable, and false if the associate of X is printable.

We have now given a precise definition of truth and falsity for sentences of all four types, and from this it follows that, for any expression X:

Law 1: P – X is true if and only if X is printable (by the machine).

Law 2: PA – X is true if and only if X – X is printable.

Law 3: NP – X is true if and only if X is not printable.

Law 4: NPA – X is true if and only if X – X is not printable.

We have here a curious loop! The machine is printing out sentences that make assertions about what the machine can and cannot print! In this sense, the machine is talking about itself (or, more accurately, printing out sentences about itself).

We are now given that the machine is a hundred percent accurate—that is, it never prints out any false sentence; it prints out only true sentences. This fact has several ramifications: As an example, if it ever prints out P – X, then it must also print out X, because, since it prints out P – X, then P – X must be true, which means that X is printable, and hence the machine must sooner or later print X.

It follows as well that if the machine should print out PA – X, then (since PA – X must be true), the machine must also print out X – X. In addition, if the machine prints out NP – X, then it *cannot* also print P – X, since these two sentences can't both be true—the first says that the machine doesn't print X, and the second says that the machine does print X.

The following problem puts Gödel's idea into as clear a light as any problem I can imagine.

1 ✦ A Singularly Gödelian Challenge

Find a true sentence that the machine cannot print!

2 ◆ A Doubly Gödelian Puzzle

We continue to assume the same conditions—and, in particular, that the machine is accurate.

There is a sentence X and a sentence Y such that one of the sentences X or Y must be true but not printable, but it is impossible to tell, from the given conditions embodied in Laws 1 through 4, which one it is. Can you find such an X and Y? (Hint: Find sentences X and Y such that X says that Y is printable and Y says that X is not printable. There are two different ways of doing this, and both relate to Fergusson's laws!)

3 ◆ A Triply Gödelian Problem

Construct sentences X, Y, and Z such that X says that Y is printable, Y says that Z is not printable, and Z says that X is printable, and show that at least one of these three sentences (though it can't be determined which) must be true but not printable by the machine.

TWO MACHINES THAT TALK ABOUT THEMSELVES AND ABOUT EACH OTHER

Let us now add a fifth symbol, R. We thus have the symbols P,R,N,A, –, and are now given two machines M1 and M2, each of which prints out various expressions composed of these five symbols. We now interpret "P" to mean "printable by the first machine," and we interpret "R" to mean "printable by the second machine." Thus, P – X now means that X is printable by the first machine, and R – X means that X is printable by the second machine. Also, PA – X means that the associate of X is printable by the first machine, RA – X that the associate of X is printable by the second machine. Also, NP – X, NR – X, NPA – X, NRA – X respectively mean: X is not printable by the first machine; X is not printable by the second machine; X – X is not printable by the first machine; X – X is not printable by the second machine. By a *sentence* is now meant any expression of one of the eight types P – X, R – X, NP – X, NR – X, PA – X, RA – X, NPA – X, or NRA – X, and we are given that the first machine prints out only true sentences, and the second machine prints out only false sentences. Let us call a sentence *provable* if and only if it is printable by the first machine and *refutable* if and only if it is printable by the second machine. Therefore, P can be read as "provable" and R can be read as "refutable."

4

Find a sentence which is false but not refutable.

5

There are sentences X and Y such that one of the two (we don't know which) must be either true but not provable or false but not refutable, and again we don't know which. This can be done in either of two ways, and I accordingly pose two problems:

(a) Find sentences X and Y such that X says that Y is provable and Y says that X is refutable. Then show that one of the sentences X or Y (we can't determine which) is either true and not provable or false but not refutable.

(b) Find sentences X and Y such that X says that Y is not provable and Y says that X is not refutable. Then show that for this X and Y, one of them (we can't determine which) is either true and not provable or false and not refutable.

6

Now let's try a quadruplicate! Find sentences X, Y, Z, and W such that X says that Y is provable, Y says that Z is refutable, Z says that W is refutable, and W says that X is not refutable. Show that one of these four sentences must be either true and not provable or false and not refutable (though there is no way to tell which of the four it is!).

McCULLOCH'S MACHINE AND GÖDEL'S THEOREM

The reader may have noticed certain similarities of some of the preceding problems to certain features of McCulloch's first machine. Indeed, this machine can be related to Gödel's theorem in the following manner:

7

Suppose we have a mathematical system with sentences certain ones of which are called *true* and certain of which are called *provable*. We assume the system is correct—every provable sentence is true. To each number N is assigned a sentence that we call *Sentence N*. Suppose the system satisfies the following two conditions:

Mc1: For any numbers X and Y, if X produces Y in McCulloch's first machine, then Sentence 8X is true if and only if Sentence Y is provable. (8X, remember, means 8 followed by X, not 8 times X.)

Mc2: For any number X, Sentence 9X is true if and only if Sentence X is not true.

Find a number N such that Sentence N is true but not provable in the system.

8

Suppose that in condition Mc1 of the last problem, we replace "McCulloch's first machine" by "McCulloch's third machine." *Now* find an N such that Sentence N is true but not provable!

9 ♦ Paradoxical?

Let's return again to Problem 1, but with these differences: Instead of using the symbol "P," we will use "B" (for psychological reasons which will appear later). We define *sentence* as before, only this time using "B" in place of "P." Thus, our sentences are now B – X, NB – X, BA – X, and NBA – X. Sentences are, as before, classified into two groups— *true* sentences and *false* sentences—but we are not told which sentences are which. Now, instead of having a machine that prints out various sentences, we have a logician present who *believes* some of the sentences but not others. When we say that the logician *doesn't* believe a sentence, we don't mean that he *disbelieves* it; we merely mean that it is not the case that he believes it; in other words, he either believes it false or he has no opinion about it one way or the other. Now the symbol "B" stands for "believed by the logician," and so we are given that the following four conditions hold for any expression X:

B1: B – X is true if and only if the logician believes X.

B2: NB – X is true if and only if it is not the case that the logician believes X.

B3: BA – X is true if and only if the logician believes X – X.

B4: NBA – X is true if and only if it is not the case that the logician believes X – X.

Assuming that the logician is accurate—i.e., that he does not believe any false sentence—then we can, of course, find a sentence that is true but that the logician does not know to be true; namely, NBA – NBA (which says that the logician does not believe the associate of NBA, which is NBA – NBA).

Now comes something interesting. Suppose we are given the following facts about the logician:

Fact 1: The logician knows logic at least as well as you or I; in fact, we will assume that he is a perfect logician: given any premises, he can deduce all propositions that logically follow.

Fact 2: The logician knows that condition B1, B2, B3, and B4 all hold.

Fact 3: The logician is always accurate; he doesn't believe any false sentences.

Now, since the logician knows that conditions B1, B2, B3, and B4 all hold, and he can reason as well as you or I, what is to prevent *him* from going through the same reasoning process that we went through to prove that the sentence NBA – NBA must be true? It would appear that he can do this, and having done it, he will then believe the sentence

NBA – NBA. But the moment he believes it, the sentence will be falsified, since the sentence says that he doesn't believe it, which will make the logician inaccurate after all!

So, don't we get a paradox if we assume Facts 1, 2, and 3? The answer is that we don't; there is a deliberate flaw in my argument in this last paragraph! Can you find the flaw?

◆ SOLUTIONS ◆

1 ◆ For any expression X, the sentence NPA – X says that the associate of X is not printable. In particular, NPA – NPA says that the associate of NPA is not printable. But the associate of NPA is the very sentence NPA – NPA! Hence, NPA – NPA asserts its own nonprintability; in other words, the sentence is true if and only if it is not printable. This means that either it is true and not printable or it is not true but printable. The latter cannot be, since the machine is accurate. Hence, it must be the former; the sentence is true but not printable by the machine.

2 ◆ Let X be the sentence P – NPA – P – NPA and Y be the sentence NPA – P – NPA. The sentence X (which is P – Y) says that Y is printable. The sentence Y (crudely read as "not printable the associate of P – NPA") says that the associate of P – NPA is not printable. But the associate of P – NPA is X, so Y says that X is not printable. (Incidentally, there is another way of constructing such an X and Y: take X to be PA – NP – PA, and Y to be NP – PA – NP – PA.)

We thus have two sentences X and Y such that X says that Y is printable and Y says that X is not printable.

Now, suppose X were printable. Then it would be true, which would mean that Y is printable. Then Y would be true, which means that X is not printable. This is a contradiction, since X in this case would be both printable and not printable; hence X cannot be printable. Since X is not printable and Y says that X is not printable, then Y must be true. Therefore, we know:

(1) X is not printable;

(2) Y is true.

Now, X is either true or it isn't. If X is true, then, by (1), X is true but not printable. If X is false, then Y is not printable, since X says that Y *is* printable; and so in this case, Y is true—by (2)—and not printable. So either X is true and not printable or Y is true and not printable, but there is no way to tell which.

Discussion: The above situation is analogous to a knight-knave island on which there are two inhabitants X and Y, with X claiming that Y is an established knight and Y claiming that X is not an established knight. All that can be inferred is that at least one of them is an unestablished knight, but there is no way to tell which.

I deal with this situation in *What Is the Name of This Book?* in a section in the last chapter called "Doubly Gödelian Islands."

3 ♦ We let Z = PA – P – NP – PA.

We let Y = NP – Z (which is NP – PA – P – NP – PA).

We let X = P – Y (which is P – NP – PA – P – NP – PA).

It is immediate that X says that Y is printable and Y says that Z is not printable. As for Z, Z says that the associate of P – NP – PA is printable, but the associate of P – NP – PA is P – NP – PA – P – NP – PA, which is X! So Z says that X is printable.

Thus X says Y is printable, Y says Z is not printable, and Z says X is printable. Now let us see what follows from this:

Suppose Z is printable. Then Z is true, which means that X

is printable, hence true, which means that Y is printable, hence true, which means that Z is not printable. So if Z is printable, it is not printable, which is a contradiction. Therefore, Z is not printable, and therefore Y is true. So we know:

(1) Z is not printable;

(2) Y is true.

Now, X is either true or false. Suppose X is true. If Z is false, then X is not printable, which means that X is true but not printable. If Z is true, then, since by (1) it is not printable, Z is true but not printable. So if X is true, then either X or Z is true but not printable. If X is false, then Y is not printable, hence Y is true—by (2)—and not printable.

In summary, if X is true, then at least one of the two sentences X and Z is true but not printable. If X is false, then it is Y that is true but not printable.

4 ◆ Let S be the sentence RA – RA. It says that the associate of RA—which is S itself—is refutable; hence S is true if and only if S is refutable. Since S can't be true and refutable, it is therefore false but not refutable.

5 ◆ (a) Take P – RA – P – RA for X and RA – P – RA for Y. Clearly, X says that Y is provable, and Y says that the associate of P – RA (which happens to be X) is refutable. So X says that Y is provable and Y says that X is refutable. (If we had taken PA – R – PA for X and R – PA – R – PA for Y, we would have had an alternative solution.)

Now, if Y is provable, then Y is true, which means that X is refutable, hence false, which means that Y is not provable. Thus we get a contradiction from the assumption that Y is provable, and therefore Y is not provable. Since Y is not provable, then X is false. And so we know:

(1) X is false;

(2) Y is not provable.

If Y is true, then Y is true and not provable. If Y is false, then X is not refutable (since Y says that X *is* refutable), and so in this case, X is false but not refutable. Therefore, either Y is true and not provable or X is false and not refutable.

(b) Take NP – NRA – NP – NRA for X, and NRA – NP – NRA for Y (or, alternatively, NPA – NR – NPA for X, and NR – NPA – NR – NPA for Y) and, as the reader can verify, X says that Y is not provable and Y says that X is not refutable. If X is refutable, X is false, Y is provable, Y is true, X is not refutable. Hence X is not refutable, and also Y is true. If X is false, X is false and not refutable. If X is true, Y is not provable; hence in this case Y would be true and not provable.

Discussion: Analogously, suppose we have inhabitants X and Y of a knight-knave island where X claims that Y is an established knight and Y claims that X is an established knave. All that can be deduced is that one of the two (we don't know which) must be either an unestablished knight or an unestablished knave. The same thing holds if X claims that Y is not an established knight and Y claims that X is not an established knave.

6 ◆ Let W = NPA – P – R – R – NPA;

Z = R – W (which is R – NPA – P – R – R – NPA);
Y = R – Z (which is R – R – NPA – P – R – R – NPA);
X = P – Y (which is P – R – R – NPA – P – R – R – NPA).

X says that Y is provable, Y says that Z is refutable, Z says that W is refutable, and W says that X is not provable (W says that the associate of P – R – R – NPA, which is X, is not provable).

If W is refutable, W is false; hence X is provable, hence true; hence Y is provable, hence true; hence Z is refutable, hence false; hence W is not refutable. Therefore, it cannot be that W is refutable. So W is not refutable, and Z is therefore false.

Now, if W is false, then W is false but not refutable. Suppose W is true. Then X is not provable. If X is true, X is true and not provable. Suppose X is false. Then Y is not provable. If Y is true, then Y is true but not provable. Suppose Y is false. Then Z is not refutable; so in this case Z is false but not refutable.

This shows that either W is false and not refutable, or X is true and not provable, or Y is true and not provable, or Z is false and not refutable.

7 ♦ This situation is little more than a notational variant of this chapter's Problem 1!

We know that 32983 produces 9832983 (in McCulloch's first machine); hence by Mc1, Sentence 832983 is true if and only if Sentence 9832983 is provable. Also, by Mc2, Sentence 9832983 is true if and only if Sentence 832983 is not true; so, combining these last two facts, we see that Sentence 9832983 is true if and only if it is not provable. So the solution is 9832983.

If we compare this with Problem 1, we see that obviously, 9 plays the role of N, 8 plays the role of P, 3 plays the role of A, and 2 plays the role of the dash. Indeed, if we replace the symbols P,N,A,– by the respective numerals 8,9,3,2, the sentence NPA–NPA (which is the solution of Problem 1) becomes the number 9832983 (the solution of the present problem!).

8 ♦ To begin with, McCulloch's third machine also obeys McCulloch's Law—i.e., for any number A, there must be some X that produces AX. We prove this as follows: We know from Chapter 13 that there is a number H—namely,

5464—such that for any number X, H2X2 produces X2X2. (Recall that H2H2 then produces itself, but this is not relevant to the present problem.) Now, take any number A. Let X = H2AH2. Then X produces AH2AH2, which is AX. Thus X produces AX. And so for any number A, a number X that produces AX is 54642A54642.

We need an X that produces 98X: Suppose X does produce 98X. Then Sentence 8X is true if and only if Sentence 98X is provable (by Mc1); hence Sentence 98X is true if and only if Sentence 98X is not provable (by Mc2). Then Sentence 98X is true but not provable in the system (since the system is correct).

Now, from the last paragraph, taking 98 for A, we see that an X which produces 98X is 546429854642. Hence Sentence 98546429854642 is true but not provable in the system.

9 ♦ I told you that the logician was accurate, but I never told you that he *knew* he was accurate! If he knew he was accurate, then the situation *would* lead to a paradox! Therefore, what properly follows from Facts 1, 2, and 3 is not a contradiction but simply that the logician, though accurate, cannot know that he is accurate.

This situation is not totally unrelated to another theorem of Gödel's, known as *Gödel's Second Incompleteness Theorem,* which (roughly speaking) states that for systems with a sufficiently rich structure (and this includes the systems treated in Gödel's original paper), if the system is consistent, then it cannot prove its own consistency. This is a profound matter, which I plan to discuss further in a sequel to this book.

Mortal
and Immortal
Numbers

It had been some time since Craig had last seen McCulloch or Fergusson, when he met the two of them quite unexpectedly one late afternoon and the three happily went off to dine together.

"You know," said McCulloch, after the meal, "there is one problem that has baffled me for quite a while."

"And what is that?" asked Fergusson.

"Well," replied McCulloch, "I have studied several machines, and with each one I run into the same problem: In each of the machines, certain numbers are acceptable and others are not. Now, suppose I feed an acceptable number X into the machine. The number Y that X produces is either unacceptable or acceptable. If Y is unacceptable, the process terminates; if Y is acceptable, I feed Y back into the machine to see what number Z is produced by Y. If Z is unacceptable, then the process terminates; if Z is acceptable, I feed it back into the machine, and so the process continues for at least one more cycle. I repeat this over and over again, and there are two possibilities: one, I eventually get an unacceptable number; two, the process goes on forever. If the former, then I call X a *mortal* number, with respect to the machine in question, and if the latter, I call X an *immortal* number. Of course, a given number might be mortal for one machine and immortal for another machine."

"Let's consider your first machine," said Craig. "I can think of plenty of mortal numbers, but can you give me an example of an immortal number?"

"Obviously, 323," replied McCulloch. "323 produces itself, so if I put 323 into the machine, out comes 323. I put 323 back, and again out comes 323. So, in this case, the process clearly never terminates."

"Oh, of course!" laughed Craig. "Are there other immortal numbers?"

1

"Well," replied McCulloch, "what would you say about the number 3223? Is it mortal or not?"

2

"What about the number 32223?" asked Fergusson. "Is it mortal or immortal for your first machine?"

McCulloch thought about this for a bit. "Oh, that's not too difficult to settle," he replied. "I think you might enjoy trying your hand at it."

3

"You might also try the number 3232," said McCulloch. "Is this number mortal or immortal?"

4

"What about the number 32323?" asked Craig. "Mortal or immortal?"

5

"These are all fine questions," said McCulloch, "but I haven't yet come to the main problem. A friend of mine has constructed a rather elaborate number machine, which he claims can do anything that any machine can do; he calls it a *universal* machine. Now, there are several numbers of which neither he nor I can tell whether they are mortal or immortal, and I would like to devise some purely mechanical test to determine which numbers are which, but so far I have not succeeded. Specifically, I am trying to find a number H such that for any acceptable number X, if X is immortal then HX is mortal, and if X is mortal then HX is immortal. If I could find such a number H, then I could decide for any acceptable number X whether X is mortal or immortal."

"How would finding such an H enable you to do that?" asked Craig.

"If I had such a number H," replied McCulloch, "I would first build a duplicate of my friend's machine. Then, given any acceptable number X, I would feed X into one of the machines, and at the same time my friend would feed HX into the other machine. One and only one of the processes would terminate; if the first process terminated, then I would know that X is mortal; if the second process terminated, then I would know that X is immortal."

"You wouldn't actually have to build a second machine,"

said Fergusson. "You could alternate the stages of the two processes."

"True," replied McCulloch, "but this is all hypothetical, since I have not been able to find such a number H. Perhaps this machine *can't* solve its own mortality problem—that is, perhaps there *is* no such number H. Then again, maybe I just haven't been clever enough to find it. This is the problem about which I would like to consult you gentlemen."

"Well," replied Fergusson, "we must know the rules of this machine. What are they?"

"There are twenty-five rules," began McCulloch. "The first two are the same as those of my first machine."

"Just a moment," said Fergusson. "Are you saying that your friend's machine obeys your Rules 1 and 2?"

"Yes," replied McCulloch.

"Well, that settles the matter!" replied Fergusson. "No machine obeying Rules 1 and 2 can possibly solve its own mortality problem!"

"How can you have determined that so quickly?" asked Craig.

"Oh, this isn't new to me," replied Fergusson. "A similar problem came up in my own work some time ago."

How *did* Fergusson know that no machine obeying Rules 1 and 2 can solve its own mortality problem?

✦ SOLUTIONS ✦

1 ✦ We recall that 3223 produces 23223, and of course 23223 produces 3223. So, we have the two numbers 3223 and 23223, each of which produces the other. So, they are both immortal: Put one of them into the machine and the other

comes out; put the second back into the machine and the first comes out. The process clearly never terminates.

2 ♦ For any two numbers X and Y, let us say that X *leads to* Y if either X produces Y, or X produces some number that produces Y, or X produces some number that produces some number that produces Y, or X produces some number that produces some number that . . . that produces some number that produces Y. Stated otherwise, if starting the process with X we get Y at some state or other, then we will say that X leads to Y. As an example, 22222278 leads to 78—after six stages, in fact. More generally, if T is any string of 2's, then for any number X, TX leads to X.

Now, 32223 does not produce itself, but it does lead to itself, because it produces 2232223, which in turn produces 232223, which in turn produces 32223. Since 32223 leads to itself, it must be immortal.

The reader might note the following more general fact: For *any* number T that consists entirely of 2's, the number 3T3 must lead to itself, and hence must be immortal.

3 ♦ The only way I know to solve this problem is to show the more general fact that for any T consisting entirely of 2's, the number 3T32 is immortal, and that therefore the specific instance 3232 is immortal. And this illustrates a still more general principle which will also be used in the solution of the next problem.

Suppose we have a class of numbers (whether the class is finite or infinite makes no difference), and the class is such that every member of the class leads to some member of the class (either itself or some other member). Then every member of the class must be immortal.

To apply this principle to the problem at hand, let us consider the class of all numbers of the form 3T32, where T is a string of 2's. We will show that 3T32 must lead to another number of this class.

Let us first consider the number in question, 3232. It produces 32232, which is a member of this class. What about 32232? It produces 2322232, which in turn produces 322232, which is a member of this class. What about 322232? It produces 223222232, which produces 23222232, which produces 3222232, so we are again back in this class. More generally, for any string T of 2's, 32T32 produces T322T32, which leads to 322T32, which is again a member of this class. So all members of this class are immortal.

4 ♦ The number 32323 produces 3232323, which produces 32323232323, which produces 323232323232323232323. The pattern should be obvious: any number consisting of 32 repeated some number of times and then followed by 3 produces another number of this form (a longer one, in fact), and so all such numbers are immortal.

5 ♦ We first observe the following fact: Suppose X and Y are numbers such that X produces Y. Then if Y is mortal, X must also be mortal, because if Y leads to an unacceptable number Z in n stages, then X will lead to Z in $n + 1$ stages. Also, if Y is immortal, it never leads to any unacceptable number; hence X cannot lead to an unacceptable number, since the only way X can lead to a number is via Y. So, if X produces Y, then the mortality of X is the same as the mortality of Y (i.e., they are either both mortal or both immortal).

Now, consider any machine that obeys at least Rules 1 and 2 (and possibly others). Take any number H. We know that by Rules 1 and 2, there must be a number X that produces HX (indeed, we recall that H32H3 is such a number). Since X produces HX, then the numbers X and HX are either both mortal or both immortal (as we showed in the last paragraph). So there cannot be any number H such that for *every* X, one of the numbers H or HX is mortal and the other immortal, because for the particular number X = H32H3, it is not the case that one of the numbers X or HX is mortal and the other immortal. Therefore, no machine obeying Rules 1 and 2 can solve its own mortality problem.

We might remark that the same goes for any machine obeying Rules 1 and 4, or indeed for any machine obeying McCulloch's Law. (This whole problem, incidentally, is closely related to a famous *halting problem* of Turing machines, whose solution is also negative.)

◆ 18 ◆

The Machine
That Never
Got Built

Shortly after the last episode, Craig was sitting quietly in his study one early afternoon. There was a timid knock at the door.

"Pray come in, Mrs. Hoffman," said Craig to his landlady.

"There is a wild, eccentric-looking gentleman to see you, sir," said Mrs. Hoffman. "He claims to be on the verge of the greatest mathematical discovery of all time! He says it would interest you *enormously* and insists on seeing you immediately. What should I do?"

"Well," replied Craig judiciously, "you might as well send him up; I have about half an hour to spare."

A few seconds later, the door of Craig's study burst open, and a distracted, frenzied inventor (for an inventor he was) practically flew into the room, flung his briefcase on a nearby sofa, threw up his hands, danced wildly around the room, shouting, "Eureka! Eureka! I'm about to find it! It will make me the greatest mathematician of all time! Why, the names of Euclid, Archimedes, Gauss will pale into insignificance! The names of Newton, Lobochevski, Bolyai, Riemann . . ."

"Now, now!" interrupted Craig, in a quiet but firm voice, "just what is it that you have found?"

"I haven't exactly *found* it yet," replied the stranger, in a somewhat more subdued tone. "But I'm *about* to find it, and when I do, I'll be the greatest mathematician who ever lived! Why, the names of Galois, Cauchy, Dirichlet, Cantor ..."

"Enough!" interrupted Craig. "Please tell me just what it is you are trying to find."

"*Trying* to find?" said the stranger, with a somewhat hurt expression. "Why, I tell you, I've *almost* found it! A universal machine which can solve *all* mathematical problems! Why, with this machine, I'll be omniscient! I'll be able to ..."

"Ah, Leibniz's dream!" said Craig. "Leibniz also had such a dream, but I doubt that the dream is realizable."

"Leibniz!" said the stranger, contemptuously. "Leibniz! He just didn't know how to go about it! But I practically *have* such a machine! All I need is a couple of details—but here, let me give you a concrete idea of what I am after:

"I am looking for a machine M," explained the stranger (whose name, it turned out, was Walton), "with certain properties: To begin with, you put a natural number x into the machine and after that a natural number y; then the machine goes into operation and out comes a natural number which we'll call $M(x,y)$. So $M(x,y)$ is the output of M when the input is x as the first number and y as the second number."

"I'm with you so far," said Craig.

"Now, then," continued Walton, "I shall use the word *number* to mean *positive integers*, since the positive integers are the only numbers I will be considering. As you may know, two natural numbers are said to have the same parity if they are either both even or both odd, and they are said to be of different parities if one of them is even and the other one is odd.

"For every x, let $x^{\#}$ be the number $M(x,x)$. Now, here are the three properties I want my machine to have:

"*Property 1:* For every number a, I want there to be a number b such that for every number x, $M(x,b)$ has the same parity as $M(x^{\#},a)$.

"*Property 2:* For every number b, I want there to be a number a such that for every x, $M(x,a)$ has a different parity than $M(x,b)$.

"*Property 3:* I want there to be a number h such that for every x, $M(x,h)$ has the same parity as x.

"These are the three properties I want my machine to have," concluded Walton.

Inspector Craig thought about this for some time.

"Then what is your problem?" he finally asked.

"Alas," replied Walton. "I have built a machine having Properties 1 and 2, and another having Properties 1 and 3, and a third having Properties 2 and 3. All these machines work perfectly—indeed, I have complete plans for them in my briefcase over there—but when I try to put the three properties together in one machine, something goes wrong!"

"Just what is it that goes wrong?" asked Craig.

"Why, the machine doesn't work at all!" cried Walton, with an air of desperation. "When I put in a pair (x,y) of numbers, instead of getting an output, I get a strange buzzing sound—something like a short circuit! Do you have any idea why that is?"

"Well, well!" said Craig. "This is something I'll have to think about. I must be off now on a case, but if you'll leave your card—or, if you haven't one, your name and address—I will let you know if I can arrive at any solution."

Several days later, Inspector Craig wrote a letter to Walton that began as follows:

My dear Mr. Walton:

I thank you for your visit and for calling my attention to the machine that you are trying to build. To be perfectly honest, I cannot quite see how, even if you actually constructed such a machine, it would be capable of solving *all* mathematical problems, but doubtless you understand this matter better than I. More to the point, however, I must tell you that your project is much like trying to build a perpetual-motion machine: it simply cannot be done! Indeed, the situation here is even worse—for a perpetual-motion machine, though not possible in this physical world, is not *logically* impossible; whereas such a machine as you propose is not merely physically impossible, but logically impossible, since the three properties you mention conceal a logical contradiction.

Craig's letter then went on to explain just why the existence of such a machine is a logical impossibility. Can you see why?

It will be helpful to break up the solution into three steps:

(1) Show that for any machine having Property 1, for any number a, there must be at least one number x such that $M(x,a)$ has the same parity as x.

(2) Show that for any machine having Properties 1 and 2, for any number b, there is some number x such that $M(x,b)$ has a different parity from x.

(3) No machine can have Properties 1, 2, and 3 combined.

◆ SOLUTION ◆

(a) Consider a machine with Property 1. Take any number a. By Property 1 there is a number b such that for every x, $M(x,b)$ has the same parity as $M(x^{\#},a)$. In particular, with b taken for x, $M(b,b)$ has the same parity as $M(b^{\#},a)$. However

$M(b,b)$ is the number $b^{\#}$, so $b^{\#}$ has the same parity as $M(b^{\#},a)$. So, letting x be the number $b^{\#}$, we see that $M(x,a)$ has the same parity as x.

(b) Consider now any machine having properties 1 and 2. Take any number b. By Property 2 there is some a such that for every x, $M(x,a)$ has different parity than $M(x,b)$. And, by Property 1, there is at least one x such that $M(x,a)$ has the same parity as x, as we proved in (a) above. Such an x must then have different parity from $M(x,b)$—because it has the same parity as $M(x,a)$, which has different parity from $M(x,b)$.

(c) Again consider a machine having properties 1 and 2. Take any number h. According to (b) above, (reading "h" for "b") there is at least one x such that $M(x,h)$ has different parity than x. Therefore, it cannot be that for *all* numbers x, $M(x,h)$ has the same parity as x; in other words, Property 3 cannot hold. Thus, Properties 1, 2, and 3 are "incomposible" (to use Ambrose Bierce's lovely term!).

Note: The impossibility of Walton's machine is closely related to Tarski's theorem (Chapter 15), and it is not difficult to prove the theorem and the machine's impossibility by a common argument.

◈ 19 ◈

Leibniz's
Dream

Fergusson (as well as Walton, in his own peculiar way) was attempting something which, if successful, would fulfil one of Leibniz's most fervent dreams: Leibniz envisioned the possibility of a calculating machine that could solve all mathematical problems—and all philosophical ones as well! Leaving aside the philosophical problems, it appears that for even the mathematical ones, Leibniz's dream is not feasible. This follows from the results of Gödel, Rosser, Church, Kleene, Turing, and Post, to whose work we now turn.

There is a type of computing machine whose function is to calculate a mathematical operation on the positive integers. For such a machine, you feed in a number x (the input) and out comes a number y (the output). For example, you can easily design a machine (not a very interesting one, to be sure!) such that whenever a number x is fed in, out comes the number $x + 1$. Such a machine may be said to *compute* the operation of adding 1. Or we might have a machine that computes an operation, on two numbers, such as addition. For such a machine, you first feed in a number x, then a number y; then you press a button and, after a while, out comes the number $x + y$. (There is a technical name for such machines, of course—I believe they are called *adding machines!*)

There is another type of machine that might be called a *generating* or *enumerating* machine, which will play a more fundamental role in the approach we will take here (it follows the theories of Post). Such a machine has no inputs; it is programmed to generate a set of positive integers. For example, we might have one machine to generate the set of even numbers, another to generate the set of odd numbers, another to generate the set of prime numbers, and so forth. A typical program for a machine to generate the even numbers might run something like the following.

We give the machine two instructions: (1) that it print out the number 2; (2) that if ever it prints out a number n it may also print out $n + 2$. (You also give auxiliary rules that *systematize* following the instructions, so that anything the machine *can* do, it eventually *will* do.) Such a machine, obeying Instruction (1), will sooner or later print out 2, and having printed 2, it will sooner or later, by Instruction (2), print out 4, and having printed 4 will sooner or later print 6, again by Instruction (2), then 8, then 10, and so forth. This machine, then, will generate the set of even numbers. (Without further instructions, it could never come out with 1, 3, 5, or any of the odd numbers.) To program a machine to generate the set of odd numbers, of course, we need merely change the first instruction to: "Print out 1." Sometimes two or more machines are coupled so that the output of one machine can be used by one of the other machines. For example, suppose we have two machines, A and B, and program them as follows: To A we give two instructions: "(1) Print out 1; (2) if ever Machine B prints out n, then print out $n + 1$." To Machine B we give only one instruction: "(1) If ever Machine A prints out n, then print out $n + 1$." What set will A generate, and what set will B generate? The answer is that A will generate the set of odd numbers and B will generate the set of even numbers.

Now, a program for a generating machine, instead of being given in English, is coded into a positive integer (in the form of a string of digits) and matters can be arranged so that every positive integer is the number of some program. We let M_n be the machine whose program has code number n. We now think of all generating machines as listed in the infinite sequence M_1, M_2, ..., M_n, ... (M_1 is the machine whose program number is 1, M_2 the machine whose program number is 2, and so forth.)

For any number set A (set of positive integers, that is) and any machine M, we shall say that M *generates* A or, alternatively, that M *enumerates* A, if every number in A is eventually printed out by M; but no number outside A ever gets printed out by M. We shall say that A is *effectively enumerable* (another technical term is *recursively enumerable*) if there is at least one machine M_i that enumerates A. We shall say that A is *solvable* (another technical term is *recursive*) if there is one machine M_i that enumerates A and another machine M_j that enumerates the set of all numbers that are not in A. Thus, A is solvable if and only if both A and its complement Ā are effectively enumerable.

Suppose A *is* solvable, and we are given a machine M_i that generates A and a machine M_j that generates the complement of A. Then we have an effective procedure to determine whether any number n lies inside A or outside A: Suppose, for example, we wish to know whether the number 10 is in A or not. We set both machines, M_i and M_j, going simultaneously and wait. If 10 lies inside A, then sooner or later M_i will print out 10, and we will know that 10 belongs to A. If 10 lies outside A, then sooner or later machine M_j will print out

10, and we will know that 10 doesn't belong to A. So, eventually and inevitably, we will know whether 10 belong to A or whether it doesn't. (Of course, we have no idea in advance of how long we will have to wait; all we know is that in *some* finite time we will know the answer.)

Now, suppose a set A is effectively enumerable but not solvable. Then we have a machine M_i that generates A, but we have no machine to generate the complement of A. Suppose again we would like to know whether a given number—say, 10—is or is not in A. The best we can do in this case is to set the machine M_i going and hope for the best! We now have only a 50 percent chance of ever learning the answer. If 10 *is* in A, then sooner or later we will know it, because sooner or later M_i will print out 10. If 10 is not in A, however, M_i will never print out 10, but no matter how long we wait, we will have no assurance that M_i might not print out 10 at some later time. So if 10 is in A, we will sooner or later know that it is, but if 10 isn't in A, then at no time can we definitely know that it isn't (at least by observing only the machine M_i). We might aptly call such a set A *semisolvable.*

The first important feature of these generating machines is that it is possible to design a so-called *universal* machine U whose function is to observe systematically the behavior of all the machines M_1, M_2, . . ., M_n, . . ., and whenever a machine M_x prints out a number y, U is to report the fact. How does it make this report? By printing out a number: for any x and y we again let $x*y$ be the number, which consists of a string of 1's of length x followed by a string of 0's of length y. Our principal instruction to U is: "Whenever M_x prints out y, then print out $x*y$."

Suppose, for example, that M_a is programmed to generate the set of odd numbers, and M_b is programmed to generate the set of even numbers. Then U will print out all the numbers $a*1$, $a*3$, $a*5$, $a*7$, etc., and also all the numbers $b*2$, $b*4$, $b*6$, $b*8$, etc., but U will never print out $a*4$ (since M_a never prints out 4), nor $b*3$ (since M_b never prints out 3).

Now, the machine U itself has a program, hence is one of the programmable machines M_1, M_2, . . ., M_n, . . . Thus, there is a number k such that M_k is the very machine U! (In a more complete technical account of the matter, I could tell you what the number k is.)

We might note that this universal machine M_k observes and reports its own behavior as well as that of all the other machines. So whenever M_k prints out a number n, it must also print out $k*n$, hence also $k*(k*n)$, hence also $k*[k*(k*n)]$, and so forth.

A second important feature of these machines is that for any machine M_a we can program a machine M_b to print out those and only those numbers x such that M_a prints out $x*x$. (M_b, so to speak, "keeps watch" on M_a and is instructed to print out x whenever M_a prints $x*x$.) It is possible to code programs in such a way that for each a, $2a$ is such a number b; that is, for every a, M_{2a} prints out those and only those numbers x such that M_a prints out $x*x$. We will assume this done, and so let us record two basic facts that will be used in what follows:

Fact 1: The universal machine U prints out those and only those numbers $x*y$ such that M_x prints out y.

Fact 2: For every number a, the machine M_{2a} prints out those and only those numbers x such that M_a prints out $x*x$.

We now come to the central issue: Any formal mathematical problem can be translated into a question of whether a machine M_a does or does not print out a number b. That is, given any formal axiom system, one can assign Gödel numbers to all the sentences of the system and find a number a

such that the machine M_a prints out the Gödel numbers of the provable sentences of the system, and no other numbers. So to find out whether a given sentence is or is not provable in the system, we take its Gödel number b and ask whether the machine M_a does or does not print out b. Thus, if we had some effective method of deciding which machines print out which numbers, we could then effectively decide which sentences are provable in which axiom systems. This would constitute a realization of Leibniz's dream. Moreover, the question of which machines print out which numbers can be reduced to the question of which numbers are printed out by the universal machine U, because the question of whether or not machine M_a prints out b is equivalent to the question of whether or not U prints out the number $a \ast b$. Therefore, a complete knowledge of U would entail a complete knowledge of all the machines, and hence of all mathematical systems. Conversely, any question of whether a given machine prints out a given number can be reduced to a question of whether a certain sentence is provable in a certain mathematical system, and so a complete knowledge of all formal mathematical systems would imply a complete knowledge of the universal machine.

The key question, then, is this: Let V be the set of numbers printed out by the universal machine U (this set V is sometimes called the *universal set*). Is this set V solvable or not? If it is, then Leibniz's dream is realized; if it isn't, then Leibniz's dream cannot ever be realized. Since V is effectively enumerable (it is generated by the machine U), the question boils down to whether or not there is some machine M_a that prints out the *complement* $\bar{V}$ of V; that is, is there a machine M_a which prints out those and only those numbers that U does *not* print? This question can be completely answered just on the basis of the given conditions Facts 1 and 2 above.

Theorem L: The set $\bar{V}$ is not effectively enumerable: Given any machine M_a, either there is some number in $\bar{V}$ that M_a fails to print, or $\bar{M}$ prints at least one number that is in V rather than $\bar{V}$.

Can the reader see how to prove Theorem L? To take a special case, suppose the claim were made that the machine M_5 enumerated $\bar{V}$. To disprove this claim, it would suffice to exhibit a number n and show that either n is in $\bar{V}$ and M_5 fails to print n or n is in V and M_5 prints n. Can you find such a number n?

I shall give the solution now rather than at the end of the chapter. The solution is really Gödel's argument over again:

Take any number a. By Fact 2, for every number x, M_a prints $x*x$ if and only if M_{2a} prints x. But, also by Fact 1, M_{2a} prints x if and only if the universal machine U prints $2a*x$, or, what is the same thing, if and only if $2a*x$ is in the set V. Therefore, M_a prints $x*x$ if and only if $2a*x$ is in V. In particular (taking $2a$ for x), M_a prints the number $2a*2a$ if and only if $2a*2a$ is in V. So either: (1) M_a prints $2a*2a$ and $2a*2a$ is in V; (2) M_a doesn't print $2a*2a$ and $2a*2a$ is in $\bar{V}$. If (1) holds, then M_a prints out the number $2a*2a$, which is not in $\bar{V}$ but in V; this means that M_a does not generate the set $\bar{V}$, because it prints out at least one number ($2a*2a$), which is not in $\bar{V}$. If (2) holds, then again M_a fails to generate the set $\bar{V}$, because the number $2a*2a$ is in $\bar{V}$ but fails to get printed by M_a. So in neither case does M_a generate the set $\bar{V}$. Since no machine can generate $\bar{V}$, the set $\bar{V}$ is not effectively enumerable.

Of course, for the special case $a = 5$, the number n is $10*10$.

Now, what does all this mean with respect to Leibniz's dream? Strictly speaking, one cannot prove or disprove the feasibility of Leibniz's hope, because it was not stated in an exact form. Indeed, no precise notion of a "calculating machine" or "generating machine" existed in Leibniz's day; these notions have been rigorously defined only in this century. They have been defined in many different ways (by Gödel, Herbrand, Kleene, Church, Turing, Post, Smullyan, Markov, and many others), but all these definitions have been shown to be equivalent. If by "solvable" is meant solvable according to any of these equivalent definitions, then Leibniz's dream is not feasible, because the simple fact is that the machines can be numbered in such a way that Facts 1 and 2 do hold. Then, by Theorem L, the set V generated by the universal machine is not solvable; it is only semisolvable. Therefore, there is no purely "mechanical" procedure for finding out which sentences are provable in which axiom systems and which ones are not. Thus, any attempt to invent a clever "mechanism" that will solve all mathematical problems for us is simply doomed to failure.

In the prophetic words of the logician Emil Post (1944), this means that mathematical thinking is, and must remain, essentially creative. Or, in the witty comment of the mathematician Paul Rosenbloom, it means that man can never eliminate the necessity of using his own intelligence, regardless of how cleverly he tries.

"Haley? Are you feeling ill?"

In an instant her eyes lost the hollow look and began to spark blue fire. "I'm fine," she said. "I'm not sick. But some jerk woke me up last night and opened a box of memories I'd safely put away under lock and key for almost twenty-five years."

Roger hesitated, waiting, giving her a chance to continue. Then, wondering if he was prying, he asked the question boldly. "Your kidnapping?"

"Yes." She snapped the word.

"I never heard much about it," he said. "I was too young, nobody said anything to me and I just picked up that it had happened. But it was over quickly, right?"

Something in her posture eased. Her face and tone quieted a bit. "That didn't make it much better."

"I don't imagine it would. I can't conceive of anything more terrifying no matter how long it lasted."

"It wasn't just the terror," she said slowly. Then she seemed to shake herself. "It's in the past," she said, as if reminding herself.

"Maybe not far enough in the past," he remarked.

* * *

Be sure to check out the rest of the Conard County: The Next Generation miniseries!

* * *

If you're on Twitter, tell us what you think of Harlequin Romantic Suspense! #harlequinromsuspense

Dear Reader,

Traumatic events from our childhood can affect us for a long time, possibly throughout the rest of our lives. They can affect our perceptions of events in the present and our emotional well-being. They should never be minimized. While therapy can help, it cannot erase, and many will be haunted forever.

A single event can trigger us. We may experience paranoia and fear that we might once again experience terrible things. A hurricane, a tornado and other severe traumas may sometimes not be recognized as such until much later when we find ourselves lost in a cold sweat and an unwilling trip down the rabbit hole of memory.

We can also try to dismiss our current reactions as out of proportion to what is actually happening. We may be right about that or we may be wrong. Regardless, we have had our brains imprinted with a terrible experience. It will not go away.

In this story, Haley McKinsey falls into that rabbit hole of her past abduction. She doubts her own fears, doubts her own interpretation, tries to tell herself she is overreacting. Roger McLeod doesn't think she is and becomes her ally as she faces the moment when present and past combine to create terror.

Rachel Lee

STALKED IN
CONARD COUNTY

Rachel Lee

HARLEQUIN® ROMANTIC SUSPENSE

Recycling programs
for this product may
not exist in your area.

ISBN-13: 978-1-335-62638-7
ISBN-13: 978-1-335-08181-0 (DTC Edition)

Stalked in Conard County

HARLEQUIN®
™ www.Harlequin.com

Printed in U.S.A.

Rachel Lee was hooked on writing by the age of twelve and practiced her craft as she moved from place to place all over the United States. This *New York Times* bestselling author now resides in Florida and has the joy of writing full-time.

Books by Rachel Lee

Harlequin Romantic Suspense

Conard County: The Next Generation

Guardian in Disguise
The Widow's Protector
Rancher's Deadly Risk
What She Saw
Rocky Mountain Lawman
Killer's Prey
Deadly Hunter
Snowstorm Confessions
Undercover Hunter
Playing with Fire
Conard County Witness
A Secret in Conard County
A Conard County Spy
Conard County Marine
Undercover in Conard County
Conard County Revenge
Conard County Watch
Stalked in Conard County

Harlequin Intrigue

Conard County: The Next Generation

Cornered in Conard County
Missing in Conard County
Murdered in Conard County

Visit the Author Profile page at Harlequin.com for more titles.

Chapter 1

The full moon glowed almost as bright as an icy sun. It poured through the window in Haley McKinsey's bedroom, reaching through her eyelids and gently prompting her to wake.

As her eyes fluttered open, she stared with amazement at the brilliance of the silvery orb. A small smile curved her lips as she drank in the rare beauty. She'd never seen this from her apartment in Baltimore. Just another thing to make her think more seriously about moving to Wyoming. Inheriting her grandmother's house in Conard City had initially seemed like a generous gift. She could sell it and use the money for a great many things. Nurses weren't exactly overpaid.

But since arriving two days ago, she'd begun to remember the occasional summer visits here, and as the memories came back to her, the house began to feel like it might be her new home.

Seeing the moon now, enjoying the magic of being awakened by its silvery light, she found another reason to want to remain. There hadn't been very many vacations here, but there had been enough to give her a stack of good memories.

Such a beautiful place!

Lying there in a drowsy, pleasant place, the worries of the world and the past seemed far away.

Until the face appeared at the lower ledge of her window. She couldn't see it clearly because of the moon's brightness behind it, but her heart slammed into high gear and she sat up immediately, trying to think of what she could use for a weapon.

Even as she had the thought, the face dropped from view. Had someone really been there? Had she imagined it in the hinterland between waking and sleeping?

With her heart in her throat, her mouth as dry as sand, she wondered if she should even move. Should she go out and look? Should she call the police?

A Peeping Tom. Maybe only a nuisance and not a threat.

It didn't matter. She jumped up like a child scared of the monster under the bed or in the closet. The window was open a crack to let in the cool night air, and she slammed it and locked it. Then she pulled the heavy insulated curtains closed, shutting out the moonlight.

Resentment filled her. Hard on its heels came anger and fear. Resentment because she so much enjoyed sleeping in her grandmother's room. As a child, when she'd visited, she had often shared the bed with her grandmother. It was a sacred place.

Anger because her privacy had been invaded. Lying in the moonlight, she must have been easily visible to the voyeur.

Fear because as a five-year-old child she had been kidnapped through her bedroom window by a faceless man who had just two days later deposited her on a deserted road outside Gillette, where she had eventually been discovered by a roughneck on the way to work.

She hurried through the house, checking every window and door to ensure it was locked. Even on the second floor, she drew the curtains against the moon's beauty. Feeling chilled, she pulled on her red velour robe. Then she sat curled up on the living room sofa, trying to deal with the emotional storm that had been unleashed within her.

With her knees tucked under her chin, she practiced the breathing exercises her childhood therapist had taught her, at least as well as she could when curled up. Her mind bounced around between calling the sheriff, who wouldn't be able to do anything because the guy was gone, an urgent but unsuccessful desire to believe it had been a trick of her sleepy mind, and waiting for morning to release her from her dark cave.

Because, suddenly, this beloved house *felt* like a cave and she felt trapped in it.

Don't be silly, she argued with herself. Just because something bad happened to you over twenty years ago doesn't mean it will happen again.

But memories she had buried long ago bubbled up

like a hot tar pit, black and ugly. She'd been lucky, she reminded herself. Lucky that her kidnapper had released her unharmed after only two days. Lucky that she had grown up with a protective father and mother, and a grandmother who had given her magical experiences.

Reminded herself of how the therapist had insisted that she had done nothing wrong, that she had nothing to feel guilty about.

That she wasn't a bad girl.

She thought she'd moved past that. *Believed* she had moved past that. Then in one split second some jerk had brought it all back.

She couldn't allow this. But she still sat in the dark with all the curtains drawn, straining to hear any untoward sound. The prized clock, a genuine Regulator, kept ticking as normal from the dining room wall, a familiar sound from happy times. The scent of her grandmother's beloved lavender sachets filled the house. No unfamiliar odors, no unusual sounds, crept through the darkened house. It was so quiet, in fact, that her heartbeat sounded loud in her ears.

She supposed someone else would have the nerve to go outside to see if the guy was still there. She couldn't bring herself to do that. It wasn't that she was a coward; it was that his appearance at her bedroom window had cast her back to her abduction as a child.

Somewhere inside her, that little girl still resided.

But as her fear began to ease, her ire began to rise. She'd been enjoying a beautiful gift from nature, the biggest, brightest full moon she'd ever seen. That invader had ruined it.

Hell, he'd ruined more than that, she thought grimly. Would she ever again feel comfortable with sleeping in this house when a window was cracked open as she had tonight? Would she feel she needed to keep the heavy curtains drawn all the time now? That she had to sell this house or live in a cave as long as she stayed?

Finding that her strength had returned, she rose from the sofa and made her way to the kitchen. Grandma had believed in insulated curtains to save on heat, and she certainly hadn't shorted the kitchen windows. As Haley turned on the light, she looked at a line of navy-blue curtains that skimmed the top of the backsplash over the sink and completely sealed out the night. She put the battered whistling teakettle on the stove and began to heat water. The ginger jar, a delightful blue-and-white copy of some original, still held Grandma's favorite green tea. A cup of that ought to return the night to normal familiarity.

She decided against calling the police before the day completely dawned because the guy was gone, and a bunch of strobing blue, white and red lights on the street might disturb her neighbors. Morning was soon enough.

She was safe. Of course she was safe. She'd just arrived in this town and there was no reason for anyone to want to disturb her in any way. So what if some guy had looked in her window, probably out of curiosity. If he was interested in something else, he was in for a surprise. The self-defense classes she'd been taking for years, to deal with the sense of helplessness her abduction had given her, were at the ready.

Next time, if there was a next time, she wouldn't

allow fear to overwhelm her before she could react. She'd be ready.

The teakettle shrieked its tuneless note as steam poured out the spout. She rose, spooned some tea leaves into a china cup and filled it with hot water. That brought back memories, too, of how her grandmother would finish a cup of tea and turn the cup upside down on the saucer, spinning it three times. Then Grandma would enchant her by "reading" the leaves that adhered inside the bottom of the teacup. As Haley grew older, she understood it was just a game, but one she'd always enjoyed.

She wondered if she could read the leaves for herself. That might distract her until the sun replaced the moon in the sky.

She was beginning to feel foolish for the strength of her reaction to the Peeping Tom. She was safe and snug in a house full of good memories, and she shouldn't allow anyone to ruin that.

Determination mostly replaced her instinctive fear, and the soothing ritual of making tea helped considerably. The fragrance of the green tea filled her with warm memories. Memories of her grandma telling her how all tea came from one kind of plant in Southeast China. Of how the difference in flavors was made by how the tea was cured. Of course, Grandma had told her scrupulously, all teas started from the same plant but over centuries the transplanting of those plants had resulted in a few different varietals. But still, she said firmly, tea all goes back to the same plant.

When they went to the store to buy more tea, young Haley had stared in fascination at all the boxes announcing different names and tried to imagine the old times when tea had to cross perilous mountain routes to reach the rest of the world.

She could understand, even at a young age, why tea had been so important to so many. Like spices, she thought. The harder it was to get them, the more valued they became.

The tea tasted a bit on the old side, and she promised herself she'd get a fresh box in the morning. Grandma must not have been drinking it often toward the end. But then, she'd never let anyone in the family know she was failing until the day before she died.

The trip down memory lane was relaxing her, as was the comforting tea and thoughts of her grandmother. Then, rising from the mists of childhood, she remembered Roger McLeod. He'd been a few years older than her, but it hadn't seemed to trouble him. He spent some of his free time with her, playing games or regaling her with local history. "Even grandmothers need a break," he'd joked once.

She wondered if he still lived down the street. When she'd met him, he'd been his father's apprentice, making custom saddles for the horse owners hereabouts. Once she'd been allowed into the workshop and had been amazed how many layers of leather were used, each one treated and stretched and cut to fit some part of the saddle precisely.

"It has to be comfortable," he'd explained once. "People who spend long hours riding can't afford to get sore because the saddle just doesn't fit right. And there's the horse, of course. It needs customization as much as the rider."

She smiled now, remembering that day so long ago. She'd been what, thirteen? And he'd been graduating from high school. Hadn't Grandma mentioned him occasionally in her letters?

He must still be around here. Maybe still in his father's house two doors down. She smiled at last and decided she'd overreacted to a Peeping Tom. She'd tell the cops in the morning, and they'd check it out. That alone would probably be enough to keep the guy from coming near here again.

She glanced at the clock on the wall over the free-standing stove and saw that it was shortly past four. She should try to get some more sleep, if she could.

She climbed back into her grandmother's bed, feeling its familiarity surround her like a hug. She didn't crack the window, though, or open the curtains.

That creep might still be out there.

Haley was making a breakfast of scrambled eggs and toast when she heard the knock at the door. It wasn't that early, but eight o'clock still seemed like an early hour to be knocking. She made the person wait while she scraped the eggs onto a plate so they wouldn't burn. Then, grabbing a kitchen towel, she wiped her hands as she went to answer the door.

For an instant, just an instant, she didn't recognize Roger McLeod. He'd filled out and grown quite a powerful set of shoulders in the intervening years.

"Remember me? Roger McLeod? Sorry to bother

you, Haley, but I got concerned when I saw all the curtains drawn. Your grandmother never did that."

"I know she didn't." She stepped back, tacitly inviting him inside. "And I do remember you. How's life treating you, Roger?"

He smiled, a warm expression that she remembered from years ago. She liked the way his smile reached his green eyes, crinkling them a bit in the corners. "It's going well. I'm busy, which I guess is the thing. I'm really sorry about Flora, though. She never mentioned she was getting sick."

"She never mentioned it to the family, either, until the day before she died. Come on, I just made fresh coffee if you'd like some."

Again that smile that seemed to send warmth running all the way to her toes. Was she losing her mind? He hadn't affected her that way years ago.

"I never say no to a morning cup of joe," he answered. Once in the kitchen, he sat at the table as if he had a regular place there.

She poured his coffee. "Cream? Sugar?"

"Straight, thanks. We haven't seen much of you over the last few years."

"No." She brought her plate of eggs and toast to the table. "Want me to make you some?"

"I'm fine." His eyes smiled at her over the rim of the cup.

"I feel bad that I couldn't come visit more often, but I'm a nurse. Grandma must have mentioned it."

"She did." He nodded.

"Well, my hours stink and my vacations are short

and scattered. Instead of me coming out here, she used to fly back East to visit."

"That's right. I remember. It's been a while, though."

A while. Sorrow shadowed Haley's heart. Grandma had been in the habit of flying out to visit every year, staying with Haley for a week or so. A comfortable pattern. Then Grandma had missed a summer, made some excuse Haley couldn't even remember now, and she felt guilty for not having realized that something was wrong.

Well, she could kick herself over that later, she decided as she forked some scrambled egg into her mouth then followed it with a bite of rye toast. The voyeur seemed like a more immediate issue and she wondered if she should even bring it up to Roger. He'd stopped in to offer a friendly greeting, not necessarily to get dragged into any part of her life.

"Listen," he said. "This is an old house and I used to do some work on it from time to time when Flora needed it. I was in the middle of a project to fix the ductwork in the basement when she…took ill."

She looked up from her plate. Man, she'd forgotten this guy was so attractive. Maybe he hadn't been years ago, when still a stripling. "What's wrong with the ducts?"

He put his mug down. "A little of everything. Rust, age, shrinkage, loose joints. Anyway, it was rattling enough when the heat came on that Flora finally got irritated. I can't say I blame her. She asked me to come over and listen to it. Clang, bang, rattle. And, of course, it came amplified right through the registers. Anyway,

I was replacing it a bit at a time and, unless you have an objection, I'd like to finish the job. I hate to leave work undone."

"I have no objection," she answered promptly. It would be nice to have a chance to get to know him again. "They really make a racket, huh?"

He laughed briefly. "Let me put it this way. If it hadn't happened slowly over time, I think Flora would have blown a gasket. I can't believe how much she got used to before she decided she needed to do something."

"Isn't it funny how we can do that?"

"Oh, yeah. We adapt to an awful lot. Except saddle sores, heel blisters and…well, no need to make a whole list."

It was her turn to laugh. "It's so good to see you again, Roger. It's been an age."

"Yeah, and somewhere along the way we both grew up. I'm sorry you missed Flora's memorial at the church."

"Dad didn't leave me much opportunity to get here. It's okay. Flora didn't want all that for herself."

"That sounds like Flora, all right. Go on, finish your breakfast. I don't know about you, but I hate cold eggs. Come to think of it, cold toast isn't much better."

Part of her wanted to journey down memory lane with him. Thinking back, she realized the two of them really hadn't spent that much time together those few summers she had visited. He'd been apprenticing with his father and only occasionally had time off. As for her grandmother…well, it seemed likely he'd spent more time with her than Haley ever had. They'd been neighbors, after all.

But then he asked the question that directed her to more urgent matters.

"Why do you have all the curtains closed?" he asked. "Flora only did that during the winter."

She laid her fork down on her empty plate. Had she imagined last night? It seemed so distant now, but she was still wrapped in her robe against a chill that didn't exist except inside herself and she *had* turned the house into a cave.

"Last night…" She hesitated, hoping she didn't sound fanciful or hysterical. "The moon was awfully bright. It woke me up and I was staring at it, thinking how beautiful it was when…" She sighed and pushed the words out. "Someone was looking in my window, Roger. It unnerved me." Understatement.

He was already rising from his chair. "Flora's room?"

"Yes."

Before she could say any more, he'd gone out the front door.

She rose to her feet, wondering why her legs felt wobbly. Because she'd addressed what had happened last night, hadn't just shoved it into the background to be forgotten with a million other bad things? She'd learned to do that in early childhood—a lesson she had believed was well-learned, a lesson she used often in her work.

She rinsed her dishes and put them in the dishwasher that her father had installed many years ago during one of her summer visits here. Darn thing was still working.

Then she leaned against the counter, resting her weight on the palms of her hands, and closed her eyes. The image floated up in her mind, as clear as it had been last night. Her heart pounded once, hard, then settled again. A Peeping Tom. Probably no threat at all, just a guy who got his kicks by sneaking looks at sleeping women.

Nothing, she told herself. Nothing to fear.

When Roger returned, he entered the kitchen talking on his cell phone. "Yeah, Flora McKinsey's house on Poplar—901. Her granddaughter's staying here at the moment and last night she had a Peeping Tom. There are footprints under her bedroom window." He paused. "Geez, Gage, how would I know? Probably scared the bejesus out of her. We don't have any known peepers making the rounds, do we?"

He fell silent. Then, "Yeah, I think she'd be glad to see Kelly. Someone has to come, right?"

When he disconnected, Haley let go of the counter and faced him. "I didn't want to make a federal case out of it."

He gave her a half smile. "I did it for you. It matters, it upset you, and there's not a whole lot I can do, not being a cop. Just get yourself another cup of coffee and relax. You'll like Kelly."

"Kelly?" She looked down at herself. "I should get dressed."

"You're decent. Relax. Kelly's one of our K-9 officers. She'll probably talk to you for a few minutes then try to follow the guy's trail. Her dog, by the way, is called Bugle."

"Bugle?" That surprised a small laugh out of her. This was happening too fast. She'd spent most of the night trying to regain her equilibrium, to push childhood memories back into the tar pit, and, with just one phone call, everything was awake and alive again. It didn't matter there was no kidnapper involved. It only mattered that someone at her bedroom window had shaken her life until past ugliness tumbled into the present.

She took Roger's advice and poured herself some fresh coffee before returning to her seat. "It was always odd to me how Grandma would start every day with coffee and switch to tea by midmorning."

"Yeah." He pulled out the chair he'd been sitting in earlier and sat facing her once again. "She never could persuade me about the tea. And, Lord knows, she tried." Then he eyed her straight-on. "Haley? Why didn't you call the police last night?"

The underlying truth burst out of her, shocking her as she faced it. "Because I didn't want to make it real!"

Those vehement words told Roger he'd tripped into a minefield, one he wasn't equipped to handle. Damn, he was just a guy who made saddles. He knew horses better than he knew people. Well, with the possible exception of their riders.

But the very honest anguish Haley had just displayed left him feeling helpless and as if he needed hip waders so he wouldn't get in dangerously deep. The last thing he wanted was to make some stupid comment that would exacerbate whatever Haley was experiencing.

"Sorry," she said quietly. Her gaze was now focused on the coffee mug she held in two hands before her.

"No need." Really there wasn't. His brain was on a rapid search down the halls of memory, trying to pull out some sliver that could give him a clue to this moment. Peering down those hallways, however, told him how little he truly knew about Haley, how little time they'd really spent together. Flora provided more recollections.

But then, somewhere in his mental search, he ran up hard against a nearly forgotten memory. Of course it was nearly forgotten. He'd been what? Twelve or so? At that point he wasn't sure he'd ever met Haley at all, but he'd heard her mentioned. And he suddenly remembered, although it hadn't seemed important at the time, not to a kid, something about her having been kidnapped and returned unharmed. In fact, by the time any adult had mentioned it around him, she was safely at home.

And his young mind had dismissed the event as unimportant.

After Haley's reaction just now, he realized the memory was *not* in her distant past and that at this moment it was very much present.

Calling the police would make it more real? Uh, yeah. God, she'd probably spent much of the night wrestling with recollections that should have been buried beneath a tombstone nearly a quarter century ago.

All of a sudden, the Peeping Tom no longer seemed like a minor nuisance that needed to be looked into. Suddenly he seemed like a major threat to Haley's peace of mind. Problem was, Roger didn't know what to do about it. Nor, likely, would the police.

Conard City—in fact, the whole county—was by and large a peaceful place. Oh, yeah, they had their share of loonies and wackos, but overall it was still a place where people felt safe, let their children play outside and all the Norman Rockwell rest of it.

Of course, some of that was illusion. Everyone knew it but clung to it anyway. So far, he didn't think many had paid a high price for believing everything was okay around here. People might be irritated by the idea of a Peeping Tom, but they'd be equally certain they'd figure out who it was and, between a misdemeanor charge and public disapproval, he'd get back in line or leave town.

But if the guy peeked in on kids…well, local ire might be explosive. It was something he'd seen early in life. The village would put up with the idiot because he was one of them. If the village idiot went beyond the pale, however, tolerance would evaporate.

He was just putting together careful words to ask Haley if her reaction had to do with her kidnapping when a heavy knock sounded on the front door. Police, he thought with mild amusement, were never timid about pounding for attention.

"That must be Kelly," he said, rising. "Should I ask her in or just show her where the footprints are?"

She tilted her head a little and smiled. "I'm not a hermit. I'd like to meet her. I just hope she doesn't think I'm overreacting."

"There isn't a soul around here who'd think anyone was overreacting to having someone peer into their bedroom window in the middle of the night. You can relax about that."

The front door wasn't far away. A small foyer divided the ground floor of the house, a foyer he'd helped to refinish a few years back when Flora had remarked the wood wainscoting was looking rough. Dryness had begun to crack it, so he applied sandpaper and oil and made it look as good as new. His reward had been Flora's delight. All he'd ever wanted, although she'd often drowned his bachelor self with all kinds of tasty casseroles because, according to her, cooking for one was a pain.

It was a nice excuse.

He opened the door and found Kelly Noveno there with Bugle, a Belgian Malinois. Bugle sat politely beside her, looking attentive. Kelly herself was a pleasant eyeful with dark hair and snapping dark eyes, but she was already claimed by Al Carstairs, the animal control officer. A guy could still look.

Haley herself was a lovely woman. As a rule, he didn't find blondes appealing, but Haley was different. And those blue eyes of hers looked like deep, still waters, even now. Under less stressful circumstances, she might have lit his fire.

"Come on in, Kelly. Haley's at the kitchen table and I don't think she got much sleep."

"I heard that," Haley called from the kitchen. "Caffeine helps. Want some, Deputy?"

"Kelly, please. And I'd love some." Once in the kitchen, she put Bugle at ease and invited Haley to pet him. "He's a friendly guy, but don't touch him without permission."

"I get that," Haley answered with a smile. "I feel almost silly about this," she remarked as she brought Kelly a mug of coffee and joined her and Roger at the table. Revealing more than she probably realized, she clutched her robe closer. Roger didn't overlook it, though.

"Silly?" Kelly repeated. "Some guy peers in your bedroom window in the middle of the night and you feel silly for telling the police about it? Gimme a break."

At that, Haley laughed, and Roger felt some relief. Whatever had been going on earlier, that remark about making this all *real* could wait for another time. A time when he felt he'd gleaned enough to know where it might be headed.

Flora, he knew, would want him to look out for her granddaughter, but he at least had to have some idea what she needed. That meant getting to know her better.

"Okay," Kelly said, pulling out a notebook. "About what time did you see this guy?"

Haley furrowed her brow. "I hate to say this, but I'm not exactly sure. The moon woke me up, coming through my window. It was so bright!"

"Supermoon, at its closest point to earth." Kelly nodded. "Okay, so the moon was still high enough to be visible over the rooftops of surrounding houses." She tapped her pencil a few times. "Say sometime between two and three. At three, it would have been disappearing behind everything, including the mountains to the west. What exactly did you see?"

"Nothing," Haley said, flushing faintly. "The moonlight was coming from behind him and I couldn't make out his features, just his shape."

"But he could probably see you," Kelly said.

Haley nodded slowly. "I'm pretty sure of that."

The image summoned to Roger's mind made his stomach knot tightly. Some sleaze staring in the window with Haley sound asleep and fully illuminated by the moonlight.

The picture might have been magical except for the circumstances. Instead it was creepy.

"How long was he there?" Kelly asked.

"I'm not certain. I mean, to me, it was as if he popped up, looked in, and then when I started to sit up, he just vanished. If he was there earlier, I don't know."

Roger's jaw tightened, his teeth clenched. "In other words, he might have been observing you for some time. No way to know."

Haley frowned faintly. "But then why would he just suddenly pop up?"

Kelly spoke. "Good question. Let me go outside and survey the scene." She looked at Roger. "Want to show me?"

She thanked Haley for the coffee and Roger followed Kelly and the dog out the front door. "Why," Kelly asked quietly, "would she think it was silly to call us about a Peeping Tom?"

"I'm not sure," Roger answered, although the truth felt as if it were sitting in his gut like a lead weight. He was convinced this had something to do with her kidnapping, but it wasn't his place to speculate. He trusted Kelly, so that wasn't the issue. The issue was that he didn't know for sure. To figure it out, he'd need more than a few old memories. And it still wouldn't be his place to say. "You'll have to ask her."

"Maybe I will."

They reached the spot beneath the window and Kelly studied the scuffed dirt. It was easy to tell that someone had stood there, but no print was really clear, Roger thought now.

"Well, that's not helpful," Kelly remarked. "Okay, you go back inside with Haley. Bugle and I are about to take a walk and see what we can learn. Bugle, seek."

That dog, Roger had thought more than once, understood a great deal. Without further direction, Bugle sniffed around the scuffed area then headed toward the alley behind the house. Kelly followed.

"I'll let you both know if I find anything."

"Thanks."

Back inside, he found Haley still sitting at the table with cooling coffee in front of her. Except now she looked frozen, her gaze almost hollow, haunted.

He was a man who liked to fix things, but this was something that didn't appear to be easily fixable. Whatever was going on inside that woman was clearly above his pay grade. He sat again so that he'd be at her eye level, even though his whole body wanted action right now.

"Kelly and Bugle are following a scent. She'll let us know if she finds anything."

Haley gave a brief, jerky nod.

"Haley? Are you feeling ill? Do you want to go see a doctor?"

In an instant her eyes lost the hollow look and began to spark blue fire. "I'm *fine*," she said. "I'm not sick. But some jerk woke me up last night and opened a box of memories I'd safely put away under lock and key for almost twenty-five years."

He hesitated, waiting, giving her a chance to continue. Then, wondering if he was prying, he asked the question boldly. "Your kidnapping?"

"Yes." She snapped the word.

He nodded and leaned back, half deciding to just shut his mouth. She doubtless didn't want to be poked and pried at. Remembering was probably bad enough. But people didn't really forget things, no matter how deeply they buried them. What if she needed an ear right now?

"I never heard much about it," he said "I was too young, nobody said anything to me, and I just picked up that it had happened. But it was over quickly, right?"

Something in her posture eased. Her face and tone quieted a bit. "That didn't make it much better."

"I don't imagine it would. I can't conceive of anything more terrifying, no matter how long it lasted."

"It wasn't just the terror," she said slowly. Then she seemed to shake herself. "It's in the past," she said as if reminding herself.

"Maybe not far enough in the past," he remarked, keeping his tone pleasant. "You want more coffee? Are you ready to switch to Flora's tea? Or how about a bottle of water?"

She smiled faintly. "Determined to take care of me, huh?"

"Not much I can do except play waiter and listen." He shrugged. "You can also tell me to butt out. I've even been known to pay attention."

Now her smile widened and he was relieved to see

that she seemed to be shaking off whatever nightmare had haunted her. "No need to butt out. You've been kind, but you must want to get to work."

Was that a dismissal? He decided not. "No rush. The nice thing about being my own boss is that if I need a few hours for something else, I can take them."

Just then there was a knock on the door and Kelly entered with Bugle. "Dead end," she said. "Bugle tracked him to Ash Street and then the scent vanished. Guess he drives to his little trysts. Anyway, if Bugle smells him again anywhere, he'll let me know. Listen, Haley, I'm going to file a report. If we've got a peeper, you might not be the last victim. These guys seem to like to bother more than one person."

"I hope he doesn't bother me again. Thank you, Deputy."

"Kelly. Just Kelly. Come on, Bugle."

Then, in the subsequent silence, Roger took the bull by the horns. "So what did you mean when you said calling the police would make it real?"

Chapter 2

"I was talking about my reaction," she said after several minutes. "At first it seemed like a bad dream, but then it raked up old memories. It was a childish thing to say, Roger. It happened. Reporting it has nothing to do with its reality."

She pushed back from the table and went to the refrigerator, where she pulled out a bottle of water. "Want some?"

"I'm fine, thanks."

She sat again, unscrewing the bottle cap. "I remember the tap water here being very tasty, but I've been chicken to try it. I suppose I should."

"It's good water," he agreed. "Better than some of the stuff in bottles."

Again she smiled. "I remember way back when,

when we were both kids. You were infinitely patient then, too. Remember the fishing expedition?"

He laughed. "How could I forget? I got you all excited about going to my favorite fishing hole and when we got there it was nothing but mud."

"And I wanted to know where the fish had gone since there was no water left."

He laughed again. "They had the sense to get out of Dodge."

"I guess. You must have been as disappointed as I was, but that didn't stop you. We drove up a little way into the mountains and you found us a small pool. What's more, I caught my first fish!"

At least this memory was making her smile. He was glad to see it. In terms of time, her kidnapping seemed like a lifetime ago, at least to him. Apparently not so much to her.

Then she sighed and her smile faded. "I know it was a long time ago," she said, almost as if she could read his mind. "I don't think about the kidnapping often anymore. My dad made sure I had therapy afterward, and I got over it. Mostly. But once in a while…" She trailed off and sighed again, as if some heavy weight filled her. "Once in a while… Like last night. It dragged everything up from the depths. I was kidnapped through my bedroom window, you know."

His heart lurched. God, last night must have been *Halloween*-like for her. "I didn't know."

"I guess that's why I overreacted."

He shook his head. "Waking up to find someone

looking in your bedroom window? Well, I don't think you *can* overreact."

"Maybe not." She shook her head a little, as if trying to shake off bad memories. "I'm wondering if I should sleep upstairs now. I wanted to use that room because I'd shared it with my grandma on the few occasions I came to visit here. When I was really young, before you and I met, it was such a treat to crawl into her bed and have her tease me with riddles until I fell asleep."

"And you wanted to recapture that?"

"Can you ever? But, yeah, good memories. And maybe I should just sleep upstairs, where no one can peek in the windows and I can leave the curtains open and enjoy the fresh night air."

There was a sadness to that. Maybe time to change the subject? "You can decide that later. Frankly, you look like you need a nap, but I guess you had plans for today?"

"I did, sort of. I'm sure I need a nap, but I'm too wound up. Anyway, I was going to go through some more of my grandmother's things. Looking for keepsakes and so on. But then..." She hesitated. "I came here convinced I was going back to Baltimore in a few weeks. But I started to wonder why I shouldn't just stay here. I always liked it, and it's so much quieter than my home. I called yesterday and the community hospital said they could definitely use me, so I'd even have a job."

She drummed her fingers briefly. "At least I was thinking about it until the wee hours this morning. Now I'm not so sure."

"That's understandable. But there's no reason to think the creep will bother you again. And now that he's been reported, he's going to have to be awfully careful about what he does."

"How will he know he's been reported?"

Good question. Roger resisted the impulse to reach across the table and cover her hand with his. Childhood was far behind them both and, for all intents, they were now near strangers. "You opened your eyes and sat up, right? Then he knows he was seen. He'd have no reason to think you didn't report it. Then, Kelly's car was out there this morning and she brought Bugle with her."

Haley smiled wanly. "You're right. My head is kind of foggy. But I'm not ready to take a nap. First I want some of Grandma's green tea, then I'm going to open all the curtains and let some sunlight in."

"Good idea. Then?"

"I'm going to go back to what I was doing, going through her things for keepsakes. Everything else can wait."

"Mind if I go back to work on the ducts downstairs?"

"Help yourself." Her smile widened a bit. "Sure I can't talk you into some tea?"

He laughed, feeling the atmosphere leaven. "Nope. But I'd be willing to make another pot of coffee if you don't mind."

The cup of tea helped. So did opening all the curtains downstairs and letting in the brilliant summer sun. The nightmare of the wee hours seemed to evaporate in the cleansing morning light. The dark miasma that had clung to her since she'd seen the man at the window began to slip into the background, like a bad dream. The sounds from the basement, where Roger occasionally hammered on something, or a duct clanged, helped, too.

Life had returned to this house, and she was almost ashamed of the way she had reacted during the night. Overreaction. Like a child. A hot shower helped, as did dressing in her oldest, softest jeans with threadbare knees and an old T-shirt worn thin from many washings. Age improved some things, for a fact.

She caught her wet hair back in a ponytail and tried to recall her list of tasks for today. Well, it wasn't long before she remembered she'd wanted to air the house out. Despite her grandmother's love of lavender sachets, the house still smelled musty from being closed for so long. Since she'd arrived here a couple of days ago, she'd felt chilled and had wanted to keep the windows mostly closed.

The summer here wasn't very warm. She wondered if that was typical or just a spell. At home in Baltimore, it was a great deal warmer right now, and far more humid. Wyoming felt almost bone-dry. Refreshingly so, she decided.

She put the kettle on again, trying to center herself completely in the here and now. Another cup of tea would help. It would remind her of good things. In the meantime, despite lingering wisps of fear from last night, she opened every single downstairs window and let the soft summer breeze blow through.

When she'd learned she'd inherited the house, she'd had every intention of cleaning it out, storing the important items and selling it. Her life was in Baltimore, after all. Her job, her friends and the hospital she had seemingly wrapped her whole life around. Did she know anyone these days who wasn't in the medical profession?

Anyway, she'd believed herself to be happy. Then this. Somehow over the last couple of days, she'd started thinking of staying. Maybe a crazy decision based on her childhood visits and memories, but the urge was growing. It would certainly turn her life on end, but she wasn't sure that was a bad thing. She'd been kind of digging a comfortable rut at home.

But Wyoming? The state's name could still unnerve her, if only a tiny bit. After her kidnapping, her mother had taken her away to a cousin's in Michigan, no doubt trying to remove any reminders. Her dad had eventually moved his drilling business to the Bakken oil fields in North Dakota. Far enough north to feel different. The family had come together again.

Then her brother, five years her elder, had taken off with the Marines and had become a visitor in her life when he wasn't overseas somewhere. Her mother had left, tired of the life of a woman surrounded by roughnecks, and Haley had stayed with her father because she hadn't wanted him to be all alone.

But he'd been alone eventually anyway. Those summers he'd driven her to stay with her grandmother for a few weeks, and then when she'd knuckled down on her studies, determined to enter a medical career. Like all kids, she became eighteen and moved on to bigger dreams.

Her dad had evidently had some dreams of his own.

These days he was working in the Middle East and would occasionally call her with stories of exotic places, but no, she shouldn't visit him, because life was uncomfortable there for women.

So, once in a while, like her brother, he passed through her life.

But she had a good life, she reminded herself as the kettle whistled and she made a fresh cup of tea. Maybe, however, she'd caught a touch of her dad's wanderlust. Maybe that was making her think of leaving everything behind to move to Wyoming.

Although moving here didn't sound so fantastic after last night. But stamped in her brain like a tattoo was the memory of the moon and seeing that guy peering in, silhouetted against its light. Sheesh, maybe she'd seen a werewolf or something.

The tea tasted good and energized her. There was definitely a nap in her future, but she had wanted to sort through the sideboard in the dining room, with its drawers full of treasured table linens and, once upon a time, a bag of candy corn for a little girl who could have a few if she was very good.

A smile danced across her lips as she carried her cup into the dining room and set it carefully on a hand-crocheted doily that she remembered making when she was about nine. Imagine Grandma saving that all these years. A warmth suffused her and she faced the real reason she wanted to stay. For all she'd built a life in Baltimore, this was the only place that had truly meant home to her.

Sitting cross-legged on the floor, she pulled out the

bottom drawer. Carefully folded tablecloths filled it, and the scent of lavender aroused her senses.

"Haley?"

It sounded as if Roger was at the top of the basement stairs. "I'm in here," she called back. "Need something?"

"Lunch," he admitted as he entered the dining room. She felt him stand just a little behind her. "That's beautiful," he remarked.

She reached out and touched the top layer, a carefully handcrafted lace table cover. As her hand brushed it, she heard the layers of protective tissue underneath rustle slightly. "Lots of history here," she said. "You want me to make lunch?"

"Heck no. I was thinking about running out and picking something up. You want?"

It was still early, but the egg and toast had vanished some time ago. A glance toward the Regulator caused her to wonder where the hours had gone. She hadn't done that much. Had she? Maybe dozed while she was sitting here, given last night.

"Sure," she said after a moment. She started to close the drawer, but Roger squatted beside her and surprised her. "There's a story in that drawer."

She glanced at him and saw his expectant smile. "There probably is," she admitted. "The sad thing about us when we're young is that we aren't always interested in stuff that might be important later. I have a vague memory of Grandma telling me that this drawer holds tablecloths and napkins that belonged to her mother and grandmother. Maybe her great-grandmother. I wish I remembered. Anyway, this top one? Hand-crocheted by my great-grandmother, if I remember correctly. This is a drawer full of antiques and lost memories."

"That's at once neat and sad."

"Yeah." She slowly pushed the drawer in. "She did try to tell me. The drawer above has her personal tablecloths. The ones she used frequently. They're pretty, I remember that much. And this top drawer? I believe it holds her family silver. It also held candy corn for me."

He laughed at that, bringing an answering smile to her face. "I don't suppose someone in your family would know the history of the tablecloths?"

"Not likely. I don't think my dad would have been even as interested as I was, which isn't saying much. Not guy stuff, you know?" She got herself to her feet and pulled the top drawer open. To her amazement, a small, tied-off bag of candy corn sat in one corner. She touched it with a fingertip and felt her eyes burn as she blinked back a few tears. "Aww, Grandma." After all these years. Then her gaze fell on some ceramic squares, maybe an inch-and-a-half on each side, the glaze crazed from the years, but not so much that the brown pattern wasn't visible. "Butter dishes," she said. "Now, those *did* belong to my great-great-grandmother. I think Grandma said they were well over a hundred years old when she showed them to me. See, I do remember something."

Beside them was the big, flat, wooden box that held silverware. The silver was probably tarnished and in need of good cleaning by now. Flora had let some things go over time.

Haley slid the drawer closed and when it stuck just a bit, she decided she needed to wax the runners. "This house is full of treasures," she told Roger. "I just wish I knew more."

"Maybe some of her friends know something. She had a pretty tight-knit group at the church. I'm sure they'd be glad to share anything they know."

"Good idea." She faced him. "Do I need to change into something that doesn't look like it came from a rag bin?"

He laughed. "For around here, you look fine, like any other hard worker. Grab whatever you need. Did Flora ever take you to Maude's diner?"

"Probably." She shook her head a little as if trying to free a memory. "Is that the one called the City Diner now? Just off Main?"

"The same."

That brought another smile to Haley's face. "Now, there's another story. I guess I should close the windows."

Roger hesitated. "Usually, I'd say it's not necessary. But after last night…yeah. I'll go around and help you."

Though it was only a few blocks to the diner, Roger insisted on driving. "You had a rough night. A walk might really wake you up, but a good meal might help you nap."

She certainly didn't feel like arguing. She'd been feeling like a squirrel on high alert since the middle of the night, and no matter how much she thought she was relaxing, even having slept briefly shortly after four, part of her clung to a deep tension. Man, she had to get over this. So some random creep had peered in her window. He'd leave her alone if she kept the curtains closed, and eventually he'd peep in a window where someone would recognize him. Anonymity, she remembered her grandmother saying, didn't come easily in these parts.

The streets looked so familiar to her, though, and soon she forgot the night and began remembering being outside on a breezy summer afternoon, jumping rope, playing hopscotch, or just sitting on the grass and looking up through leafy trees at the bottomless blue of the sky. When Roger'd had some free time, he was kind and would bring over a board game. Together they'd sit on the porch for hours playing Parcheesi, backgammon or checkers. Often her grandmother had brought them a pitcher of fresh-made lemonade, tart and sweet all at once.

She glanced his way again and noted once more how the gangly kid had filled out. In all the right ways, too. A surreptitious smile caught her mouth as she quickly looked away.

"You said there was a story about this diner," Roger remarked as he steered them into a parking place almost directly in front of it.

Haley noted that it hadn't changed much in the intervening years. "Yeah," she said after a moment. "Way back when, around the time this place was first being settled, my great-great-grandmother—at least I think it was, I keep losing track of the greats."

"Can't imagine why," he answered lightly as he turned off his truck's ignition.

She laughed. "There's a lot of them. Anyway, about

the turn of the twentieth century, or just before, my ancestors settled here. Grandad opened an apothecary and, right off it, my grandmother at the time opened a lunch counter. I hear it was quite busy with folks who traveled through by train. The tracks aren't that far from here, as I recall."

"They're near, not that you can tell that often anymore. Few enough trains come through here."

She nodded and pointed at the diner. "It was right there. Anyway, Grandma said they retired just before the war and their son sold it to whoever Maude inherited it from."

"Your roots go deep around here."

"Some of them. Others kind of sprang up elsewhere. Grandma didn't talk a lot about it, but you know Miss Emma, right? The librarian?"

"Doesn't everyone?" he asked wryly. "Founding family."

"Exactly. The McKinseys weren't far behind."

"Another reason to stay," he remarked lightly. Then he climbed out and came around to open her door for her. "Eat well," he said as he helped her down. "Food is good and plentiful and, with any luck, you'll be lights out by sunset so you can catch up on your sleep."

"That'd be nice." Fatigue hadn't reached her yet, but she figured her nursing schedule had made her reasonably immune to the occasional long stint. She could handle it for a while. Tonight she would probably crash into a dead sleep, disturbed by nothing short of an emergency.

Inside, the diner was reasonably quiet, just a few of

the tables busy. Either they were ahead of the lunch rush or behind it, but they had no trouble getting a table in the back. Haley had little desire at the moment to sit in front of a window. Sheesh, she thought, that needed to stop before the fear dug in.

Maude, who looked as if she hadn't changed a bit in twenty years, slapped menus in front of them and filled coffee cups without asking. "Got fancier stuff now, if you want one of them lattes." Then she peered at Haley. "Well, well, well. Heard you was in town. Wondered when you'd show up."

"It's been a while, hasn't it? How are you doing, Maude?"

"Same as usual. Mavis is helping me out these days, but she's got a lot to learn."

Haley figured Mavis would never learn enough to suit her mother. Maude was born to be a dragon.

"Sorry about Flora," Maude added, surprising her. "A good woman." Then, "Order up. The grill's still hot."

Amusement caused Haley to look down at the menu. Some things never changed, like the menu here and Maude's crusty attitude. Of course the grill was still hot. It'd be hot until close of business tonight. Although that seemed a gentler than usual way for Maude to hurry them along.

"Is the steak sandwich still as big as I remember?" she asked Roger.

"Big enough for two meals, you mean? Easily. And as tasty as ever."

She settled on that, thinking it would save her having

to worry about making a meal this evening, assuming she was still awake.

"I'm hardly settled," she remarked to Roger as they waited for their orders to arrive. "I'm twixt and tween, mainly because I can't make up my mind. Am I cleaning Grandma's house to ready it for sale? Or getting it ready to move into? I think that's a question I need to answer."

"It might help with what you're doing."

Of course it would. Then it struck her that she'd dumped all over him about the Peeping Tom, she'd shared her family's history, had let him work in her basement without making any arrangement to pay him...and she hadn't even been polite enough to ask about him or his family.

"I was thinking earlier," she began cautiously and then paused as their lunch platters were slammed in front of them and the coffee cups refilled. The banging platters was a Maude-ism she'd never forgotten. It would be easy to think the woman was always angry.

"You were thinking what?" Roger asked as he lifted half the huge sandwich in hands that were big enough to handle it easily.

"About you. We hardly know each other after all this time, but you were one of the bright spots in the summers when I visited Grandma. Awfully patient with a young girl."

One corner of his mouth crooked upward and his green eyes crinkled at the corners. "First of all, I was only a few years older. That probably seemed bigger back then than it really was. And second, you were someone new, which was nice, and you were good at board games, which I used to love. Why wouldn't I hang with you when I could find time?"

"You must have been working awfully hard with your dad, though. And how's he?"

"Retired. He's living in Oregon now with his brother Tim's family, working a small horse-rescue facility."

She laughed. "He calls that *retired*?"

"It's different," Roger pointed out, returning her laugh with a chuckle. "Now eat."

She was only too happy to take a bite of the sandwich. It was every bit as good as she remembered, with impossibly tender steak. She had to grab a napkin as juice ran down her chin. "You must be awfully busy running the business by yourself now."

"Not as busy as I could be, I guess. I get orders from all over for custom saddles these days. It depends on how much I want to travel and how long I want to be away. And that's good because there are other things I like to do."

"Like fishing?" she asked, and they both shared a laugh.

"Like fishing. Like hiking in the mountains. Sometimes I even want to go cross-country skiing. I can work those things in if I'm careful about the jobs I take."

"So I take it there's no one else you have to report to?" That was the most indirect way she could ask if he had his own family. A question that suddenly seemed of burning interest to her.

"Just myself. Only child. My mother died long ago in a riding accident. I don't think you ever met her."

Haley racked her brains while eating another mouthful of the heavenly sandwich. "If I did, I don't remember."

"She wasn't easy to meet," he offered. "She used to help Gideon Ironheart with training horses. That man's a genius with it. Unfortunately, my mother decided to saddle-break a mustang, and the horse wanted no part of it. Or her."

"I'm sorry."

He tilted his head a little, a mild shrug. "It's been a while."

"I think I'm living proof that some things don't stay in the distant past." She looked down, wondering why she was casting a shadow over this meal.

"No," he agreed, "they don't."

Change the subject, she advised herself. She could get gloomy later on her own time. "How'd you guys get into making saddles? It's not the first occupation that would spring to the top of my mind. Of course, my dad was a wildcatter before he settled into contracting with larger oil companies, an independent who drilled exploratory wells, and I don't suppose that would be at the forefront of anyone's mind, either."

He laughed. "Maybe in this part of the country it might. But as for saddles? Well, we get back to grandparents and even greats again. My family were shoemakers back East. My great-grandfather was a very young guy, maybe eighteen, when he decided he was bored with making shoes. He was working for his uncle, who reminded him that people always needed new shoes or shoe repairs, and thus there was always plenty of work.

My great-grandad didn't care. He wanted something different, maybe with a dash of adventure. So he apprenticed to a saddle maker, where his leather skills were useful. When he struck out on his own, he settled here, repairing saddles back in the days when ranches were thriving and there were plenty of cowboys. Eventually he found plenty of work making custom saddles and here we are. I repair them, I build them from the very bottom up, and make tack, as well. Keeps me busy enough."

"I can't imagine what goes into that."

"Layers and layers," he said jokingly. "If you have time one day, stop by. I've got three in the works right now."

"Three?" The idea surprised her. She guessed she had imagined him working one from start to finish.

"All at different points in the process. More efficient if I can swing it. It helps to take my time, too. The most important thing is the horse's comfort, so every fit is custom. If I hurry anything, I might blow it."

"And when you finish one?"

"Me and the saddle pay a visit to the horse to make any adjustments necessary. Usually there aren't many because I start off taking care with my measurements."

That fascinated Haley. "I never thought of saddles as being a custom fit."

"Any owner who can afford it, and who gives a damn about the horse, sees to it. Horses don't all come in the same size, and an ill-fitting saddle can cause problems. But when the horse is no longer being ridden, for whatever reason, the saddle doesn't have to be ditched. I can modify it to fit another equine."

So complicated. Her initial interest had arisen from the unusual nature of his work. Now she began to imagine just how complex it could be, and how much knowledge might be necessary. "Like being a doctor," she said slowly.

That caused him to laugh. "I don't know that I'd go that far."

After lunch, with their leftovers in insulated containers, they drove back to her grandmother's house. The sun was still high, the day warm, and the streets active with kids and adults engaged in everything from play to shopping to yard work.

Bucolic. Perfect. She closed her eyes, breathing in the fresh air that blew through the window, and let her thoughts drift to dreams of staying here.

But as soon as they pulled into the driveway, all of that washed away. Little prickles of fear returned, but she tried to quash them ruthlessly. A stupid Peeping Tom. Was she going to let that pervert ruin everything?

No, she told herself. *Absolutely not.*

But the discomfort wouldn't quite leave her. Even as she went back to looking through drawers and closets, it pursued her.

She hoped they'd catch the guy soon, or she might be hightailing it back to Baltimore. Even though she was now not at all sure that was what she wanted.

Downstairs in the basement, working on the last of the ducts, Roger thought over all he'd learned from Haley. Given that she'd been abducted through her bedroom window as a small girl, he was kind of surprised she wasn't ready to pack and leave.

He hated to think of how she must have felt here alone in this house after seeing the peeper at her window. She sure as hell should have called the police rather than suffer through agonizing hours of memory and most likely overwhelming fear.

Anyone would have been unnerved but, given her past, it had to have been truly awful.

Just how awful had been revealed by her statement that reporting the matter to the police would make it all real. He wondered how hard she had clung to the idea that she'd imagined the man at her window. How much effort she had spent controlling her fear and trying to tell herself it hadn't really happened, that it wasn't going to happen again as it had when she was a child. That it *couldn't* happen now that she was grown.

Son of a… He bit the cusswords back before they could begin to emerge. The idea of a Peeping Tom was bad enough. No one wanted to think their privacy was being invaded while they slept, all so some sicko could get a charge. Yeah, windows would get locked and curtains drawn. Anyone would do that. But add to that a past kidnapping and the whole ballpark changed.

He bit off another cussword as a piece of metal duct slipped and sliced his finger. Being experienced with home repair—his own and Flora's—he'd come prepared and was able to get a bandage out of his tool kit.

He liked this kind of work. It used his body and mind in a different way from saddlery, gave him a different kind of workout. It was almost fun. Well, mostly fun, especially as a change of pace. There were occasional tasks that were just plain irritating, but most of the time he liked working with his hands.

Finally he had to call it quits for the day. He needed an elbow joint and another three more feet of ducting to make everything fit tightly. When he finished, he wanted the heat to come on without all that rattling. Yeah, the ductwork would tick as it heated, but it shouldn't shake and bang as if it was about to fall apart.

Which it had been, he acknowledged as he packed up his tools. Flora had let it go way too long, probably because it had become background noise. Or maybe because she didn't want to impose. God, he hoped not. He'd tried over the years to make it clear to her that he didn't at all mind doing odd jobs around her house.

Roger supposed he needed to make that clear to Haley, too. If she didn't hightail it back to Baltimore after last night.

He hoped she wouldn't. He'd enjoyed their time together and, in the privacy of his own mind, he could even admit she was one sexy woman. Regardless of his own feelings, the decision would be hers, and he had the sense that right now she was fragile.

Well, why not?

Picking up his tool kit, he headed up the stairs and turned the lights off behind him. The basement stairs opened onto a mudroom just off the kitchen. As he walked through it, he saw Haley standing by the counter with a box in front of her.

"Find something interesting?" he asked.

She looked over her shoulder at him. "Photos. I've

been pulling them out one at a time and trying to figure out who everyone is."

"Oh, man," he remarked. He put his kit on the floor against the wall and came to join her at the counter. A big stack of photos, all right, most of them black-and-white, indicating age.

She gave him a rueful smile. "Why don't people ever think of labeling?"

"Oh, I don't know. Maybe because the people at the time knew who everyone was. Why would they consider that fifty or more years down the road someone who hadn't even been born yet might want to know?"

"Probably."

He spied one that he recognized. "Hey, that's my granddad. I didn't know Flora had that."

He lifted it from the box. "Man, he was young then. Look at him."

Haley leaned in closer. "You look a lot like him."

"Maybe that's why I recognize him. He was a lot older when I came along."

She pointed to a corner of the photo. "That looks like part of a sign."

"Yup. It's still there, much older and painted different colors. *McLeod's Saddlery and Tack.*"

"You should keep this, then. One mystery solved."

He didn't argue, merely slipped the photo into his breast pocket. "I'd be happy to go through those with you. Maybe some of them will ring a bell for me."

"Thanks, I'd like that."

So, apparently she hadn't decided to leave just yet. He gave her points for courage.

"You know," she said after a moment, "this whole day there's been an undercurrent of sadness for me."

He leaned back against the counter so he could see her face better. "Sorrow?" And here he'd been thinking of her fear.

"Yeah, but not exactly. That's a strong word. It's just that I'm going through things that people considered important enough to keep, but I don't know why. So much is lost."

"Maybe your dad could help? Flora was his mother, right?"

"Yeah." She left the box on the counter and went to put the kettle on. "Maybe I can persuade him to come home for a visit. He's awfully busy, especially after he fell behind on drilling because of Flora's funeral."

"How do you fall behind on drilling?"

She surprised him by laughing. "Danged if I know. I just know when he kissed me goodbye before getting on the plane, he said he had a backlog he needed to catch up on, so he might miss a few phone calls. Can I make you some fresh coffee?"

"I need to run to the store to get a few more things for the ductwork. How about I do that and come back after?"

"I'd like that, Roger. I can't tell you how nice it is to reconnect with you."

"Same here. Okay then, I'll be back as soon as I get all the parts."

She was still smiling when he left. He almost felt like whistling.

* * *

Across the street, the beefy man walking a white Yorkie watched Roger pull out of the driveway, then stared at the house for a few minutes before moving on. Edgar Metzler was a regular sight at this end of town, although usually he walked Puddles, his dog, in the early morning or evening, varying according to his schedule.

Haley McKinsey was still there. Maybe that McLeod guy was making her feel safe...

Edgar would give it another day or two, but if she didn't leave town, he was going to have to do something stronger than look in her window.

He was almost positive she couldn't identify him. She hadn't been able to do that right after he'd kidnapped her, mostly because he'd taken care not to show his face, except once by accident when he'd returned her.

He didn't really have a criminal nature, he assured himself. Yeah, he'd made a big mistake stealing six hundred bucks from her dad and getting himself fired. He'd known he'd been stupid, but the way Jack McKinsey had treated him—as if he were poop to be scraped off the bottom of his boot—that had rankled.

It wasn't like he hadn't found another job. Of course he had, up in Alberta, far away from the scene of his crimes. But McKinsey's treatment of him had been like a constant irritation until he'd decided to teach the man a lesson.

So he'd stolen the guy's daughter. Okay, he'd been young and stupid, and it had taken him only two days to realize just how stupid. Taking a man's daughter and demanding a hundred thousand in ransom? Made him look like a pettier crook than he actually was and had walked him into deeper trouble than he'd even thought about until he'd done it and seen the reports on the news. Kidnapping. To this day he couldn't figure out how he'd come to the conclusion that would be a good idea. It was like that ad he saw on TV about diamonds: kidnapping is forever.

But as soon as the light bulb had turned on, he'd dumped the evidence where he was sure she would be found and fled back to Alberta.

For a long time he'd felt safe. A quarter century safe. He'd retired from the oil fields and had been drawn here by a job teaching about drilling equipment for a vocational program at the community college. Less than two years ago.

Then he'd heard that Haley McKinsey was in town to take care of her grandmother's house. All of a sudden he didn't feel quite so safe. What if she remembered him even after all this time?

Going by the house last night to look in on her while she was sleeping had been a test as much as anything. Yeah, he'd wanted to scare her a bit if she woke, but mostly he'd wanted to know if he could remember her. She'd been a kid when he'd last seen her, but if he could recognize *her*...well, buried somewhere deep in that blond head there might be a memory of him. He'd recognized her. She was just an older version of the kid.

So she might recognize him. But apparently she hadn't because if she had, she surely would've called the cops pronto. Still, that didn't make him feel terribly safe because she hadn't gotten a good look at him, what with it being dark, and how fast he had ducked when her eyes opened. But she'd get a really good look if she ran into him on any street in this town.

Obviously, he hadn't learned to restrain his impulsiveness, though he'd been working on it for years. Looking in that window might have been royally stupid, might have dredged up memories. On the other hand, it might have told him that he needed to hightail it to some other part of the country.

He'd never been a settled man. Half-unpacked wherever he went, ready to go at a moment's notice.

Regardless, he had to hurry her back to wherever she'd come from so he could bury all that stuff in the grave where he'd been keeping it for a long time. He couldn't live on the edge of fear for long. He'd figured that out when he'd kidnapped her.

He'd also learned over the years that he was capable of a lot worse than kidnapping if his blood got riled enough, so that woman better not recognize him. She might wind up dead, and while he assured himself he wasn't a murderer, it wouldn't be the first time if he got upset enough. Worse, whatever he told himself about everything being the fault of circumstances and his own impulsiveness, not some rooted evil, he couldn't escape the shiver of pleasure than ran through him when thinking about killing Haley.

She'd been stalking his nightmares and dreams for a whole bunch of years. He didn't deserve that. He'd returned her safe and sound, after all. He deserved some peace after all this time. He'd built a respectable life for the most part. Look at him now. He didn't need that woman's ghost sitting on his shoulder all the time.

Word making the rounds was that she'd be here only a few weeks. Sure, so what was she doing hanging out with that saddle-making dude?

But given the assumption that she was going to clean house, put the place on the market and leave, the local "welcomers" hadn't tried to make an appearance yet. No casseroles arriving. No pies or plates of cookies. Just the saddler who was often at that house anyway, doing odd jobs from the look of it.

Maybe that was the only reason McLeod was there now.

That didn't make Edgar feel a whole lot better, though. Now he had to waste time figuring out if he needed to do something else, like peep in a few more windows so the attention wouldn't be drawn to Haley and create the impression someone was interested in her especially. Someone might well put two and two together if she was the only one visited.

Hell. He rubbed his face and looked down at Puddles. Small enough to fit in his tote when needed, and about the best companion he'd ever had. He wished the dog could give him some answers.

Because if there was one thing life had taught Edgar, it was that he wasn't much of a thinker. Plotting, planning... Damn, what a waste of time and effort. And now he might be stuck needing to do it.

"Come on, Puddles," he said. "Let's go home."

Puddles wagged her tail happily and continued to trot at Edgar's side. Why couldn't everything be as easy as this dog?

* * *

Ridiculously—or so Haley told herself—being alone in the house after Roger left really bothered her. She'd been alone here for most of the last two days, working her way through mementos, treasures and trash, and thinking almost constantly of her grandmother. She'd felt comforted then by being so close to the woman she had loved as only a child can love.

Now she was uncomfortable?

She shook herself and gathered some boxes she'd purchased two days ago, spending a few minutes to fold them into shape. Most of her grandmother's clothes would have to be donated, at least the ones in good enough condition. It seemed she, like her granddaughter, occasionally like to wear a pair of pants or a shirt until it was just shy of falling apart.

Slowly she began to empty drawers, first from Grandma's bedroom. Later she'd gather from upstairs, where a whole lot seemed to have accumulated. Proof, she supposed, that stuff filled the space available. Then she'd have to start on the books. Maybe she ought to call the local librarian—Miss Emma, she recalled—and ask if she wanted donations, possibly for a fundraising sale. To judge by the creaking and overflowing bookcases upstairs, Flora had bought nearly as many books as she'd read.

That made Haley smile at last. She had the book bug, too, but avoided needing yards of shelf space with her e-reader. Great invention, especially for someone living in a small apartment.

She did, however, miss the smell and feel of books. Her memory reached into her younger days, summoning the remembrance of getting a new book, opening it, smelling the ink and feeling the paper, seeing those tightly bound pages as a mystery to be explored. The e-reader just didn't give her those tactile sensations, nor quite the sense of adventure. Once in a while she went to the library just so she could feel the weight of a book in her hands.

Flora had never wanted to give up on that from the looks of the upstairs.

But first the clothes. Undergarments went into the first box. Most of what she found approached pristine condition, almost as if Flora had bought it all then had scant opportunity to use it. Or maybe when she'd grown ill, she had started to wonder what her granddaughter would find in these drawers and had replaced the most intimate items. That would be like her, all right. She wouldn't want to leave anything tattered or stained behind her.

In the next drawer she found neatly folded nightgowns, but one in particular caused her breath to catch and her throat to tighten. It was almost threadbare now, but the pale green flowers stamped on the white background, an old-fashioned look, carried her back to her visits. Grandma had often worn that when Haley stayed with her and, holding it now close to her face, Haley could almost feel her presence.

That one was not going to charity. It was too old and worn to begin with, but it was also loaded with memories. Little Haley had loved it and Grandma knew it, which was probably the only reason she'd kept it all this time.

Blinking back tears, Haley folded it carefully and put it on the end of the bed. For now, at least, it was a treasure she would keep.

She paused, looking out the open window to see that the day had begun to dim. Where had all the time gone? She glanced at the digital alarm clock beside the bed and saw that it was still early. Then she remembered. When the sun fell behind the mountains, the light changed, not exactly darkening, but losing some of its depth and brightness. A long twilight had just begun. Only slowly, and much later, would real darkness begin to approach. She had hours left.

She released a sigh and got back to work. It didn't take long to finish emptying the bureau drawers. Next came the closet. Flora had church clothes in there and two heavy winter coats. Someone would be happy to receive them.

As she finished folding dresses into a box and started on the hats on the top shelf, she wondered how many dressers upstairs held more clothing. She hadn't really looked closely, and while Flora had never been a hoarder, who knew how many generations had been carefully laid away up there? If only because no one had looked for many years.

She guessed she was going to find out.

She glanced at the clock again and wondered where Roger was. That peeper last night had left an impression she just couldn't shake. The sooner she got done here, the sooner she could escape back to Baltimore and forget that voyeur.

She paused as she stacked the last hatbox on top of

the boxes full of clothes. Had she made up her mind? Just like that? All because of some creep?

That didn't sit well with her. Not at all. Not since childhood had she allowed fear to drive her decisions. She was no coward. Not like that.

But now, as she stood in a bedroom that had once been full of cherished memories, feeling as if someone had flung dirt all over the place, she wondered.

After Grandpa's death, when Haley had been too young to have more than the vaguest memory of the man, Grandma's life had become limited to the bottom floor of this house, almost as if she had cut something off. Yeah, on the occasions when Haley's dad came to visit, he'd taken an upstairs bedroom. Other than that, however, those rooms had remained untouched.

Maybe as a result of heartbreak, Flora had narrowed her life down to one floor of this house and her church. Haley, who would have been too young to know this, had heard her father talking about it once with her mother. How they should insist Flora sell the house and come to live with them.

Haley had no idea why her mother had opposed the idea. Maybe because her mother hadn't been happy living in the oil fields. Or maybe whatever her mother had thought hadn't mattered. Maybe Flora had just refused to give up her home.

Shaking her head at the way her thoughts were wandering, realizing she was trying to avoid thinking about the fact that another night was approaching, she carried the boxes into the foyer. She needed to call around to find who might want them and would pick them up.

Her little rental car wasn't really designed to carry much beyond her and a couple of suitcases.

Just then, much to her relief, the front door opened, revealing Roger with his arms full of ducting and a paper bag with handles hanging from his arm.

"Need help?" she asked swiftly.

"Grab the plastic bag?" he asked. "I thought salad would go well with our leftovers for dinner."

So he was planning to be here at least that long. Her heart lifted for the first time all afternoon. Smiling, she took the bag from him and carried it into the kitchen. Inside she found not only two containers holding chef salads, but two tall lattes, still piping hot.

Roger was already clattering down the basement steps with his armload of galvanized steel, or whatever it was, and she hurried after him. "Do you want me to bring down the coffee?"

"Nah. Thanks. I'll be up just as soon as I unload."

She placed the coffee cups side by side on the table, unsure if he wanted both himself, and set the containers with salad beside them. She glanced at the clock, surprised to see it was nearly five.

Man, she must have gotten lost in memories, or even her fearful thoughts. It felt as if one second she had hours of the day ahead of her and the next the afternoon was gone.

Roger emerged at the top of the basement stairs and closed the door behind him. "I didn't expect to be gone so long," he said. "I know I told you just a few minutes, but I always underestimate." He flashed a grin. "Besides,

I ran into one of my customers and he wants an adjustment to the saddle I made for him a couple of years ago."

He stepped to the table, passing her one of the coffees before pulling out a chair and sitting. She liked the way he settled into this house as if he belonged. After all these years, he probably belonged here more than she did. "What was wrong?"

"That remains to be seen." Again another grin. "He may have lost his own padding. The saddle sure shouldn't have broken down, but as we get older..." He winked at her.

Haley laughed. "I keep hearing that. My dad started carrying a pillow with him a few years ago. He swears they don't make a chair soft enough."

"He might be right." He snapped open the lid on his coffee and took a sip. "Ahh. Maude, when you learn to do something new, you learn to do it right."

She had to agree. "I've never had a better latte."

He leaned back in his chair, holding his cup. "You can tell me to skedaddle if you want some private time. I'm done with the basement for today."

Private time. No, she didn't want any. At this moment she wondered how she was going to handle the evening and mostly the night. "You know," she said slowly, "closed curtains have two purposes."

"Yes?"

"They keep anyone from looking in, but they also keep me from looking out."

He sipped his coffee and she could tell he was thinking. "I understand," he said after a minute or so. "You're going to be wondering if that Peeping Tom is creeping around the house out there tonight."

Haley hated to admit it, but it was true, so she nodded. She couldn't lie to herself and could see no reason to lie to him. "It's stupid."

"I don't think so. You're alone here and that would scare the bejesus out of just about anyone, having someone peer through their window in the middle of the night. I know I wouldn't like it."

She thought that was very generous of him. She somehow had the feeling that little would scare this man. Too big, too competent. She sipped more of the coffee he'd generously provided and wondered if she could change the subject to something that sounded more rational than she was feeling right then. Her next words told her she couldn't.

"Something happened to me today," she offered honestly. "And I don't like it. Today this house became less welcoming and warm. Just now, as I was packing things, I realized that the charm I'd always felt here in Conard City was evaporating. That's what I mean by stupid. One creep shouldn't be able to change my feelings about this whole town. I used to love to play out in front, you remember?"

"I remember."

"The streets, in my memory at least, are always warm and friendly. Not so much this afternoon. And the house is full of some of my best childhood memories. I love it. But now I no longer feel comfortable here. A huge part of me just wants to call someone in to empty out the house while I go back to Baltimore."

He looked down at his lap, nodding slowly. "If that's what you want to do, I can take care of the house. But I wish you wouldn't, Haley."

"Why?"

"Because I'd hate for you to leave here with a bad taste instead of those warm memories."

He had a point. She didn't think of herself as someone who ran from things, but maybe some vestiges of that five-year-old kidnapping victim remained in her. Some deep-seated fear she didn't often have to face, if ever. At work, she was fearless. Among her friends at home, she was fearless.

Or so she had believed. She remembered how her mother had taken her to Michigan after the kidnapping, to get her away from reminders. Maybe she'd learned the wrong lesson from that: run.

"A penny for your thoughts?" Roger asked. "Or has inflation raised it to a buck?"

She had to laugh, disturbed as she felt. "I was just thinking. They teach you to do that in therapy, you know, and I had lots of therapy after I was kidnapped."

"I should hope so."

She half smiled. "I learned not to lie to myself, for one thing. Which doesn't mean I never do. I've built quite a sense of my own strength and the belief in my ability to handle anything. Then I come here and discover I can't handle a Peeping Tom because the child is still alive and well inside this adult, and she still remembers the stark terror of a man coming through her window and carrying her away. That child isn't fearless."

Something in Roger's face gentled. He had a man's

face, marked by sun and wind, with a square jaw and crinkles around his green eyes, but right then it looked less like granite and more like something far softer. "I'd be shocked if that child weren't still with you."

"I thought she'd given up her grip."

"She probably has, mostly. Then this. How could it not stir things up?"

She gave a wan, mirthless smile. "Resurrection?"

"Not completely. I'm sure you haven't forgotten all the things you learned and practiced over the years. But a whisper? A ghostly reminder? Hell, yeah. Who wouldn't be disturbed?"

She sipped more of the coffee, savoring its milky, bitter heat, and thought over what he'd said. She reached one conclusion swiftly, however. "I can't give in to it."

"Maybe, maybe not."

She raised her gaze to his. "Meaning?"

"How important is it to you to fight it? I mean, there's no reason to face it down all over again, is there?"

That hardened her resolve. "Sure there is. That man soiled my memories of this house and this town. They were good memories, all of them. I don't want to let him taint them."

He tipped his head back to drink more coffee, then he gave her a heart-melting smile. "You're tough, Haley. Know that?"

She blinked. "I don't think so. I've been thinking about turning tail for hours now."

"That makes you all the tougher. You're refusing to give ground to your past. As for this creep…" He shrugged. "I don't know the stats, but I imagine Peeping Toms don't often do more than look. Want me to check that out online?"

She had to laugh. "Would you believe the first thing I really noticed when I got here was that Grandma didn't have a computer and doesn't have internet? I may start suffering withdrawal soon."

"Your smartphone can pick up some of the slack if you want. We have good reception here in town."

She shook her head a little. "I think it'll do me good to break the habit." Then her stomach rumbled, startling her. She glanced at the clock. "Has it really been that long since lunch?"

"We ate early," he reminded her.

"Well, if you're hungry, I'll get out the leftovers."

She even went as far as to bring out the crockery. Flora would never have considered serving anything in containers, not even leftovers. A nice touch. Also another journey down memory lane.

She skipped serving it in the dining room, however. Grandma considered the kitchen table to be for working on, not eating on, but Haley changed all that in just a few minutes. She'd never had a separate dining room in all her life except when she was here.

Inevitably, though, night drew close and Roger, nice as he'd been all day, had to get home. He had stuff in his own life to take care of.

He stayed long enough, however, to help her draw all the curtains once again and to check all the locks.

Then she was alone with the ticking Regulator, the otherwise silent house, and memories she wished would return to their mausoleums.

They were just memories now, she reminded herself. They'd lost the power to hurt her unless she let them.

The guy at the window was another matter, but he wouldn't even be able to peek in tonight, if he bothered to return.

With that in mind, she determined she'd spend the night in Grandma's room. It was where she wanted to be, and it even had a small television on the bureau, something that had surprised her. Maybe an addition when her grandmother had started to become ill.

Soon she was settled in, wrapped comfortably in blankets and surrounded by good memories. The best memories.

To hell with the creep.

Chapter 3

The church ladies started to show up, casseroles in hand, Edgar noticed. Hell. Nearly a week had passed and Haley showed no sign of heading back to wherever she'd come from. Boxes had been picked up by charities and carted away, but still the woman remained.

He tried to tell himself he was getting wound up for no reason, but that didn't help. He was seldom successful at calming his own anxieties, and this one was growing.

He told himself if he just stayed out of Haley's way, she never had to see him, and there'd be no risk that she'd recognize him. He couldn't make himself believe it, most especially if she decided to stay.

He could stay out of her sight line for another week or two, but not indefinitely. He reminded himself that he could always pack up and leave—his usual method for dealing with matters he couldn't control—but a couple of things made him truly reluctant to do that now.

For one thing, he was now in his fifties. Finding a job wouldn't be all that easy. Second, he was heavily invested in his current job at the vocational school. He liked the work, liked his colleagues, liked his students… and for the first time in his adult life he felt as if he truly belonged somewhere.

Was he supposed to throw that all away because some woman might remember him from a quarter century ago? He thought not. In fact, he rather thought he might kill her before he allowed that. He hadn't had much in his life, working as a roughneck in the oil fields, but now he had something important to lose.

Respect. He was *respected* in his current position. He'd never felt that way before. People sometimes called him *sir*. Throw that away because some twit might remember him? After all these years? The cops probably wouldn't even believe her when she hadn't been able to remember him around the time of the crime.

Nope, he assured himself, he was safe. Just keep a low profile. Because even if her identification didn't convince the cops, it could mess up his life anyway. Make people wonder. People wondering was to be avoided at all cost. He'd seen what gossip and unanswered questions could do, especially in a tight-knit area like this.

Edgar gave himself a mental pat on the back for having thought this through instead of giving in to an immediate impulse to act. He didn't often consider the possible consequences when strong emotion drove him, but this time he had.

Good man. He was getting better at this. For now... keep his head down and out of that woman's way. Easy enough to do. She had no reason to come out to the college, and he didn't need to walk Puddles anywhere near her house.

But if something went wrong, he didn't doubt his ability to deal with her. She'd never testify against him. He wouldn't allow it.

Once again calmed down, he put Puddles in her backyard kennel and headed out to work at the college. Friday, his favorite day of the class week because Fridays were when he tested his students on what they'd learned during the week.

Handling drilling equipment required more than brawn, it required knowledge and understanding what each nut, bolt and pipe joint did. Well blowouts were anathema, and he made sure his students understood that before they left with their certificates for oil fields.

He even enjoyed showing them film of what happened when someone cut a corner, whether the oil company or some worker. He loved watching the violence of the results, but he never wanted to be the cause. A man would never work again if it got pinned on him, so he'd better hope he was a casualty.

Whistling tunelessly under his breath, he pulled out of his driveway and headed toward work. He couldn't resist passing by the McKinsey house, though.

Yup, the woman was still there. Anxiety crawled

along his nerve endings anew. She'd better go soon or he'd have to protect himself.

Yeah, protect himself. That made him feel better about what he might have to do. Nothing pointless, something essential.

Yeah. Protection. Self-defense.

Roger needed to get back to finish that ductwork for Haley but, more important, he needed to get back to check on her. He'd gotten caught up in some pressing work that hadn't left him with a whole lot of time to spare. He'd glanced toward the house when he'd needed to run out for supplies and had seen that she was still pulling all the curtains closed at night. Probably wise. She didn't need another shock like that.

He'd also noted when he was out back getting the hose to bring water into his work shed that some of the church ladies were beginning to show up. So Haley wasn't completely alone, and he was sure those women were full of stories about Flora that must entertain her.

But she was still too much alone, he didn't know what she'd decided about remaining here, and at some level he felt he was falling down on his job. A self-imposed job, maybe, but he'd known Flora well. She'd count on him to keep an eye on her granddaughter.

On those occasions when Haley had come to visit as a child and young teen, they'd had a lot of fun together. Sure, he'd been older, but being an older guy meant being able to relax a bit when he was away from other guys his age. No comparisons. No showing off. No "I'm better than you are" stuff. Male competition. He'd always competed as well as anyone, but he'd worked hard for his father and being able to relax with Haley over a board game had felt almost tranquil, more relaxing than the boys' club that had surrounded him for so long.

He'd thoroughly enjoyed every one of her visits until she'd stopped coming and Flora had started to go visit her and her mother. He had little idea what had happened to her all those years, except tidbits dropped by Flora in passing. One thing you could say for Flora, she was never a gossip and friendship had given Roger no special entrée.

When he'd finished stretching carefully cut leather pieces onto a rack to dry into proper shape, he decided he was done for the day. He ran upstairs to his living quarters to take a shower and find some clothes that didn't smell like the saddles he was making or the chemicals he used on the leather. Then he hopped into his truck and headed the few doors down to see Haley. He could have walked, but on the off chance she needed to make a grocery run or something, he took his wheels.

She was slow to answer his knock and while he waited, he looked up and down the street. The early evening was beginning to quiet as families settled in for supper and television. Or video gaming, he'd learned. The thought brought an amused quirk to his mouth. Did anyone talk to anyone face-to-face anymore?

When Haley opened the door, she appeared flushed and a little breathless. "Sorry I kept you waiting. I was up in the attic."

He lifted a brow. "Let me guess. You found a dusty treasure trove."

She laughed. "Basically. Come on in."

"First, I wanted to ask if you'd like me to go get something for dinner, since I'm bold enough to invite myself."

She laughed again. "Beat you. I'm making Flora's goulash."

He leaned in a little, sniffing. "You mean with hamburger, tomatoes, celery, macaroni…"

"Her recipe exactly. You a fan?"

"The biggest."

"Well, as is necessary with this dish, I have enough for an army. Come on in."

"What were you going to do with the rest?" he asked curiously.

"Fridge. Freezer. Whatever. I never feel like cooking every night. And despite all the casseroles I've been receiving, I occasionally develop a craving for comfort food."

He closed the door behind him. Then, seeing her hesitation, he turned to lock it. "Still uneasy?"

"I feel like a fool, but yes. It's awful. I love fresh air but I'm keeping this place buttoned up except for a little while each day. A couple of hours while I'm downstairs, then a few while I'm upstairs."

As they entered the kitchen, she faced him. "I'm beginning to wonder if I'm losing it, Roger. After all these years, the man in my nightmares couldn't possibly come after me again. Why would he? As for the guy the other night…"

"Probably a harmless creep." But not exactly harmless, Roger thought. He'd brought nightmares back to this woman—nightmares she couldn't quite seem to shake. Like post-traumatic stress disorder.

The idea gave him a mental jerk. He hadn't thought of it that way, but he knew plenty of people who suffered from it, not all of them vets. A guy peeking in her window… A guy had kidnapped her through her bedroom window all those years ago…

Hell, this was no mere problem of memory. This ran deeper and, from his experience with some of his friends, he wasn't sure there was enough therapy to get rid of it. Maybe therapy had helped her move on but hadn't removed all the baggage. Well, how could it? She been through an event so terrifying he couldn't imagine it. Kidnapped by a stranger as a child, right out of the safety of her own bed.

His hands clenched into fists, then he forced them to relax. Too late now to wrap them around the perp's throat.

But it couldn't be helping her at all that they'd never caught the guy who'd taken her. No closure there. No sense of him being gone for good.

"Haley…"

She shrugged and looked rueful. "I'm feeling like a big baby."

"I don't think you should."

"Very kind of you."

He shook his head sharply. "I'm not being kind. Just honest. What happened to you all those years ago isn't something anyone could just sweep under a rug permanently. Then this jerk, this *creep*, does that? You'd be nuts not to react this way."

She stirred the tall pot on the stove, releasing more delicious aromas, then turned to the fridge. "Beer? I felt a need today."

"Beer sounds great."

She pulled out two longnecks and handed him one. It felt frosty in his hand. She turned the top on hers and removed it, tossing it into the trash. "I'm more of a wine drinker when I drink at all, but for some reason this sounded awfully good today. Lots of B vitamins, you know."

She winked at him and he gave her high marks for her guts. "I like one myself after a long, dusty day, and I suspect that attic is dusty."

"Dusty and hot. I need to get a new exhaust fan in there. The current one is anemic."

"Well, that's something I can do, right after I finish the ducts. And by the way, I didn't mean to abandon the job—I had a hurry-up order I needed to get going on."

She pulled out a chair, waving him to join her. "No apology necessary. I'm not even sure I can afford you."

That drew a laugh from him. "Sure you can. I'm cheap. I never took a dime from Flora and I'm not about to start."

He swung the chair around and straddled it, resting his elbows on its back. The icy beer went down like ambrosia.

He spoke again when her thoughts appeared to be tugging her down a dark path. "Flora used to send me her home cooking all the time or invite me to supper. I figure I got amply paid."

That brought her back into the moment. Her smile returned. "Her cooking was to die for."

"No kidding." He cast his mind back to a happier time for her. "She was teaching you, wasn't she?"

"When she could get my attention. I always wanted to be doing something else, and that didn't much change as I grew up." Her smile grew a little wistful. "She'd come visit me in Baltimore after I started my nursing career, and when she could nail me down at the right time of day, she tried to teach me again. I kept complaining that my hours were weird and I was too tired. No excuses for her, though. She argued that having a lot of home-cooked food in my freezer would make life easier."

A laugh escaped her. "Roger? Have you ever seen the average refrigerator in an apartment? The freezer will hold two ice trays and a few boxes of frozen veggies. I don't know where I was supposed to put all the bounty."

He laughed with her, imagining. "When she got her mind set on something, no deterring her. Have her friends from church been stopping by?"

"Some of them. Flora's chest freezer is big enough to hold all those casseroles. I suppose I should have heated one, but then I got this craving."

"I'm glad you did. I love this meal." But his mind kept dancing back to his thoughts about deep scars and PTSD. He wondered if he should even mention it. This woman was still afraid because of the Peeping Tom, and if that fear cut really deep, it could become a serious problem for her. But what did he know? He had no training. Best not to stir things up.

She spoke. "So what have you been doing?"

"Well, I had this rush repair I mentioned, and while I was waiting for things to soak and glue to harden, a little of this and a little of that. I think I told you, I don't work just one job at a time. There are a whole lot of steps involved, and a lot of soaking and shaping of leather, so I have things in various stages. Today, I was working on fixing a saddle. God knows what the owner did to it, or maybe it was just lousy work, but I'm glad I don't have to take responsibility for the way it's falling apart."

"Were you serious about custom measurements?"

"Yeah, I was. There are other saddle makers who rely on the fact that eighty percent of horses can wear standard measurements, but I don't like to do that. Horses matter, too. Then there's the rider. Some folks know how to measure the seat they like, but if I'm going to go to all the trouble to make a custom fit for the horse, I'd prefer to make a custom fit for the rider, too."

"So you're like the Bentley of saddle makers?"

He had to grin. "I pat my own back sometimes. No, I wouldn't go that far. Details are important to me, is all. I'm fussy about it."

Her eyes danced, a sight he remembered from when they'd played games years ago. He liked seeing it again. "Fussy explains why those ducts in the basement look like perfection."

"You've looked? But I haven't finished."

"I was curious." Her face was shadowing again, however, and she revealed something that slammed his attention into high gear. "When I went down there, I remembered something from my abduction. The guy kept me in a basement at least part of the time. I kinda ran back up those stairs today."

"I guess so." The urge to reach over became almost overwhelming, but he didn't have the right to do so, and he didn't want to make her jumpy about him being around. Heaven knew what opinion of men she might have been subconsciously harboring all these years. Here she was, thirty, but he'd never heard of her in a serious relationship. While Flora had never been a gossip, he thought such a development would have made her happy enough to share the news.

But what did he know? He could almost sigh at the gaps in his knowledge of every kind. He might create a wonderful saddle, but people were more of a mystery.

"You know," he said presently, "this is a helluva mess that jerk put you in."

She nodded slightly. "You could say that."

"I *am* saying it. He raked up all kinds of bad memories, he's taken your pleasure out of this house, you're living in a cave because of it, and I can't imagine why you just don't put it all up for auction and go home to where you at least feel safe." Saying it made him realize how much he'd been hoping she'd stay. Too bad. This was about what was best for her, not some half-formed dream on his part.

He missed Flora. Surely he didn't want to replace her with her granddaughter? That wouldn't be fair.

"I wonder," she said slowly, "if it would have been any easier if they'd caught the guy. At least I'd have no reason to be thinking of him now."

His chest tightened as he listened to her and he realized how deeply involved he was becoming. Yeah, he'd known her years ago, sort of, but she was nearly a stranger now. He shouldn't be getting so tangled up with her situation. But he was. He gave one great big damn about this.

"You might not. On the other hand, Haley, you suffered a huge trauma. That's going to leave scars that never quite erase. Even if they'd caught that guy, it still leaves *this* guy."

"True." She fell silent and he let her be, wishing there was something he could do to be truly helpful. He liked to be helpful. It gave him purpose and justification. He also liked to fix things, but this was clearly beyond his ability to fix.

Haley stood and went to stir the pot simmering on the stove. "Not much longer," she remarked as she returned to the table. "The attic was interesting. I'm not sure Flora went up there for years. I'm looking at stuff that's probably a lot older than she was. Somehow, though, it doesn't strike me as hoarding."

"A lot of people who went through hard times find it difficult to let go of possessions they might need someday. And maybe some of what's up there held memories for her."

"I'll never know now. I honestly wish I'd listened more carefully and asked more questions. Especially when I was here visiting. Part of me is reluctant to get rid of anything because it might have had meaning to her." She shrugged. "I'm beginning to sound like a broken record. If wishes were horses, beggars would ride, as a lot of people say. And this other thing…" Her gaze lifted. "I'm sorry, Roger. I keep harping on the same old things. I've become boring."

"You've had a shock. Anyway, it's not always the same thing. I learned a lot about your family when we went out to lunch. I shared some about mine. See, we have more than one topic of conversation."

He was glad to see her expression lightening. Then, making a clear effort, she said, "So, eighty percent of horses can wear the same saddles?"

"In theory."

"Then why a customized saddle?"

"For comfort. For decoration and flash. Basically, for show. Most of the time fit doesn't cause problems if you have a good saddle blanket. But, like I told you, I feel different. It's like buying shoes. Most people can walk in and buy off the rack. They may get blisters, or may get pinched a little while they break them in, but it's not enough of a problem to pay for custom shoes. That's expensive. Same with a saddle. My feeling is that a saddle will last a horse's entire lifetime. Why stint and take the chance of an uncomfortable horse?"

"I can see that. But later, do you just have to hang that saddle up?"

"When the horse dies, you mean? Nope. Send it back to me and I can make a bunch of adjustments to fit a different horse. No saddle made of decent materials needs to wind up on the junk heap."

She put her chin in her hand. "I'm getting more and more interested."

"Then come over to the shop when you can fit it in. I've got saddles in every stage of development."

"I'd like that. But first this house."

He leaned forward, feeling suddenly intent. "Have you decided?"

"Whether I'm going home or staying? I don't know yet. Part of me just wants to run. Another part of me wants to stand my ground. Am I going to give in to a Peeping Tom?" She waved her arm. "But I already have, haven't I? All the windows covered and locked. I'm giving ground. I don't like that."

Then she hopped up. "It's time. I hope you're hungry."

Her grandmother's goulash was one of Haley's favorite comfort foods, although she so seldom made it because it was one of those dishes that just didn't work well in small quantities. She saved it for times when she was having a bunch of friends over to demolish it.

So what had possessed her to make it today? Because her grandmother's freezer was big enough for leftovers? As she ladled it into two big bowls, however, she understood something.

She carried the bowls to the table and, before she got the flatware and napkins, announced, "I guess I'm going to stay here."

He looked up and she thought she saw a spark of pleasure in his green eyes. "Did you just decide that?"

"I think I decided it without realizing it before I made the goulash. That's an awful lot for one person." Turning, she retrieved the rest of the table settings and a couple of fresh beers. "I don't know how I'm going to do it, but I will. I already sounded out the community hospital and they have an opening, but I think I told you I looked into that when I arrived. Before…all this stuff. I was up in the air then. I guess I'm not now."

"What happened?"

Her smile was crooked. "Darned if I know. Howdy, neighbor."

After dinner, Roger helped Haley clean up and then suggested they take advantage of the porch swing out front.

It was one of the charming features that Haley had loved on her visits here as a child. When she wasn't playing with Roger or running around or skipping rope, she had been able to sit for what seemed like hours, at least at her young age, swinging back and forth. In the evenings, Grandma had often joined her with tall glasses of homemade lemonade and a small dish of walnuts to munch on. Even on the hottest of summer days, the porch enjoyed the cool touch of the breeze in those early-evening hours. They'd sit and swing, and exchange pleasantries with neighbors out strolling. Grandma had seemed to know everyone.

Haley had a yearning for that feeling; she had never found it anywhere else. Maybe that was part of the reason she wanted to stay: maybe she could find that sense of home she'd experienced at Grandma's side.

Roger used his foot to push them gently. The chains creaked a bit, as did the swing itself. Pleasant, familiar sounds.

"I used to sit here with Grandma," she told him. "A lot of evenings. You?"

"Once in a while, when I had time. The front porch swing seems to have become a relic of the past. Replaced by television, I guess."

"Or missing because newer houses don't have much in the way of a front porch."

He gave a brief laugh. "Point taken. I'm glad I didn't make my career in building wooden front porch swings. Mostly what you see now are those freestanding ones with metal poles and plastic seats. No more painting, sanding or creaking. At least, not like this." He lifted a hand and waved to a couple walking on the other side of the street. When they waved back, Haley responded in kind.

"Grandma used to know everyone," Haley remarked. "A lot of times people would stop to talk. I always liked that."

"Soon they'll be stopping to chat with you, just the way they did with Flora."

Almost as if in answer to his words, an older woman, with short, graying hair, who was walking a harlequin Great Dane, appeared around the corner and approached.

"Hey, Rog," she called. Then, as she drew closer, her bright eyes lit on Haley. "You must be Flora's granddaughter, Haley, right? Believe it or not, I remember you visiting way back when. Don't let me count the years. My heart wouldn't survive the shock. By the way, my companion is called Bailey. He might be big, but he's a lamb."

The Great Dane proved it. As his owner sat on the

top porch step, he stretched out to the end of his leash and sniffed around Haley's and Roger's feet.

"I'm Edith Jasper," the woman said, looking at her from eyes as blue as a slice of Heaven. "Since Rog isn't going to introduce me. I'm sure you don't remember me at all."

"Oops," said Roger. "I'm so used to everyone knowing everyone that common courtesies can skip my mind."

"You're a man," Edith said as if that explained it all.

Roger leaned forward. "Why don't you sit on the swing, Edie?"

"Because this is my porch step. Where I sat when I was chatting with Flora. It ought to have my name on it."

Haley was glad Roger didn't leave her side. It wasn't as if there was anything threatening about either Edith or her dog, but she liked having Roger nearby. Maybe that was a problem?

"So," Edie asked bluntly, "are you selling the house or staying?"

Haley opened her mouth to answer then hesitated. "I'm dithering. I make up my mind then unmake it," she said after a few beats. "Most of me wants to stay. I loved the time I spent here with my grandmother."

"Well, I don't want to be pushy or anything, but a lot of us miss Flora and we'd be delighted to welcome you. Not that you're Flora." She paused. "That came out wrong, didn't it?"

Haley had to laugh. She was beginning to like this

woman a whole lot and it wasn't taking long. "I understood what you meant. I'm not that touchy, I hope."

Edith nodded approvingly. "You sound a little like her, too. She'd have said that. So you're dithering?"

"Yeah," said Roger. "Just before we ate dinner, she sounded like she'd decided to stay."

Haley looked at him, feeling her cheeks heat a little. "I did, didn't I? Well, maybe my mind's made up and I'm just not ready to believe it."

Both Roger and Edith laughed. "Been there," said Edith. "You should have listened to me trying to make up my mind whether to get Bailey here. I'm lucky someone else didn't adopt him while I was flipping back and forth."

"And now?" Haley asked, charmed.

"I wouldn't part with this dog for anything. I was just worried about how big he was going to get, whether I'd be able to walk through my own house without tripping, how I was going to pay for dog chow. Well, it all worked out, didn't it, big boy?"

The dog climbed down the steps and sat on the sidewalk. Even then his head was higher than Edith's.

"He *is* big," Haley agreed.

Edith reached out and scratched Bailey's neck. "My advice? Get a cat."

A peal of laughter escaped Haley. How could she even think about leaving this place? This was the kind of thing she'd been weighing in her mind against returning to her small apartment in a busy city. Evenings on the front porch. Oh, yeah.

"I was wondering…" Haley asked, "Did my grandmother tell you any of the history of the things she saved here? She tried to share it, but I was just a kid, and interested like a kid."

"Well, she did talk about some of it. You want me to help?" Edith raised her brows questioningly.

"Any information I can get would be greatly appreciated."

"My pleasure. Of course, you may have to put up with some of my memories in the process. Flora and I would talk about the past a lot. Happens when you get older, so look out."

"I'll be grateful for all the stories." Haley hesitated, hoping she wouldn't sound as if she were criticizing her parents. "I don't know a whole lot about my family's past. Dad probably knows more about Flora, but he's half a world away. And Mom had no family, so her memories were limited to various distant relatives I never met. She didn't have many happy memories of her childhood."

"That's sad," Edith remarked. "I met your mom just once. She only came out here for one visit and, considering that for a while she was living in Gillette with your dad, I wondered about it."

Haley nodded. "Mom hated Gillette, or at least life around roughnecks. It got worse when Dad moved his operation to the Bakken oil fields and, finally, she divorced him. Anyway, I think she extended her dislike to this entire state." She'd also wondered if her mom's problems had arisen partly from her abduction. No way to know now, since her mother had passed two years before of an aneurysm.

Edith nodded. "Not the place or the life for a lot of people. It's a shame, though. It's pretty around Gillette."

"I think I could get to love it *here*." Deep inside, she was feeling the shift continuing toward a strengthening desire to remain here.

Roger spoke. "I'll drink to that."

Edith laughed then stirred as Bailey made a small sound in his throat, almost a whine. "Time to continue the walk. Big dog, long walks. Good for both of us. You ought to join us sometime."

Edith rose and, with a wave, returned to walking Bailey.

"Darn," Haley said. "His head reaches her shoulder!"

"Get a cat," Roger said, causing her to laugh anew. "Maybe a Maine coon. Thirty pounds of loving fur ball."

"Is that all?" She just shook her head. Then a thought struck her. "Roger? I'm wondering if things between my parents weren't good. I mean… Was it just the oil fields that drove her to leave? Why wouldn't she come visit her mother-in-law?"

He shrugged. "I hear mothers-in-law aren't always popular."

"Yeah. Funny how things I haven't thought about much are starting to come to me now. As if being here in Flora's house is reminding me of puzzles in my past. Was it really the oil field that my mother hated or that being around them and roughnecks always reminded her of my abduction?"

He turned on the swing, causing it to creak a protest, until he was leaning in the corner between back and arm and able to look almost straight at her. "I'm getting a crick in my neck and this seems too important for me to be staring at the street while you talk."

"Want to go inside? Or I could just change topics."

"No." He shook his head. "Talk all you want. I'm definitely not bored, and we're getting to know each other better. So you think your mom could have been wrecked by your abduction? That wouldn't be astonishing."

"I guess not." But the pieces of her life were shifting, coming together in a different picture. Memory was an unreliable thing, as well she knew from her studies, so any picture she had or made could be a fantasy. But she looked at the puzzle and found impressions changing. "I just said my mother had a terrible childhood."

"You did. How so?"

"She was orphaned. Distant relatives took her in, sending her from one place to another when they decided they'd had enough. I'm not sure she wouldn't have been better off in foster care. Anyway, some treated her like a servant, some like unwanted trash and one of them was actually kind. I met her just once. Mom didn't have very many happy stories to tell about growing up, so that was pretty much a mystery to me. She just didn't say much about it."

"That sounds rough."

She didn't mind that he leaned toward her and took her hand, holding it gently. She wasn't inclined to much physical affection, not a hugger by nature, but she liked his kind touch. "I'm sure it was."

"It would hardly be surprising if that continued to affect her into adulthood."

"Likely, I suppose. But I was just wondering… I mean, after I…was recovered from the kidnapper, she took off for Michigan immediately. I heard her tell Dad she wanted me away from all those rough people. She didn't trust them."

"But they have no idea who kidnapped you?"

"None. I was so young, I couldn't even give a description. Plus, he wore a ski mask almost all the time. That didn't help. Mostly I remember that mask to this day." Something in her chest was tightening. She hadn't talked about this in a long, long time. Far from freeing her, it seemed to be tightening its grip, those memories. "Anyway, she had a cousin in Michigan and we stayed there for almost a year, I guess. Then Dad moved his operation to the Bakken oil fields."

He waited then asked, "Because of you, do you think?"

"Maybe. How much do you think they were telling me at that age? But it's possible, since she had such a distaste for Gillette after that, that he thought she might be more comfortable at Bakken. She rejoined him and, about a year later, took off for good."

"And you?"

"She left me with him."

"Hmm."

She watched his face darken a little and wished she could read his mind. "What are you thinking, Roger?"

The simple question suddenly seemed potentially treacherous. Her heart skipped a beat as she realized she was worried about what he might say. Why? God, all her reactions were messed up. She was out of her element, out of the world she had built for herself where she worked herself to near exhaustion and spent free time with people from her job. A very tight club.

Now she was in a place where few of her familiar things supported her. Even memories of Flora couldn't ease her path into a different life. And that voyeur hadn't helped one bit.

"I'm just thinking that maybe your mom, given her upbringing, didn't feel she could be a good mother. Your kidnapping might have made that worse. Do you feel she abandoned you when she left?"

"Good question. You don't need to help me sort this out, Roger." She smiled to take any possible sting from the words that came next. "You're not my therapist."

Evidently, he didn't take it wrong, because he squeezed her hand. "Didn't think I was. Just asking because I give a damn. I also have two good ears and the ability to keep my mouth shut. But let me add a caveat. I know horses better than people."

His expression turned crooked in a way that might have been wry, and it caused the corners of her mouth to lift higher. "You think so?"

"I'm pretty sure. Lots of horse sense and slightly less people sense. Anyway, I was just wondering how all that made you feel. I can't imagine and it would be stupid to assume I know what you think about anything. So, see? You have to tell me."

Now she had to laugh. Dang, he was making her feel good in the midst of this trip down memory lane, a trip filled with pitfalls and old sorrows and fears. "You're a good friend, Roger McLeod. I'm so very glad I'm getting to know you again. And maybe now I could beat you at Scrabble."

That made him laugh, too, and they decided to go inside to play a game. Haley remembered exactly the shelf on which Flora had kept her collection of board games, a collection gathered over a lifetime. Some of them were probably antiques, but all were in impeccable condition.

As they spread the letter tiles on the table and compared them to the list on the side of the board, Haley said, "Have you ever known anyone who could keep this game so long and never lose a tile?"

"Not me. I had to order a whole set of replacements years ago."

This was good. This was okay. Everything felt right again.

Everything, that was, except wondering about the *real* reason her mother had left her behind.

Chapter 4

Since that first night after the creep had showed up at her window, Haley had insisted she was fine being alone at night.

Roger had no earthly reason to argue with her, but he was still uneasy. He called the sheriff's department in the morning to ask if there'd been any other reports of voyeurs looking in windows, but there had been none.

Maybe it was mere curiosity about a house that had been empty for a few months before Haley had returned. A one-off. Except, Roger couldn't quite believe that. He was normally pretty laid-back, but he just couldn't get there with this incident.

For reasons he couldn't even explain to himself, he was concerned about Haley. She'd come out here with every intention of selling Flora's house and going back to her job in Baltimore. But that had already been changing the first time he'd dropped in. Now she was bouncing back and forth like a rubber ball. Leave, stay. Stay, leave.

He wondered how much of that was ghosts from her past. She didn't strike him as an indecisive woman. Of course, how long had he known her? Childhood didn't count.

He visited his shop, as he did every morning, to check out the progress of leather curing, then decided there was nothing that couldn't hold for a few hours or even a few days.

And he couldn't stop thinking about Haley. Last night, sitting on that porch swing with her, he'd badly wanted to draw her close to his side and wrap one arm around her. An innocent hug. Except, his thoughts about her were becoming a whole lot less than innocent.

The more time he spent with her, the more his attraction to her grew. He was getting to the point where he wanted to weigh in on her decision about staying because he sure as hell didn't want her to leave.

But there were no guarantees that, even if she stayed, anything enduring would grow between them. His own life was spattered with broken relationships that had seemed great at first but had withered either quickly or slowly. That was one of the reasons he thought he knew horses better than people. One misjudgment after another on his part.

At least with horses he felt as if he always knew where he stood. Not so much with women.

That was okay, though. He was fairly content with

his life, and only the pull he felt toward Haley was disturbing anything now. It certainly wasn't enough to risk upending his life over. Or hers. No, she had to make her own decision about remaining here.

He locked up then headed over toward Flora's house. Maybe Haley's house now. He was antsy, wondering if she'd been okay last night. Or if something had frightened her.

He still couldn't believe she'd spent the entire night sitting up, frightened by that Peeping Tom, and hadn't called the cops. Now he wondered every night if she was doing it again. His problem, not hers. Grown woman, yadda yadda.

But she sure brought out his protective side. He wondered if that would annoy her if she knew.

Yeah, probably. She'd been independent for years now.

Shaking his head at himself, he drove down to her place, taking the truck in case she had boxes to be donated or taken to the landfill. He never wondered if he should call first. She always seemed glad when he arrived.

Once again she greeted him warmly, but this time he noticed that she looked a little frazzled around the edges, and there were circles under her eyes. Stepping inside at her invitation, he followed her to the kitchen, where she offered him coffee. He waited, hoping she'd tell him what was wrong, but he watched her gather herself, drawing on the inner strength that must have carried her through all the difficulties in life, from her abduction to her parents' divorce, to her nursing career.

She sat across from him at the table. "How's the saddle-making going?"

"Peachy," he answered. "Leather soaking, leather drying into necessary shapes. Some pieces in place on a new saddle. Yeah, it's going. What about you?"

"Packing, cleaning. The same."

"You look like you could use a break."

"Maybe. It needs to be done, though."

He watched her sip coffee, closing her eyes while she did so. She looked so weary that he couldn't keep silent anymore. "Tell me to shut up if it's none of my business, but…did you get any sleep last night? If not, why not? You look exhausted."

Her eyes opened slowly. "Sleep was full of nightmares. And I kept hearing noises, probably my imagination. That damn peeper apparently stirred things up really good, and arguing with myself isn't helping a whole lot."

"Ah, hell." He'd been hoping she'd been able to move beyond that creep, but instead she'd moved into the past. He wished he knew of some way to be useful in helping her deal with her memories, but his own past was uncomplicated by comparison. Yeah, he had memories that could make him unhappy or even squirm, but nothing, not even remotely, approaching what she had suffered as a child.

"I keep telling myself I'm being silly," she said after a few more sips of coffee.

"Why? It's been my observation that traumas may ease with time but they never quite go away. Given the right trigger, they can pop up again. But I'm no psychologist. Did you think someone was actually out there last night? Old houses can makes noises sometimes."

Haley shrugged one shoulder. "I don't know. Chicken that I am, I didn't go out and look. But I'll tell you how ridiculous it got. At one point I thought someone was in the attic. That's impossible. Just plain impossible."

"It should be," he agreed. Someone would need a three-story ladder. Carrying that and leaning it against the house without waking someone would be impossible. Then there was prying open wood-framed windows that over the years had probably welded themselves to the house. Small windows. "It's sure not likely."

"I know. But I still went up first thing this morning to make sure the two small windows up there are locked. They are. No sign they'd budged." She gave an embarrassed laugh. "Tells you the kind of housekeeping I've been doing. The sills are thick with dust. Unmoved dust. I don't even have a rat or mouse up there."

"And nobody could come through the attic vent without breaking it."

"Exactly." She sighed, shaking her head. "I lost it, I guess."

"Did you run screaming out into the street?"

Her head lifted sharply. "What?"

"I'm just saying, if you didn't run screaming into the street, you were far from losing it."

At least that drew a weary, reluctant chuckle from her. "I kept telling myself to quit imagining things, but I swear I heard scratching at the window, as if something was out there, but I couldn't bring myself to look."

"Which window? Want me to check for fresh disturbance? Although it might be hard because it hasn't rained."

"No," she said quietly. "There's no need. What I imagined was probably not important. A small animal. No human would scratch at a window."

Probably not. He wished, however, that he was sure of that. If some creep wanted her to peek out the window, that might do it. At least she hadn't looked.

He rubbed his chin, thinking hard. Could there be a reason that guy had looked in her window in the middle of the night? It appeared odd that there hadn't been any other reports of a Peeping Tom. He was no expert, but it seemed unlikely to him that a guy who got his kicks from looking in on sleeping women would quit after one instance.

It was always possible, though, that the guy hadn't been noticed by other women. Compared to other things that popped into his head, that seemed benign.

Because surely her kidnapper wouldn't have returned after all these years. It just didn't make sense. She hadn't been able to describe him as a child and the guy had gotten away free of all consequences.

No, Haley had been left with all the consequences. Every last damn one of them.

"Roger?"

He looked at Haley. "Hmm?"

"He touched me, you know."

Everything in him stiffened and then coiled like a snake ready to strike. "The kidnapper?" His stomach turned over as he thought of a five-year-old, stolen from her own bed, terrified and then treated that way.

"Yeah." She closed her eyes. "I couldn't make myself tell anyone back then. I felt so dirty. It was all dirty."

"God in Heaven," he said almost inaudibly.

"It was more than the kidnapping," she continued after a couple of minutes. "That was scary. What came after was scarier in a different way."

He didn't know what to say. Just couldn't find words as horror filled him.

After a while she seemed to shake herself. "I don't know why any of it happened. I wish I knew. But in retrospect, what he did…that was a long way from what happens to children with a pedophile. It was almost like he was trying it out, then changed his mind."

"Bad enough. Ugly enough. I am so sorry you had to go through that, too."

"I was lucky compared to some."

It almost sounded like a mantra, something she had been telling herself forever. Maybe it was true, but that didn't make what she'd endured any less awful. Try as he might, he couldn't summon the imagination to fully understand what all that must have been like for her. Just couldn't. And the last thing he wanted to do was serve up platitudes that she'd probably heard countless times.

Damn, he thought. He felt as useless as teats on a bull, and he didn't like that feeling at all. Usually there was something he could do to help. This time he felt so far out of his depth it was unpleasant. No fancy saddle, no stubborn horse, no lunch disagreement or bar argument had taught him anything about this. Yeah, he knew some vets who were struggling with post-traumatic stress, but they had support groups and infrequently leaned on him a bit by confiding. But a woman whose childhood had been scarred by a kidnapping and a sexual assault?

Yeah. He stifled a sigh because she might misread it. He just wanted to make her feel safer here, but if she couldn't feel safe, she'd probably head back to Baltimore. Regardless of how he might feel about her leaving, she ought to if it would give her peace of mind.

Finally he spoke. "Thinking about moving back to Baltimore?"

"Because of this?" She tilted her head quizzically.

"Why else?" he asked.

She shook her head. "I was talking to one of my friends back home earlier. I told her pretty much what I told you, only I must have bored on about it for twenty minutes. She told me to just make up my mind, that I had enough spine to go whichever way I chose, but I needed to find my spine."

He arched his brows. "Doesn't sound supportive."

She bit her lip, shaking her head a tiny bit at the same time. Her hands curled around her coffee cup. "She was right. I'm being a nervous wreck for no earthly reason. It probably has to do with not making up my mind."

He leaned forward, placing his elbows on the table. "How so?"

"Because my subconscious has joined the game. Can't decide? Well, let's imagine some strange noises in the middle of the night, so I can come up with a million reasons to leave. Freda was right. I have more backbone than that. I'm just unsettled."

Her subconscious playing games? Well, he supposed it was possible. It was also possible that some creature of the night had been interested in a reflection on glass. After a moment he told her that.

She perked a little. "That makes sense. It could have been almost any critter, and the moon is still amazingly bright."

He nodded, finally feeling that he might have helped a bit. "You should take a nap."

She shook her head. "I want to go totally lights-out at nine. Get a solid night, regardless of everything. A nap might get in my way."

"Then I have a suggestion. Let's go take a walk. It's beautiful out today and stretching your legs instead of your back and arms trying to sort and pack might actually feel good."

"I'm sure it would. In my job I'm on my feet most of the time." She lifted an arm and crooked it, as if she were making a muscle for him. "Of course, the other parts get quite a workout, too. You should see me slinging patients around."

That drew a laugh from him. "I hope you don't let go when you fling."

"Seriously not. I might damage a wall."

Just like that the whole mood had changed. He hoped she wasn't just boxing her fears up, the way she was boxing things up in this house, because boxes had a way of springing open with a little pressure.

"A walk sounds great," she declared. "I need to get out of here. I've been so focused on getting this place shipshape, and I don't know who I'm shaping it up for.

Which may be part of the reason I'm having crazy experiences at night."

He wasn't prepared to dismiss her experiences as crazy, but it was so easy, when alone in the dark, to become uneasy because of strange noises. He'd outgrown that years ago, but he could remember it, and she'd already been shaken by the Peeping Tom.

She stuffed her stockinged feet into some jogging shoes and together they walked out into the pleasant midmorning. The sun was bright, the breeze light, and birds seemed to be singing from every direction. In short, it was the kind of morning that ought to make anyone feel good.

He spoke as they walked in the general direction of downtown. "Not knowing your ultimate goal has got to make all this sorting rough to do."

"No kidding," Haley answered. "I'm dithering, like I said. I'm not usually a ditherer, but I find I can sit with something in my hands for ten or fifteen minutes trying to decide if I want to keep it or donate it. Really. Wasted mental effort."

"Any emotional connections? That would make it clearer about some things."

"I've already found those things. Now I'm working on the *what the heck was this saved for and what kind of history might I be throwing away.* I hope Edith can help. She said she'd come over tomorrow afternoon."

"You want me to look around to see if I recognize anything? Flora *did* talk to me about things other than repairs."

"That would be wonderful, Roger. I'll take all the

help I can get. Sometimes I feel as if I'm ransacking a museum."

He laughed. "I guess Flora kept just about everything. But that's understandable. Her family lived in that house for generations."

"That would probably do it. You know, I always wondered why she didn't have much of a family herself."

"She was lesbian," he said bluntly. "And living in a small town like this, she probably figured she'd be better off not letting it be known. I mean, she even married and had your dad."

"God! That must have felt lonely. So she told you that?"

"Some years ago, when she was poisoning me with tea. It was kind of like she felt the need to tell someone. I know she didn't want you or your parents to know. She feared they wouldn't let you come visit."

She exhaled slowly. "That's awful. And she's right, they probably wouldn't have."

"Like it's a contagious disease."

"You'll never convince some people it isn't. Thanks for telling me, Roger. Oh, man, I feel so bad for her."

"She seemed to think she had a good life. If she had regrets, she never mentioned any, at least not to me."

"I hope she didn't. But you know, that kind of makes her amazing."

He glanced down at her as they turned a corner onto Front Street. "How so?"

"You have no idea how many women I've met who married first, just because that's the way it was, then ten or twelve years later discovered they didn't fit the cookie mold."

"Now *that* would be regrettable."

She shrugged. "Depends. Those who had kids were grateful for them. But it was a painful struggle to realize who they really were."

She fell into thought as they strolled along the leafy street. Being midmorning on a workday, they didn't see too many people, but when they did Roger was able to greet most of them by name and make a quick introduction to Haley. While he linked her to Flora for them, he offered no assumptions about whether she was staying or going.

One middle-aged woman with hennaed hair wanted to talk about Flora, though, in some depth, so Haley invited her over to have tea in a few days.

"Roots," she said as they walked away. "Flora certainly had them and I'm beginning to feel mine starting to grow. Is everyone here this friendly?"

"You've got to be kidding me."

She laughed. "There are problems here, too?"

"Every village has an idiot or a hundred. Careless, thoughtless, not especially nice. We're definitely not a painting from Currier and Ives or Norman Rockwell. But most of the time...? Yeah, most of the time people are at least friendly, and in times of trouble they'd give you more help than you'd probably believe. The first settlers out here wouldn't have made it if they hadn't stuck together. Some of that has certainly passed down."

He spied a man in the blue uniform of the city police just ahead of them. Jake Madison owned a cattle

ranch some distance from town but, like many ranchers
these days, he was having trouble making ends meet.
A number of years ago, he'd begun to supplement his
income by becoming a part-time deputy because he'd
wanted to be sure of paying his ranch hand. Then a few
years back, the city council had received a government
grant for law enforcement and decided they needed a
city police force in addition to the coverage provided
by the sheriff's department. Jake had been chosen to
become the new chief of police.

It created an interesting situation in one respect: Jake
had married Nora Loftis, the daughter of a fundamen-
talist preacher who sometimes angered town residents
when he stepped out of his role as pharmacist at the
drugstore he owned. Jake, as chief, had been able to
avert trouble more than once with Loftis's followers.

"Come on," he said to Haley. "I want you to meet
Jake. He's a good friend and I think you'll like him."

He called out Jake's name and the other man turned,
smiled and walked toward them. Roger stepped forward
then suddenly realized Haley wasn't moving with him.
About two steps away, he turned to looked at her, wondering what was wrong.

What he saw chilled him. She had halted and was
staring at the far side of the street where a chunky man
was walking a small dog.

At once he stepped back to her side. "Haley? Is something wrong?"

She shook herself but never took her gaze from the
receding man. "I thought for a moment…he looked familiar."

If her face hadn't turned so pale, he might have dismissed the guy as someone she'd seen on one of her visits to Flora.

No, that man had reminded her of someone else. He stared at the man, almost failing to note when Jake reached them.

"Something wrong?" Jake asked.

Haley answered, "I don't know. I really don't know."

Then Haley dragged her gaze back to Roger and Jake and smiled slightly. "I'm sorry. Everything's fine." She eyed his police uniform. "It's been a long time since I visited Flora, but I don't remember blue uniforms."

"We now have a police force," Jake said. "And, since Roger seems to have lost his tongue, I'm Chief Jake Madison. And you are?"

"Haley McKinsey, Flora McKinsey's granddaughter… Roger?"

But Roger's gaze was following that chunky man down the street. Something had disturbed Haley. He wasn't going to overlook it. No way. Then, when she called his name, he forced his attention back to Haley and Jake.

The way she had looked at him. Edgar's uneasiness exploded until he had trouble walking steadily. How could she have recognized him? Of course, he had recognized her, but had been helped by knowing all along what her name was. She didn't know anything about him and hadn't even been able to describe him to police. So what had that look been about?

He'd feared this. He'd feared she would somehow remember him even after all these years. Hell, wasn't that why he was trying to scare her back to Baltimore? To get her out of here before she *did* remember something?

Maybe the dog had attracted her attention. Puddles always drew attention. There was something about the way the Yorkie walked and wagged its tail that seemed to draw women especially.

Yeah, maybe that was it. Or maybe his time to act was evaporating. Maybe he had to step it up somehow. He wouldn't be able to breathe quite right again until she was gone.

Gone one way or another. Since she kept the windows firmly covered and closed at night, he couldn't scare her in the guise of a Peeping Tom again. Hence the scratching last night, to let her know she wasn't alone.

Maybe that hadn't been strong enough. He'd have to find something better. Something good enough to really scare her on her way, and something that wouldn't let her know her kidnapper was hanging around. If she ever guessed that, she'd probably head straight for the police.

When he reached the corner, he dared to glance back to see her talking with Chief Madison. Edgar's stomach sank into his shoes. Was she telling Madison she'd just seen her kidnapper?

He dared another look, but saw Madison laughing.

Okay. Edgar took some deep breaths and kept walking until houses concealed him from their sight.

Okay, he told himself again. Why ever she'd looked at him, she evidently wasn't saying anything important about him.

Good. He still had time to figure out something.

* * *

Roger realized as he returned his attention to Jake and Haley that Jake hadn't missed the little moment, either. His gaze followed the walking man, as well, but only briefly. There was no break in his conversation, however.

"Say," Jake said, "you might like to meet my wife, Nora. You could also see the ranch at the same time, because she's kind of stuck out there."

Haley arched her brows. "Stuck?"

"Two preschoolers. She insists she wants to care for them herself, and not put them in pre-K, but getting it all together to come to town is limited to once a week. By her decision. I think riding herd on them in the grocery or some other place is trying. Active little buggers. Anyway, she could come see you and bring them with her, but..." He shrugged with a smile. "Are you kid-proofed?"

That elicited a laugh from Haley and everything about her relaxed to normal, much to Roger's relief. He'd ask her what had struck her later, but he'd let it go for now, rather than risk bringing her tension back. Anything that made her feel better.

"Anyway," Jake said, "gotta run, I'm on duty in ten minutes. Nice meeting you, Haley, and if you want to make the trip out to the ranch sometime, let Roger know. He can show you the way and how to get in touch with Nora. See you."

"Nice man," Haley remarked as he walked away.

Roger decided to gossip, thinking it might distract Haley completely from whatever had disturbed her. "Interesting story there," he said as they resumed walking. "Nora is the daughter of a local preacher whose following is more like a cult. Anyway, Pastor Loftis…who also owns the town's pharmacy…didn't want his daughter dating Jake, and one of his followers played nasty. You don't need the details. What I'm leading up to is, I think the main reason Nora doesn't want to put her kids in pre-K is because of those followers. She doesn't want her kids exposed."

"Oh, man," Haley said. "And what about when it's time to start kindergarten?"

Roger shrugged. "Nora's tough. When she thinks it's time, she'll loosen the reins. I'm sure the kids being so young is what makes her pause now."

"That would make sense. Bad experiences at an early age can stick."

As she would know, Roger thought. He could have kicked himself for reminding her of that. "Is there any shopping you want to do here in town? Or should we go back and get my truck for a grocery run? I'm just suggesting here. If all you want to do is get back to the hoard, I won't stop you."

She laughed again. "Groceries would actually be good."

"Then I'll take you. Gotta keep up your energy for all that sorting." And gotta keep her away from the house at least for a while. The way she had looked when he first dropped by this morning had him seriously concerned. Fear was wearing on her. Maybe staying in Conard County wouldn't be the best thing for her.

He knew he didn't want her to leave, ridiculous as

that was. Their friendship from a long time ago didn't carry over much, and their friendship now was really new. Too new to form any kind of deep attachment. Besides, she was entitled to make whatever decision she felt best suited her, and that didn't include any input from him unless it was asked for.

But that didn't keep him from wanting to give it. His mama had raised him to stay out of other people's business, but he sometimes suspected there was an alpha male lodged deep inside him. His impulses would sometimes fit. His actions rarely did.

He shook his head at himself and kept walking beside Haley as a slow smile creased his face. All his mother's rules about respecting others had been branded on him. His dad had added to it, reminding him that a businessman couldn't afford to offend people. *Keep your mouth shut unless you have something nice to say and be helpful when you have the chance.*

Right now, his desire to help could lead him down a path that might not be welcome.

They took his truck because he had more load space and needed to pick up a few things himself. Not that she suggested taking the little car she had rented. It would barely have been big enough to fit him.

After that sticky bit on their walk, her spirits seemed to have improved greatly. The walk must have done her good, because her color had returned and the pinching around her eyes had vanished. All good.

At the store he saw the nurse in her. Watching her fill her basket, he finally said, "Are you following the food pyramid exactly?"

She glanced at him. "No, why?"

"Because I don't think I've ever seen a cart so full of healthy foods."

A grin began to dawn on her face. "What would you like to see?"

He pointed to his cart, which at this point mainly held some cleaning supplies. His home was stocked with enough food to carry him through another four or five days. "Not that."

She chuckled. "What, then?"

He leaned over her basket. "Lots of veggies. That's good. Boneless, skinless, chicken breasts. Okay. But where's the beef? And don't you ever snack?"

"On cheese and whole wheat crackers."

He pretended to groan. "I'm surprised you let yourself have cheese. Fatty."

"Calcium without milk sugars."

"God help me." He pretended to frown. "How come you offered me sweet rolls, then?"

She outright laughed. "Because I like bad things, too. I just try not to overdo it."

He shook his head a little, enjoying the exchange. "What bad stuff?"

"I have a thing for potato chips."

"Oh, now, that's bad. What else?"

"Cookies. Don't bring me anywhere near chocolate chips or sandwich cookies. Then there are candy bars. Hate to admit it, but I keep one in my bag for quick energy on a long shift."

"You're going to hell."

Her laughter was glorious. People nearby smiled as they turned to look.

"And cheesecake?" he added hopefully.

"Depends on what kind of pants it's wearing."

Roger almost lost his breath as he looked into her dancing eyes. Man, she was beautiful. "All right. You got me."

"For real?" she asked pertly as she pushed her cart down the frozen food aisle.

Dang, she was flirting. What a change from earlier. He liked this side of her, too. Grinning, he followed with his cart and pulled some frozen fish out of one of the freezers. "I need to go fishing for fresh," he remarked.

"We tried that once, remember?"

Yeah, he definitely remembered, and also remembered feeling a bit stupid when the fishing hole was dry. It had been a fun day, though.

Haley pulled out some tilapia and cod to join the chicken in her basket and added some frozen Brussels sprouts.

In fact, from the look of her purchases, she was in no hurry to skip town. The realization settled warmly in him.

"Why don't you come to dinner tonight," she asked when they finally headed for the checkout. "I've been sick of cooking for one for a long time. My friends and I would try to get together for big dinners where we had fun cooking for each other, but our schedules didn't often mesh. So…I cooked for one."

"With your job, I'm surprised you didn't wind up on fast food."

"I don't want the health results."

He laughed. "I would have guessed that from your cart. I'd love to stay for dinner, but only if I can help. And, by the way, I'm tired of cooking for one, too."

And maybe over dinner he could find out what had disturbed her on their walk. He was certain it had something to do with that man who had passed on the other side of the street but couldn't imagine what. Maybe she thought she remembered him from childhood visits here.

He hoped that was all it was.

Haley was glad Roger decided to accept her dinner invitation. Truth was, she didn't want to be alone. She never felt that way in her snug Baltimore apartment, and she certainly hadn't expected to feel that way in her grandmother's house. Damn that Peeping Tom for stirring up memories best left in a deep hole.

Since the fish was vacuum-sealed in pouches, she could thaw it in cold water and, frankly, fish sounded yummy. She asked Roger and he agreed.

"Which kind?"

"I like both, so whichever."

She chose the cod and left it to thaw before making fresh coffee. She'd need it to get through this day, but was afraid if she napped she might not get a full night's sleep.

As a nurse she was used to crazy schedules and had no doubt that if she stretched out on a bed she'd probably sleep for six uninterrupted hours. Then she'd be up all night. No thanks. She wanted to be so far out of it that the house could scream at her and she wouldn't wake.

Last night had been awful. All of it, she assured herself, the result of an overactive imagination thanks to that creep peering in her window. Still she'd wrestled with memory and the fear that was surprisingly strong after so many years.

While the coffee brewed, she threw together a plate of cheese and crackers for a light lunch for the two of them, then filled mugs and placed it all on the dinette. "Help yourself."

"Thanks." He reached for a napkin from the holder on the table and placed a cracker and a slice of cheddar cheese on it. "So…I'm gathering that last night was hell for you."

She hated to admit it. "My self-image doesn't include becoming terrified by bumps in the night."

"If that guy hadn't looked in your window, you might not have been." He popped the entire cracker with cheese in his mouth and chewed, eyes gazing at her. He said nothing, as if he waited for her to speak.

But what could she say? "I'm embarrassed," she confessed. "The only thing I didn't do last night was hide under the covers or look under the bed."

He nodded. "Don't be embarrassed. Your worry was provoked, and unusual noises are hard to take, especially in an environment you're not used to. Heck, even at your place in Baltimore you'd probably get at least a bit weirded by strange noises."

She tilted her head to one side. "Are you always so kind, understanding and patient?"

He appeared startled. "Hell, no."

"Well, you've been incredible to me. By now, I might be getting impatient with me. Heck, I *am* getting impatient with myself."

He smiled with his eyes, crinkling the corners. "Be kind to yourself. Eat. You look worn to the bone."

"Okay, you're not always nice."

He laughed. "I'm serious. Eat. As for the rest, you haven't given me any reason to be impatient. I'm doing my best to understand what I'll never understand."

"What's that?" she asked, wondering if she were beginning to step into dangerous territory. There were things she simply didn't talk about for her own peace of mind.

"What happened to you when you were a kid. The words all fit together. I know what they mean. But as for your *experience* of it…" He just shook his head. "Even if you were to share every detail, I hope I'm smart enough to know that would never be like walking in your shoes."

For an instant, her eyes stung as tears tried to well up. She blinked rapidly. Fatigue, she told herself. But it wasn't just fatigue and she recognized it. Roger had just expressed a level of understanding different from walking in her shoes. He understood that he couldn't *know*. Even her own mother had held her while she'd cried and dared to say, *I know, I know.* At the young age of five, Haley understood that wasn't true. *Nobody* knew.

Meant to be comforting. Useless, really. She took care never to say that to a patient or family member.

She released a sigh and finally took a cracker and

some cheese. He was right; she needed to eat. She hadn't even bothered with breakfast this morning. As if waking up at last, her stomach gave a little growl. It didn't embarrass her. Everyone's stomach growled.

This morning she'd barely tasted the coffee she'd made, but now it tasted hot and bitter and oh, so good.

They had nearly cleared the plate when Roger spoke again. "What happened this morning?"

She knew what he meant and, all of a sudden, her heart galloped. "What?"

"When you stared across the street at that man. Was it his dog? Cute little thing."

He'd given her an out. She could say it was the dog. But lying didn't come naturally to her. Her best escape would be to say it didn't matter. But it *had* mattered and she wondered if it was a sign of a crumbling mind. Strange noises at night kept her awake, and now some guy walking down the street had frightened her? Because he had, and he'd barely glanced at her.

She decided to be truthful. Roger might as well know all her craziness. If he couldn't take it, then he wasn't a friend.

"The guy," she said. "The guy bothered me for some reason." Skimming over it.

"Did you meet him when you were a kid?"

"Maybe, I don't know. Did he always live here?"

"I don't know. I could find out."

"It doesn't matter."

For the first time she got treated to another side of Roger. He wasn't one to be dismissed. "It *does* matter. You froze like a deer in the headlights. That wasn't the reaction of thinking you might have met someone as a kid. Although, it passed fast, but even Jake noticed."

"Oh, God." She wanted to bury her face in her hands. Welcome home, Haley. Your slip is showing. "Damn. I'm too tired. I thought…for some reason his walk looked familiar. But only briefly. Then he started walking unevenly and it didn't seem familiar at all. So I can't really tell you what happened or why. Just a fanciful moment like last night when I imagined someone in the attic or scratching at my window. I should just go back to Baltimore and come back to deal with this house later when I won't make a fool of myself."

"You're not making a fool of yourself."

"I know I am, Roger! Damn, stop being so nice. I'm acting crazy today."

"You're not acting crazy, but I'm not going to argue with you. Pointless. If you want to think you're losing your mind or being foolish, nothing I say is going to change that."

She thought she heard a thread of steel in his voice. She dared to look at him and saw his expression had grown grim. What had she said to put that look on his face? She didn't like it, but didn't know what to do about it. She sure as heck wasn't going to apologize for arguing with him. What she knew about herself and what he thought of it were two entirely different things.

But she regretted making him feel bad. "Roger?"

He drew a deep breath and his expression eased. "Sorry. I suppose I shouldn't get frustrated when I can't help in any way."

That's how she was making him feel? Not good.

"You've helped a lot. Really. You've been calming my fears since the guy looked in at me."

"Yeah, but I can't help at all when you're determined to believe you're flipping out. That guy set off a firestorm inside you, and you should give yourself space to feel whatever you feel and stop worrying you're crazy. But it's your head, not mine, and I'm no shrink to be giving advice like that. All I can say is that *I* don't think you're crazy."

She was grateful for that. She had begun to think she was teetering in a way she hadn't in years. There'd been plenty of therapy to teach her coping mechanisms, but that training seemed to be slipping away. "I wonder…" She trailed off.

"Wonder what?" he prompted when she said no more.

"Maybe coming back to Flora's house in some way has made me feel like a child again. Maybe I'm slipping in time a bit, emotionally speaking. Sheesh, you'd think years of therapy would have gotten me past that. Years of therapy, years of growing up, becoming independent. I'm not that little girl anymore."

"Of course not," he agreed. "You're clearly a capable woman. What does that have to do with this? Trauma is trauma, and if something happens to refresh it, life gets rough for a while. I know any number of vets who would tell you that. Other people, too. Miss Emma, the librarian. You said you remembered her, right? Emmaline Conard Dalton?"

Haley nodded. "She was always so kind to me when Flora would take me to the library."

"She's a kind woman. She survived a vicious rape and was left for dead in a dumpster."

"Oh, my God," Haley breathed. "That's beyond horrible."

"She never finished college because of it. She simply couldn't go back. But, like you, she's a strong woman and has made a life with Gage Dalton, the sheriff. I bet she still has the occasional nightmare, though. Want to talk to her?"

Haley quickly shook her head. "I wouldn't want to stir it up for her. No, I'll get past this. I always do." She straightened a bit in her chair and determination filled her. "I *will* get past this. But…why is Emma *Miss* Emma to everyone?"

Roger shrugged. "I've never heard her called anything else. I suspect it's just an old-fashioned courtesy. I wouldn't be surprised if it began with parents teaching their kids a respectful way to address her, but I don't know. It sure has stuck."

"Even my grandmother always called her that." Remembering Flora at once lightened her mood and filled her with the sorrow of loss. Odd how that seemed easier to deal with than things that went bump in the night.

She released another sigh and, with it, some of the tension that had been gripping her for so long she was aware of it only because it was slipping away. "Why did you get annoyed with me?"

"Annoyed?" He looked genuinely surprised. "I wasn't. I was frustrated with myself is all. I can't see any way to help you. I'd like to, but unless you tell me some way, I'm stuck. I don't want to come off as pushy, I don't want to tick you off or offend you, and now that I think about it, my parents might have overdone it in the courtesy department."

"What?" she said on a surprised little laugh.

"I mean it. Keep your mouth shut. Don't gossip. Don't be nosy... Oh, a whole bunch of things that are probably wise, but here I sit now and I don't even want to press you. But I will anyway. Just promise me you'll let me know if there's anything I can do."

"I will," she answered promptly, although she wasn't sure what she could ask of him. She enjoyed his company immensely and wanted to see a whole lot more of him. But as long as she was so unsettled inside herself, bouncing around about whether to change her entire life, and wondering if she should even consider staying where she felt as if threats were closing in on her...

"God," she said aloud.

"What?"

"I just had a thought that astonished me." She hesitated, but now that she was aware he was reluctant to press her out of politeness, she just went ahead and told him. "I feel like there's a threat here."

"Here? In this house? In this town?"

"Not in this house exactly, although you couldn't guess that from my reaction to strange noises last night. No, I don't know what it is. I always used to love it here. Surely, I can't be letting that voyeur get to me so strongly."

"Well, I'd agree, except you told me you were kidnapped out of your bedroom window. So this creep did exactly the right thing to upset you completely. It would be bad enough without what you went through."

"I guess. Oh, man, I'm tired of myself. I wasn't like this before. Really, Roger, I hate it. I wasn't afraid of my own shadow until the other night."

"I believe you." He rose, carrying his mug. "Want more coffee?"

"No thanks. I'm too jittery already."

He refilled his mug then returned to the table. When he'd placed it at his seat, he picked up the plate she'd used for the cheese and crackers and put it beside the sink.

Haley closed her eyes, wishing she could make the inner turmoil just vanish. This was an overreaction, certainly. A guy had looked in her window. He hadn't tried to get in, had disappeared the instant he realized she could see him. Getting his kicks out of watching sleeping women was hardly on the same level as kidnapping or physical violence.

She had to get over this. At this moment, she wondered if returning to Baltimore would really make things any better. A chest of memories had been dragged from a cave into the open, and a few of her recollections seemed as fresh as yesterday.

She absolutely couldn't allow herself to give in to this. She'd worked hard to recover from her kidnapping, to become a reasonably stable adult and nurse. She couldn't allow a creep to destroy all that.

She rose from the table. "I still have some of my grandmother's clothes to get ready for donation. Is there anywhere around here that deals in vintage clothing?

I found some outfits that people might like. It seems Flora had a taste for some finer things in her youth."

Roger nodded. "There is, and I'll help you."

Together they climbed the stairs.

Chapter 5

The next several nights passed quietly, mainly because Edgar was almost afraid to go out. He didn't need to, except to exercise Puddles, and he pretty much shortened his walk and headed away from anywhere Haley might have reason to go.

He needed to get her out of town. For now he was grateful not to be teaching a summer class. No reason to show his face again in daylight. He and Puddles could do their exercise well after nightfall. The dog made him seem so harmless that people didn't even give him a second look if he was out with her at midnight.

Getting Puddles may have been the smartest move of his life, he thought irritably.

Damn, why had he ever kidnapped that girl to begin with? His reasoning, such as it was, had grown into a muddy memory after all this time. He'd been angry with her father for firing him over a theft of just under six hundred dollars.

Furious. He'd wanted to get even. He'd never once thought how lucky he was that Jack McKinsey hadn't called the cops. He might have spent the next year in jail instead of hiding out in Alberta.

He'd asked for a paltry ransom, too. A hundred grand. But stupid as he could be, he wasn't stupid enough to think McKinsey was made of money. Wildcatting could pay a lot of money when an oil well produced, but the profits had to be shared with the landowner McKinsey leased from, and the roughnecks who did the actual drilling had to be paid. When wells came in dry…the costs were heavy. He'd heard enough wildcatters talking to know they were doing okay, but not that great.

Edgar had figured a hundred thousand might be possible. At worst, McKinsey might be forced to sell some of his drilling equipment, very expensive stuff.

Then he'd done the one thing he was sure would hurt the man: he'd taken his daughter.

Instead he'd gotten a big surprise himself when the news informed him that the FBI was on the case. The FBI? Edgar might not be brilliant, but tangling with the Feds wasn't on his bucket list. So he'd let the girl go.

He'd thought he'd been done with it after all these years, until he'd heard Flora McKinsey's granddaughter was in town. He'd snuck a look and almost wet his pants. She'd grown up, but he still recognized her. A race to a computer at the school had given him even worse news. There was no statute of limitation on kidnapping.

If Haley recognized him, he was done for. The rest of his life in prison. For kidnapping. Maybe for the way he'd touched her a couple of times out of curiosity. Shame had stopped him. One of the very few times in life when he'd been ashamed. Not that that would help him if she recognized him.

Six hundred dollars… It had seemed like a lot of money way back then, and he'd needed some hefty car repairs he couldn't quite pay for. But he'd needed the car to get to work.

He'd been aware the boss kept cash in the construction trailer. Everyone knew it, and maybe that was why he'd had a false sense of security about dipping into it. The cash was there for unexpected expenses, and Edgar hadn't taken all of it, just what he'd needed. He'd thought the boss wouldn't even notice for a while.

But two days later he'd been nailed and fired. How? Had someone seen him? Or was there a camera in the place? He never knew. Back then, security cameras had been unusual, not common at all. He hadn't even thought about the possibility.

He'd been furious. Just furious. He'd offered to pay McKinsey back in installments, but all the man had said was "I can't trust you now. I need to be able to trust the people who work for me."

An icy response. McKinsey was coldly angry, even more frightening than blowing up, at least as far as Edgar was concerned.

Out the door, into the chilly Wyoming night, with nowhere to go and no job. That's when Edgar had started to seethe. Maybe seething had gotten in the way of thinking. Hell, he'd done his job as well as anyone. He wasn't a slacker. McKinsey owed him a second chance.

Furious, not wanting to explain anything to curious friends about why he wasn't working on the rig anymore, he'd packed his measly belongings and left town. Got away from the scene and the questions. Living in his run-down car.

But he'd continued seething, wanting to get even with McKinsey more and more with each passing day. It wasn't like he hadn't offered to pay the money back out of his next several paychecks. He had, even though it would have meant withholding his rent for a little while. But no, that wasn't good enough. Trust? Trust had to be a two-way street, and if McKinsey had a camera in the construction trailer, then he wasn't very trusting of his men, was he?

Then the idea had hatched. In retrospect, it had been stupid, but at the time it had seemed brilliant. McKinsey had deprived him of his job. He wanted to deprive McKinsey of something equally important, and that obviously wasn't money or the man would have let him pay back the six hundred bucks.

He'd never intended to hurt the girl. He'd figured she might get a scare, but she'd get over it. Her father, on the other hand, would be forced to feel as helpless as he'd made Edgar feel. He'd feel the pain of losing the most important thing in his life, for just a few days. Or, at least, that's what Edgar had hoped.

Apparently the only one who had lost had been him. Again.

Now he stood to lose everything. His freedom. The job he'd come to like.

If asked, Edgar would have said that he'd been stupid in his youth but had grown considerably. He was a law-abiding, upstanding citizen now. An instructor at a junior college.

He was not the same man.

Except right now that argument was sounding awfully thin even to him. He was considering committing another crime. Hell, maybe he'd started when he'd looked in her window.

This was driving him nuts. Earlier, for a couple of minutes, he had believed she had recognized him as he'd passed her on the far side of the street with Puddles. But then she'd gone back to talking with Roger and the chief of police. She'd been smiling, he'd noted when he'd glanced over his shoulder before turning the corner.

How could she recognize him, anyway? He'd worn that damn ski mask almost every minute he'd been with her. She'd seen him only once when he'd believed her to be asleep and he'd pulled it off because it was itching. When he'd turned around, he'd been looking into her open eyes.

At the time he hadn't been sure she'd even been really awake. She'd cried herself to sleep out of exhaustion. God, that had been maddening, that unending sobbing. But when she'd seen his face, her eyes had fluttered closed again. When he read in the newspaper that she hadn't been able to describe him, he'd been relieved, then *really* put the pedal to the floor to get to Alberta. No one there would be looking for him. No one knew *who* to look for.

The articles had told him other things, too, like the fact that Jack McKinsey had a few enemies, bigger ones than a lowly roughneck. The paper had taken delight in mentioning the names of many who had been questioned. Since Edgar's name had never come up, Edgar had assumed that McKinsey had mentally dismissed him as a threat.

Which was fine. Edgar hadn't made a dime, the girl had gotten back to her family quickly and Edgar didn't feel like he'd done anything terrible enough to require prison time.

But now? Hell, *now*. Banging his fist on the arm of his chair, he vented some of his anger, fear and frustration. Any chance that woman could identify him could mess him up seriously.

Maybe the only way he could be safe would be to kill the woman. Either that or leave the new life he was building, where he felt respected and had some friends, and head out again the way he had so long ago.

He didn't want to run again, but unless he found a really good way to make Haley go home, he was going to have to do something to solve this situation before he went nuts. He didn't deserve to live the rest of his life in fear, or to lose everything he'd worked so hard for.

No. He didn't.

Puddles gave a little whimper then jumped up into his lap. The dog evidently sensed his mood. A good dog. Loyal and loving.

That's what Edgar deserved, not the terror that now loomed ahead of him.

But how could he take that woman out? It wasn't like he had ever murdered anyone. He hadn't any idea about how to start, how to get away with it.

Because if he did anything, he had to get away with it.

Well, he had once before. If he could do it once, he could do it again.

Satisfied with himself, he settled in the chair and petted Puddles. He'd figure it out. He was smarter now than all those years ago. He just needed the time to think.

One week, he decided. He'd spend the week thinking about how to handle it, and if he didn't get a clear sign she was heading back to wherever she came from, he'd have to take her out.

He had a lot to protect. And that Roger guy... If he didn't stop hanging around so much, he'd have to go, too. Damn fool was acting like a cat that smelled catnip. Regardless, he was very much in the way.

Yeah, one week.

The summer evenings were long, but as twilight deepened, Haley called a halt to sorting and packing.

"This is overwhelming," she admitted. "I had no idea how much Flora had saved. When I was a kid, I explored, but I guess I wasn't interested in how much was here stashed in drawers, closets and armoires."

"Don't forget the attic," Roger reminded her. "I never had any idea that Flora was something of a hoarder."

"I don't think I'd call her that. You can still use every

room in the house, but right now, if I hadn't cleaned a little closet space, I wouldn't have been able to hang my own clothes."

They were on the second floor. She was avoiding the attic, which, while clearly organized to some extent, held furniture items that might be antiques, and probably some stuff that someone in the past had meant to repair and had never gotten around to.

Standing and stretching to ease her back, she brushed her hands on her jeans. A glance out a nearby window told her that night was once again lurking. Only then did she realize a buzz of uneasiness was running through her.

"Damn," she said.

"What?" Roger folded the last box closed and reached for packing tape.

"I'm getting edgy again. I should be able to control it. There's no *real* reason to be afraid here. I just need to toughen up."

"Yeah." Then he snorted. "Toughening up means running until you can do a mile in five minutes, or lifting weights or…"

She almost laughed, despite her increasing uneasiness. "What exactly are you trying to say?"

"When you figure out how to lasso emotions, let me know. They pretty much happen regardless."

She couldn't much argue that. Every time she looked at this man, she felt urges and needs she couldn't seem to corral. They just washed over her and tried to force their way into her mind to push her into action. She knew it. He was probably right about all the rest of it.

"Where are you sleeping now?" he asked as they went downstairs to get a soft drink and possibly some Bagel Bites.

"In Grandma's room. I am *not* letting that creep take that away from me."

"Brave decision. Good on you."

Good on her? Maybe it was merely another thing to raise her anxiety levels. But she *did* have a backbone, and she was trying to stiffen it. Just how much of her past was she going to allow to ruin her present?

But the butterflies in her stomach warned her she might be losing the battle.

"I'm not a coward," she remarked as they reached the kitchen. "Cola or beer?"

"Beer, please. One of the major food groups."

Again a smile twitched at her mouth. Roger was good for her in a lot of ways.

As she brought the drinks to the table and sat, he asked, "How much more do you think you have to do?"

"I'm pressing it," she admitted. "There's pressure. But with each passing day, I'm wondering why. I don't think I'm leaving, Roger. I want to stay. It means up-ending my life in every way, but I have this inescapable feeling that would be good for me."

He nodded. "I like the idea of you staying. If you leave, I know I'll miss you like hell."

Her heart slammed and she dared to look into his eyes, where she could have sworn she saw heat. Did he want her? She hoped so, regardless of where it might lead. Still, even though she was working on stiffen-ing her backbone, she didn't have the courage to reach out. Not yet. Mainly because she couldn't be sure, and if she was having problems now, imagine how a rejection would make her feel. No thanks.

"I'll miss you, too," she admitted after a second or two of internal struggle. She was making herself vulnerable, something she had tried to avoid since childhood. Vulnerability was another thing that made her uneasy. So maybe her perceived toughness was merely a shell?

"You in any kind of special nursing?" he asked.

"Yeah. Registered nurse practitioner. I usually work in the ER. I can do a lot of things docs can do, but always under their supervision, which is fine. I have a lot of decision-making ability, but there are just certain areas where I have to step back and let a doctor take over."

He swallowed a sip of beer. "Long hours?"

"Depends. We tend to work twelve-hour shifts three days a week and maybe more as needed."

"Twelve hours is a long time."

"It can be. Or it can flash by, depending." She smiled, glad to be on familiar territory. "Either way, by the time I wind down after I get home, I'm exhausted."

"I bet, especially after a stint in the emergency room. I can't imagine what you see."

"Most people can't and most people shouldn't. There are enough of us who take home nightmares."

She pushed her diet cola aside and went to get herself a beer. She'd never been one to drink much, nor did the idea of relying on it for relaxation usually appeal to her, but right now it did. Besides, she *liked* beer.

She twisted the top off and drank right out of the bottle. "My back's pretty sturdy," she remarked, "but for some reason all this packing and boxing is giving me a lower back ache. I guess it's different than lifting a patient."

"Maybe it's your posture." He studied his own bottle for a minute or so, then said, "That guy who disturbed you earlier? Have you been able to put your finger on what it was?"

She snapped back to that moment, which she didn't want to do. "Damn, Roger. I'd almost forgotten."

"Sorry." But he didn't look sorry. He was genuinely seeking information, she decided.

"Okay, I'm not really sure what grabbed my attention. Maybe his stride. Except, after a few steps, it changed. I remember thinking for some reason that he was built wrong. Nothing was really familiar about him. I know I haven't been here in a few years, but I don't think anyone I met in this town would give me that feeling. It was just an instant anyway. Some little trigger flipped."

He nodded. "Built wrong how?"

"Obese."

Roger arched his brow. "He wasn't *that* big."

She forgot her nerves. "Medical term. Twenty percent overweight."

"So your usual football-watching, beer-swilling, chip-eating, middle-aged guy."

She had to laugh. "Basically. But that's not really fair. I was just making an observation about one man."

Then she glanced toward the windows over the sink. Night was falling fast now. "I need to close the curtains."

* * *

Everything about her changed in that instant, Roger noticed. Her shoulders sagged a little and her face became tense.

Damn that Peeping Tom. He rose. "I'll help. You take care of those and I'll run through the house."

She gave him an almost sad look. "This is awful. I'm sorry."

"No need," he said firmly. He got it, at least as much as he could, and he didn't blame her for growing uneasy. Not after what she had gone through as a child. She'd have to be made of stone not to react this way. He just hoped for her sake nothing more happened and that this experience would fade quickly for her.

As he walked through the house, making sure every drape and curtain was closed, leaving not even a crack for someone to peer through, he considered how brave she was. Braver than she evidently realized.

After having her past trauma raked up this way, she was making up her mind to stay anyway. That took a lot of courage when she could have easily gone back to Baltimore without excuse or explanation.

But he needed to find out who this guy was. One thing he'd noticed long ago: people could be quickly identified by their walks. Few walked precisely the same, and he'd decided some time ago that a person's gait was almost as individual as a fingerprint, if you paid attention. Not exactly as strong an identifier, but close.

Haley had recognized something in the man's stride, for just an instant. An instant wasn't enough, especially when she said that it changed thereafter. But he still wondered. It had reminded her of someone, at least. Maybe her abductor.

God! The likelihood that that man would be in this town was so low that a percentage would probably be full of zeroes on the front end.

Yet the guy had triggered something in her, however briefly. She wasn't even linking it to her abductor. In fact, she almost seemed to be trying to laugh off the whole thing.

But he'd seen the change in her, the way she had stiffened and stared. It had struck her hard.

The memory of her reaction was beginning to make Roger uneasy, too, although he was almost totally convinced that while something about the guy had struck her, it was only a similarity.

Similarity could be enough, especially when she was already uptight.

When he got back to the kitchen, he found her starting to put a lasagna in the oven.

"Did you make that?" he asked. He didn't remember it from her shopping cart. Although she might have purchased the ingredients and they hadn't added up for him.

"Yes."

"When?"

At least that brought her cheer back. "Not even by the best will in the world can I sort and pack all the time. I made a big tray and froze part of it. Plenty for two here, though."

"It looks great."

"I hope so." She closed the oven door and quickly washed her hands at the sink. In front of her, the curtains created a wall.

"Everything's buttoned up," he told her. "I checked that all the windows are locked, too. Now, what can I do to help?"

"In a little while we can make garlic bread if you want. I don't usually because it adds carbs and fat to a meal that already has plenty but…well, I love garlic bread and I might want to be bad for once."

He laughed quietly. "A sinner, huh?"

"For one night. But I also have the ingredients for a salad. I hope you like salad."

"That I do. I make them often. A little later, when the lasagna is almost ready, show me your ingredients and let me have at them."

She arched a brow. "Impressive in the kitchen, too."

"Are you making a list or something?" He'd asked teasingly, but he could have made a list of her attributes, too. Major things like trying to remain positive when she was swamped by a fear she couldn't help, because trauma stamped itself in the brain like a branding iron. Little things, like her work ethic. She just kept pushing ahead on dealing with this house, even though she could walk away at any time and hire someone to clear the place for sale. She had quite a backbone, a beautiful smile, and sometimes her eyes even seemed to dance.

What a delight she was, when the shadows left her eyes. He wished he could erase them permanently.

The way she remained in the kitchen with him when he began to make the salad signaled that she didn't want to be alone. Not at all. She wasn't being clingy, but he could sense her hesitation. Too many glances at a curtained window. A heightened awareness of any sound. Today had evidently freshened all her feelings and they were sticking with her.

After a really delicious dinner—she was a star with lasagna, and fresh garlic bread was something he never bothered with just for himself—he put the dishes in the dishwasher and then asked if she wanted coffee or something else.

She surprised him. "There's a bottle of red wine on the mud porch. I'd like some. You?"

He wasn't the world's greatest wine drinker, but he didn't want her to feel alone in any regard. Drinking coffee or beer would feel unsociable, at least to him.

The wine was sitting on the counter and he brought it in. He didn't have to ask where the corkscrew was. Unless she'd moved it for some reason, it was still in one of the drawers with odds and ends of other utensils. He removed the cork with surprising ease, considering he seldom performed the task, then pulled two of Flora's six wineglasses out of another cupboard.

He set the bottle down to let it breathe, as Flora had once told him it must… The thought trailed off and all of a sudden he was awash in memories of her. She'd been like a grandmother to him, too, in so many ways, and he missed the hell out of her.

Roger even had brief flashes of memory from when he was maybe two or three. She'd always welcomed him when he'd wandered over, and always had a cookie for him. In some ways, she'd been a great stand-in for his own mother, who was busy with her other activities.

"Flora," he said.

Haley looked up. She'd been studying her hands, laid out flat on the table in front of her. Her eyes looked a bit pinched again, and he suspected she felt another night closing in around her.

"Flora?" she asked.

"Yeah. Since I was a little kid, she was practically my grandmother, as well. Cookies, candy corn in the drawer—"

Her question interrupted him. "Did you like the candy corn?"

"When I was little. She only gave me four or five pieces."

"Me, too." A faint smile curved her mouth. "But there was another thing I liked more. She had this big glass canister where she kept brown sugar, and she sometimes would pull out the little balls of it that stuck together and give me one."

He nodded. He remembered that, too. "It took me longer to get over the brown sugar than the candy corn. I hate that stuff now."

"And I can't imagine eating that much sugar anymore."

He laughed. "Nope. Raw sugar in hand, I'd run out to play. And I probably ran it off. It was always a tank topper, and when I look back at it, I'm sure I thought those balls were bigger than they really were. My hands were smaller then."

She nodded. "Much."

A minute or two later, he poured wine into her glass until she waved her hand. He gave himself about half as much. Wine just wasn't his thing. He raised his glass in toast and tasted it. Not bad, whatever it was.

"I'll need to go back to my place shortly," he said, watching her reaction closely. The strain around her eyes deepened, but she made an effort to act as if everything was normal for her. He knew it wasn't.

"You've spent a lot of time with me today," she answered. "You must have other things to do."

"Oh, yeah, but I'm in the middle of a bunch of things in the shop that need to wait. Glue needs to set, leather needs to stretch and harden on frames. Every now and then I need to take time off to let things catch up." His fault this time. He usually sequenced the stages of his work more productively, but he was spending a lot of time worrying about Haley and wanting to be with her.

He'd need to get a rein on that, but not right away. When she'd finished half her wine, she didn't appear perceptibly more relaxed. He stood, his mind made up. "I'm going back to my place to shower and clean up. Then I'm coming back."

She craned her neck to look at him. "You are?"

"Am I wrong or would you sleep better if you're not alone in this house?"

She bit her lip, and he could almost feel her struggle. She was trying not to give in.

When he spoke again, he kept his voice low and kind. "It's not wrong to need a friend sometimes."

She stopped biting her lip and nodded. "You're right."

"So I'll be back quickly, and maybe tonight you'll actually sleep."

He wouldn't, though. He intended to be on guard. As she rose to see him out, he impulsively reached for her, risking everything given her current state of mind. But he touched her gently, drawing her into a hug. "Remember that time we promised *friends forever*?"

She relaxed into him and her head nodded against his shoulder.

"Still true," he said, then released her reluctantly. He didn't want to give her new fears or to resurrect old ones. "Be back in a few."

"Thank you, Roger."

"No problem. None at all."

He'd certainly feel better being there and making sure she got a good sleep.

As he hurried home, he wondered how he could find this guy who had scared her today. Bringing him to her, proving to her that he wasn't the man in her nightmares, could help a whole lot.

If, however, by some extraordinary chance he turned out to be that man, the cops could remove him from her life forever.

Win-win.

Or so he thought. He'd talk to Jake Madison tomorrow. Jake ought to know damn near everyone in town, given that he'd grown up in these parts and now policed the place. He might even have known this morning whom she was staring at.

Yeah. That was it.

* * *

The minute Roger walked out, the house ceased to feel friendly. To Haley it suddenly felt huge, dark, threatening. A mausoleum.

But it was none of those things. It was Grandma's house, a place of warmth and love. Like the hug Roger had just given her. As he'd gently drawn her in, she'd wondered how she would react, given all her nerves and the flashbacks she'd been having.

It had felt *good*. So good. As if his arms around her had relieved a tension deeper than she had known she was carrying.

But now that tension was back and she hated herself for the weakness. For heaven's sake, all that was in the distant past. She'd worked through it during years of therapy that must have cost her dad a small fortune. She was better.

Wasn't she?

Aww, man, how could she have backpedaled so fast?

A glance at the clock told her it was after ten. With the curtains closed so much, she'd begun to lose her moorings in time. Like when she worked several extra-long days in the ER. It could be a shock to emerge from the brightly lit clinical setting into the night, especially after she'd put in overtime on an emergency. The hours had slipped away, the darkness astonished her, or sometimes it was the early-morning light when the last she recalled she was supposed to leave at seven in the evening. The *previous* evening.

She'd noticed since her arrival in Conard City that the sun sort of set early behind the western mountains.

It was still daylight, but a different kind of light, and it would linger for hours before it really began to fade. She'd had the curtains open today because Roger had been with her, making her feel safe enough, but she had no idea what time she'd closed herself in again.

She'd noticed the deadening of the light, the loss of shadows beyond the window, and her nerves had begun to twitch uneasily. Her stomach had said it was suppertime even though they'd eaten earlier, but she wasn't at all sure that she'd adjusted yet to the time change from Baltimore.

Regardless of her mixed up *everything*, there was no escaping that now the clock said it was bedtime and her body shrieked for her to stay awake.

Because she was alone? It had begun to feel like it. It was one thing to be scared like this when she'd been little, but for goodness' sake, she'd faced and fought horrible things in an ER. She'd seen the worst that could happen to a human body, and some of the worst that people could do to each other. She'd lost her fear, though not her loathing, of terrible things.

Because she could act. She could help. Right now she felt helpless against the terrors that insisted on holding her hostage. Maybe it was helplessness that was fueling all of this.

"Ridiculous," she said to the empty house. She was overreacting to an occurrence that had happened to all too many women. A hateful but probably harmless pervert had looked in her window during the night. He'd left her feeling vulnerable.

But other women dealt with it.

Maybe she should meditate. But much as that might calm her down, Roger had said he would hurry back, and if he walked in while she was just beginning to relax—the way she felt, that might take some time—it would do her no good at all.

She at last managed to stop pacing and sit on the overstuffed living room sofa while she waited, summoning memories of her childhood in this house in the hope they would replace the bad memories.

She probably needed a break. The idea had started niggling at her mind since her arrival. The ER here couldn't be as bad as the one she worked in back home, a trauma center that drew cases from all over the city. No, here she'd still see trauma, but not in the soul-crushing numbers of her current job.

Maybe she needed some downtime, a rest from the constant barrage.

Maybe she'd been hiding in the endless press of emergencies and now that she had time on her hands, even while she packed and sorted, she couldn't hide anymore.

That notion gave Haley a serious jolt. Hiding? In that horror? But she hadn't had the opportunity to think about much else. Extra hours when there was a crisis of some kind, and breaks spent with other nurses whose shared experience bridged the nightmares.

Because there *were* nightmares. Home alone, a scene from a shift would play through her head and she'd often dream about it. The ER had haunted her, but it had filled her, too, making her too busy to remember the distant past.

Her memories of her work in Baltimore were still painfully fresh, hardly eased by the change of scenery. But now she had time, and Grandma's house was unleashing a different set of memories. That peeper had set things in motion.

Maybe she needed to return to therapy. She didn't seem to be doing a very good job on her own. At least, not right now.

It would pass, though. One sick man peeking through her window couldn't leave the kind of impression other things in her life had. No, he couldn't. He was a trigger, nothing more.

Triggers could be handled.

She eased into deep breathing just about the time there was a rap on the door and Roger strode in. He had a large bundle in his arms.

"What's that?" she asked, nearly sighing with relief as all the tormenting things eased away.

"Oh, a sleeping bag, an air mattress, a pillow."

She felt her eyes widen. "But, Roger, there are three bedrooms upstairs. You could have a *real* bed."

"I know. But I figured you'd rest easier if I was down here."

He dumped the bundle on the floor.

"But…" She hardly knew what to say. She definitely felt touched, though.

"No buts," he answered firmly. "Nobody can get in here except on the ground floor, and they're going to trip over me. I have spoken."

The way he said it drew a reluctant laugh out of her. "Your decree?"

"Absolutely." He patted the pockets of the light gray windbreaker he'd donned. His hair still gleamed from being wet. Delicious.

"Yeah, here they are," he said. "I was sure I'd tucked them somewhere." From an inside pocket he brought out a bunch of packets. "Instant hot chocolate, for the man who forgot how to make the real stuff and doesn't have the ingredients anyway. But I *did* forget to bring cream. It makes it more like the real thing."

"Better that it has no cream."

"Dang, the nurse reappears." He winked as he passed her the packets. "We don't need to make it right now. I just wanted it to be handy. Now, if you don't mind, I'm going to stroll around outside."

She tensed immediately. "Why?"

"To make sure all good people are in for the night. I'll be right back."

She supposed that should make her feel better. He'd clearly intended it to. Instead it threw her back into the dark places she'd been wandering lately.

"Oh, for Pete's sake," she said aloud and marched into the kitchen with the packets. She needed an *off* switch.

The curtains were like walls, she thought as she paused by the sink. The question was whether they were walling something out or walling her in.

Ugh.

She felt grimy from the day's hunt, searching and packing. Flora had done her best, but Haley was buried in possessions and they had naturally grown dusty. She needed a shower.

But of course she'd once again left the front door unlocked so Roger could get back in, and that proved a bridge too far. She certainly didn't want to lock him out, but disappearing into her grandmother's bedroom and showering, which she'd been doing since she got here, had become increasingly difficult. Tonight, after her being jolted by that guy's stride, it felt even harder.

Wait. Just wait until Roger returned. Then she could do it.

Tomorrow morning she was going to have a long talk with herself about backbone and the ridiculousness of letting one petty jerk resurrect a long-gone past. About letting herself become paralyzed by a fear that had no basis. At her age, who the hell was going to pull her through a bedroom window? No one.

How was anyone going to get into the house, as buttoned up and locked as it was? With a fire ax? She wished she could shake herself.

"Enough!" Only when she heard the word bounce back at her from a nearby wall did she realize she had spoken out loud. This was bad.

Just then, Roger returned. He closed the door behind himself and locked it. "All quiet except a bunch of people down the street drinking a little too much around a firepit."

"I guess I should get out soon and meet the neighbors."

He started to pull off his windbreaker. "I'd have thought most of them would already have come by. Maybe they're under the impression that you won't be here long."

"Well, I dithered enough with the ladies from Grandma's church. I still hadn't made up my mind."

"Are you changing it?"

"No. I refuse to."

"Last stand and all that?"

Damn, he always seemed able to find some humor. She was going to envy him for it if she didn't get over this hump and find her own sense of humor. "Not quite like that. Listen, I need a shower, so if you wouldn't think I'm being rude…"

"Rude? C'mon. I invited myself over for a pajama party and just moved in on you. How could it possibly be rude of you to take a shower? Don't think of me as a guest. I'm more of an invader."

He always put a smile on her face, she thought as she headed for the bathroom. Always. He made her glad she'd decided to stay.

In the small foyer that turned on one side to the living room and on the other to the kitchen, Roger waited until her door closed behind her. The room was at the back behind the stairs, rather isolated at night. It was a wonder she hadn't permanently retreated upstairs to sleep.

He looked for a convenient place to spread his air mattress out that would both allow him to prevent anyone from passing, yet not trip her if she needed to come out later. It wasn't as if there was a whole lot of room. Well, she'd see how it was laid out when she finished her shower.

He spread everything out but didn't blow up the mattress in case she wanted it elsewhere. Then he straightened again and walked around the downstairs. Like a fortress, which disturbed him.

The first couple of nights after the creep had looked in her window, it had seemed natural. But now it was passing that and driving home to him just how deep Haley's scars really were.

Setting himself up as a watchdog seemed like a basically useless role. Yeah, she'd be able to sleep without fear, knowing she wasn't alone in this house. Given the way she had looked this morning—worn out—and then the encounter with the guy on the street that had left her a bit shaken, maybe being a watchdog was the best thing he could do.

But he was itching to do more. A guy didn't get to his age, single, without learning a certain amount of self-reliance and without becoming accustomed to being in control of most things.

This was all beyond his control, from Haley's natural fears to his inability to shut down the cause of them. He definitely had to learn the identity of that guy from this morning so he could tell Haley and ask if she wanted to see him again to reassure herself.

But finding the voyeur who'd looked in her window? He reminded himself the cops were probably keeping an eye out for men who were on the streets at a late hour, watching for shadows lurking near houses or walking in the alleys between. Of course they were. He wished he could join them.

Haley had been wrecked enough by the man's sickness. He'd hate to hear that any other woman had to fear sleeping with an open window.

He ought to look into getting her security cameras. At least she could sleep better knowing that if the guy showed up again, he'd be caught on video. Security cameras. In this town? Only a few businesses had them and none of the homes. Despite occasional evidence to the contrary, people in Conard City persisted in feeling safe in their homes. Many still didn't lock their doors.

Hell, he felt safe, too. On warm summer nights he often left his inner doors open to let breezes waft through the screen doors. The only place he ever worried about was his shop. Expensive tools in there. Tempting to someone with light fingers or a need for money. Dangerous chemicals, too. He couldn't risk a kid getting hurt. He'd invested in some pretty strong locks there... but not security cameras.

There was an upside to installing cameras here, though. Gossip about it might be enough to keep the pervert away.

The thought of that guy made him sick. He'd read up on the subject online and hadn't at all liked what he'd read. Perverts indeed. Twisted minds that left their victims scarred. Some even ratcheted up to violence.

Most didn't, he reminded himself. They just took their sick thrills and fled. If they found easy prey, they'd return, but the way Haley had this place shuttered, it was unlikely this peeper would return here.

How many other women was he looking in on, women who didn't notice? That question bothered him, too. To find this guy, they'd need more than one report.

But if there were no other cases...

He stopped midstep as he walked through the kitchen

yet again. Restlessness worked on him, but as another thought struck him, it became more than restlessness.

What if, despite astronomical odds, it *was* the kidnapper of her childhood? What if…?

He shook his head, trying to move away from that thought. The kidnapper had to know from the reports following the incident that she hadn't been able to give the police any identifying information. The guy had nothing at all to fear.

So even if he was living in this town by some weird chance, he didn't even need to be worried about it.

Get real, Roger told himself. Even if she claimed her kidnapper was here, who could do anything about it? She couldn't identify him and would be dealing with a child's memory anyway. Who'd believe her, especially after all these years?

Rock meet Hard Place, he thought sardonically.

There was damn all he could do about any of this. Soon he'd absolutely have to get back to work, and while he was willing to camp out here as long as she needed him, he'd still have to leave her alone all day.

"Roger?"

He heard Haley call him from around the corner. "In the kitchen," he called back.

She appeared in the doorway, wrapped in an electric-blue terry-cloth bathrobe. Her white nightgown, buttoned to her throat, reached all the way to her ankles, nearly touching the tops of her white ballet slippers. She was hiding behind another layer. His chest tightened with the recognition.

He cleared his throat. "I wanted to check with you

before I inflate the air mattress. You need to be able to move around at night."

"Sure. Were you looking for some of that hot chocolate?"

"Not exactly, but it sounds good. How about you?"

She nodded.

"Then take a seat. I can make instant anything."

A smile flitted across her face as she pulled out a chair and sat. "You're familiar with Grandma's kitchen."

"Believe it. The woman wouldn't let me do things around here without feeding me. The last couple of years she started to want some help with what she considered to be a proper dinner."

She nodded. "I feel so bad for not getting out here."

"Don't feel guilty, Haley. She didn't let anyone know she was sick, and she wasn't all that old. Why wouldn't you expect another ten years at least?"

"I ought to have enough experience to know that's a lousy bet."

"Any of us could say that." He filled the kettle and turned it on before pulling a couple of mugs from the cupboard nearby. "You okay with the way this cocoa is?"

"Absolutely."

He brought the mixed cocoa to the table and sat facing her. "Maybe I should have offered you warm milk instead. It might help you sleep."

She regarded him from eyes rimmed with fatigue. "I'll sleep. I think I could sleep through a tornado. But I'm starting to get pretty disgusted with myself. This is a total overreaction to some creep looking in my window. It's not as if he could pull me through a six-inch crack the way the guy did when I was a kid. Nor is it likely I'd ever be kidnapped again."

"Not likely, no," he agreed. "But don't be so hard on yourself."

"Why not? I'm not this person."

He hesitated. "You had a can of worms opened and they're wriggling all over the place."

She wrinkled her face. "Ugh, what a description."

"Well, I could have said snakes."

At that, she produced a half smile. "Snakes doesn't sound so silly. Anyway, I'm starting to feel ashamed. I'm overly preoccupied with this whole thing. I need to let it go."

"Yeah?" Again he paused a moment, sipping his hot drink, framing a response. "Look it up online. Even without your past, victims of Peeping Toms can have problems for a long time. They don't feel safe. They feel their privacy has been invaded. And more."

"Really?" She frowned. "I haven't had any experience with that."

"I doubt it shows up in the ER very often."

"True." She shook her head a bit. "I also feel like I'm stealing your time. You have a life, Roger, and I'm not giving you very much room to live it."

"Quit the guilt trip. I wouldn't be here if I didn't want to be."

Then she honestly smiled. "You're a very good man, Roger."

That warmed him all the way to his toes.

Overreaction to a simple compliment? Well, it had

come from her, and maybe that was the important thing. Regardless, he enjoyed the feeling.

Edgar couldn't stay away, even though that seemed like the wisest thing to do. There were plenty of streets he could meander along with Puddles that didn't take him anywhere near Haley's house. Flora's house. Whatever.

This time he'd left Puddles at home. The dog stuck out at night, being all white. Wearing dark clothes, Edgar strolled along an empty street. On either side, a few windows still showed light, mostly from the back as if folks were tucked in. An occasional upstairs window flickered from a TV.

A nice summer night had begun. Windows were open, people enjoying the breeze, settling in for a pleasant night.

Only one house was completely dark, and that was his target's. He wanted to cuss a blue streak when he saw Roger McLeod's truck parked out front again. Didn't that man have a life?

Plus, he was getting in the way. If Haley stayed much longer, Edgar would need to act. The chance that she'd recognize him after all this time was slim, but he'd noticed the way she'd frozen for a few seconds when she'd passed on the other side of the street. Something had jogged her memory.

Therefore, she was a huge danger.

He, also, wasn't a patient man.

So how to deal with the two of them? Maybe he'd let a couple more nights pass. The grapevine didn't seem certain that she was going to remain in town. If she'd just pack and go, it would be done, and he'd much prefer that. It wasn't that he had a bloodthirsty streak. Not at all.

Here he was, standing on a darkened street in a town he'd started calling home, with a job he loved and didn't want to give up. He needed to make sure he could keep what he wanted and not lose it to the memories of a young girl.

Every time he thought of getting the hell out of Dodge, he felt sick and his stomach cramped. Leaving would remove the problem entirely. But it also would mean giving up every damn thing he cared about. He hated her for that. *Hated* her.

So Edgar stood there in the dark, trying to figure out how he could handle this threat. He wished to hell Roger would just go back to his saddlery. For crying out loud, why was he stuck to Haley like a burr? He could have had any woman in town. The county's most eligible bachelor. Well, mostly. But, no. For some reason he wasn't trailing after some other woman. For some reason he couldn't seem to stay away from this one.

The thoughts that had begun to fill his head nearly terrified him. He'd gone from thinking he could scare her away somehow to thinking of ways to kill her.

A shaped charge, maybe. He'd learned a lot about blowing things up in the Alberta tar fields, and he could make a directed charge that would blow a hole in her bedroom and not destroy much else. He knew he could.

But, man, to do that without leaving a trail? It wasn't like he could buy much in the way of explosives without proving his identity somehow, and providing a description of their use. Maybe he could steal some from a ranch around here? He didn't know, but he'd have to look into it.

Or he could set the house on fire. He'd have to think that through, but its major advantage would be that the woman would no longer have a reason to stay here.

Damn, he just wished she had gone home the night he'd scared her. That's all he wanted: for her to leave him secure in his new life. Was that so much to ask?

He was reasonably certain that she wouldn't be able to pick him out of a lineup, partly because she'd seen his face only briefly, just once. Partly because the years had changed him a lot. And partly because she hadn't been able to describe him in any useful way all those years ago.

He didn't want to kill her any more than he had wanted to kill her when she was five. But this time he would, if it appeared necessary.

Yeah, he would. Because life in prison seemed an awful heavy price for a stupid mistake when he'd been so young.

No way was he going to let that happen.

At this moment, Edgar believed he would choose killing her over anything else if she didn't leave soon. He was sick of being a virtual prisoner in his house, afraid he might run into her somewhere.

All he'd have to do was get her alone somewhere. Breaking a neck was easy. So was using a knife. He'd seen both done in the past. He could do it.

So, damn her, she'd better leave town, soon. Because he had a right to live his life unfettered by fear.

Turning to walk home, he reminded himself that no one could trace him to Gillette. He'd erased all that from his history, and no one had thought to ask what he'd done during those couple of years because he'd worked for so long in Alberta. There was nothing left to tie him to Gillette.

Except Haley McKinsey.

Chapter 6

When morning arrived, Haley stretched luxuriously, feeling more rested than she had since the night of the Peeping Tom. The room was dark because of the heavy curtains, but the clock told her it was already past seven.

Roger had been right. She had slept better knowing he was out there. She just hoped he had slept well, too.

Man, she didn't want to move. It seemed like forever since she'd felt this relaxed. Every muscle in her body had uncoiled, like one of those cold mornings under a heap of blankets when the bed felt like a heaven she didn't want to leave.

She didn't want to get up, but she knew this feeling wouldn't last long. It seldom did. Soon her mind would be sending action signals to her body and making her want to move. She'd never been very good at holding still for long. One of the main reasons she'd never want to work in surgery. The ER kept her on the move most of the time.

But gradually that wonderful relaxation began to pass and, with a sigh, she picked up the day's mantle. Memories returned, fear tried to make a comeback, but the thought of Roger spending his night on the floor to make her feel safe seemed to dispel all the bad things. At least for now.

She washed up, dressed in fresh jeans and a purple T-shirt with a green superhero on the front. Kids got a kick out of it, and she had a whole collection of such shirts she'd been building over much of her life. They amused her. Sometimes they spoke to her.

Be a superhero. Yeah. As if.

Refreshed, ready to face the day, pleasant or unpleasant, she left the bedroom and walked through the dining room around the door into the living room and foyer area. She wasn't sure the bed and bath off the dining room had been intended for that use, not with four good-size bedrooms upstairs and a full bath. Whatever, Grandma had always slept in there, maybe because it felt cozier to live on one floor.

Certainly, the upstairs wasn't cozy. Big and roomy, but not cozy. She wondered which of her ancestors had thought four bedrooms would be necessary, because she wasn't aware of any big families among the McKinseys. Somebody had been hopeful. Or maybe that's the way they had once been built.

My, wasn't she avoiding any serious thought this morning? As she rounded the corner from the living room toward the foyer, she saw that Roger's bedroll had already been folded up, the air mattress leaning against the wall. Not exactly getting ready to leave.

Her spirits lifted at once. She must have been hoping he'd stick around. But really, that wasn't fair to him. He had a career he needed to tend, saddles to make, orders to fill. He couldn't babysit her forever.

Niggling at the back of her mind was an awareness that no one else had reported a peeper. It made her feel as if she'd been personally targeted. That frightened her.

She tried to shake off returning anxieties as she followed the aroma of coffee to the kitchen. She wondered what Flora would think of all this coffee drinking. She'd been absolutely wedded to her tea, either green tea or English breakfast. Maybe she ought to brew some, just to make this house feel like her grandmother once again.

In the kitchen, she found the coffee already brewed and Roger bent into the fridge, looking around. He at once straightened and greeted her with a smile. "Good morning, sleepyhead. A good night?"

"The best since the creep. Thank you so much. But what about you?"

"I'm accustomed to air mattresses. I've reached the age where I don't go camping without one." He looked into the fridge again, still talking. "You ever do much camping?"

"Yeah, my dad liked to. Mom usually stayed home. She swore nothing could keep her warm."

"I've known some folks like that." He straightened again, bringing out the eggs. "You remember that rock? Well, it probably was bigger than a pebble, but not quite a rock."

She got it instantly and giggled. "Oh, I do. No matter how you smoothed out the area under the tent there was always one rock or root that somehow found you in the wrong place. No matter how you tried to move around."

"I finally had enough and got an air mattress. I forgot the air pump one trip. Never knew I could blow so hard."

He placed the eggs on the counter. "I've found enough for a loaded omelet. If there's anything you don't like, speak now."

"Hey, if it's in my kitchen, I like it, right?"

"Good point. Want some coffee?"

"I'd love some." What a luxury to sit at the table and be waited on. She glanced at the clock and started. "Good heavens, back home it's almost ten o'clock. I never sleep this late!"

"Enjoy it. Most of my sleeping-in days are fading into the past. I don't like it when someone points out I'm getting older."

She giggled again. "Was that a sideways remark?"

"Absolutely not." He brought her a mug and placed it in front of her. "You know, I was never able to talk Flora into insulated mugs. With one of those I can pour myself two cups in the morning and go until after lunch with hot coffee. And I hate lukewarm coffee."

"She was a traditionalist in some ways."

"In more than a few. But then she'd have these surprising moments, like when she bought a smartphone. And the smart TV in her bedroom. Almost overnight she became a streaming addict and thus came the Wi-Fi. No computer, though."

"I noticed that. If I stay, I'll have to get one."

He arched a brow at her as he whipped eggs. "*If* you stay? Are we back to that again?"

"Not really, I suppose. Roger, has anyone else reported a Peeping Tom?" She watched as he pulled out a green pepper from the vegetable drawer then added a leek.

"You don't mind if I use this?" he asked as he waved the leek at her.

"Not at all. I seem to remember a grocery not too far from here."

"Well, I can't use an entire one for an omelet. Anyway, back to other reports of Peeping Tom. I haven't heard any, but that doesn't mean much. I was going to check with the chief and the sheriff today to see if they've heard anything. I'm not plugged into *all* the tentacles of the grapevine around here."

"Thanks," she answered. "I appreciate it."

"You can come with, if you want."

"I might."

He pulled out a cutting board from a lower cabinet and the chef's knife from the knife block on the counter. My, that man was dexterous, she thought as she watched him make short work of slicing and dicing. A bit of butter went into the frying pan on the stove, followed by the veggies as it heated up.

"I saw some salsa in the fridge, and some shredded cheese. You up for either?"

"Both, actually."

"My version of huevos rancheros coming up." He gently stirred the vegetables around in the frying pan, releasing wonderful aromas. "Why'd you ask about other reports of that creep?"

"Because if there aren't any, maybe I was specifically targeted." The thought sounded ridiculous as soon as she said it, but it was out now, lying there to be criticized as it probably deserved.

"I was trying not to think about that possibility," he said after a moment. "Not worth worrying about until we talk to the cops, though. Right?"

He was right. No point in borrowing trouble. Letting go of the thought with difficulty, shunting it to the side where it was going to simmer anyway, she put her chin in her hand, sipped a little coffee and watched him finish the omelets.

"You ever think about becoming a short-order cook?" she asked.

"Hardly. These are bachelor survival skills. Easy and quick as it might be to run to Maude's or the truck stop diner, my arteries can take just so much."

"Ha. And you teased me about being a nurse."

He flashed a grin her way as he placed perfectly folded omelets on two plates and brought them to the table. "I forgot toast," he said. "Dang."

"This is fine. Eat while it's hot. Then maybe you can tell me the secret of folding an omelet like this. I always make a mess and usually just scramble the eggs."

"I'll show you next time it comes up," he promised.

Quiet settled over the table as they took turns sprinkling cheese and spooning salsa over the eggs.

"Ooh, this is good" were the only words Haley spoke. "You can make this for me anytime."

"I'll hold you to it."

She looked up from her plate and felt a blush creeping into her cheeks, something she thought she had lost the ability to do ages ago. Evidently not. This guy sure affected her, and so far only in good ways. Slowly it was beginning to occur to her that the reason she wanted to stay here was him.

Maybe that wasn't a good idea?

His eyes were smiling at her. Just his eyes. She loved their color, a mossy green, and the way they crinkled at the corners, making a friendly expression all by themselves. The corners of his mouth just barely tipped up to join them.

Warmth was filling her, a good warmth. In fact, he made her feel good all the time. Impossible for anyone to do that constantly, but for right now she wasn't going to argue with herself. He made her feel good.

They skipped toast and washed up together. When they were done, he asked, "Wanna come with me when I go see the sheriff about this voyeur and whether there have been other complaints?"

"I'd love to." Maybe that would settle her down some, if other women had lodged complaints. At least she wouldn't feel as if she had a target on her back, which was utterly ridiculous, but the fear wouldn't quite quit. Then she made a strike for her freedom.

"Let's walk," she suggested. "I need some time out of this house."

Roger was glad to see that spark. This whole incident had really gotten to her, and while he could understand why, she still needed to shake it off. He hoped they could solve the problem soon. Once the creep was caught and arrested, she was bound to feel a whole lot safer and the distant past would probably move into the past again.

What had happened to her as a child was horrifying. If that word was even adequate. It had left scars that had followed her through life like the footsteps of a stalker. He didn't blame her for that. He couldn't see how anyone could go through what she had and come out unscathed.

Yet she had made something of herself, something good and helpful. How many lives had she helped save? Probably more than even she could count. Every day at work she faced sights and the human pain of both victims and families that would mess up a lot of people. A lot of the firemen and EMTs, not to mention cops, that he knew carried similar haunting scars from the things they had seen. He'd known some to just quit because they couldn't bear the thought of ever seeing such things again. But they saw them in their nightmares anyway.

Haley had faced life head-on in one of the most difficult ways imaginable. Meanwhile, he spent his days in the mostly peaceful pastime of working with leather, cloth and wood, taking artistic and professional pride in his creations. A far cry from what she did.

He spoke as they strolled along the leafy street. This day was going to get warm. "Ever think about being a doctor?"

She turned her head, eyeing him. "Once in a while I did. But I was in a rush to go 'hands-on.' I just wanted to get into it, and it took only six years. Being a doctor would have taken a whole lot longer."

"And a whole lot more money, I suspect."

She nodded. "Of course. But that didn't hold me back. My dad's been doing well since he started taking jobs around the world. I think he would have helped me quite a bit. So, no, I wasn't thinking about money. Mostly my impatience to get on with helping people." She looked at him again. "You ever think about another line of work?"

"Nope. I guess I'm boring. I grew up in this business and I take a lot of pleasure in it. Never wanted anything else."

"I don't think that's boring. I think that's enviable."

He held out his hands. "The only scars I get come from sharp objects when I'm cutting leather."

"Plenty of those, I see."

"Oh, yeah. Got a few raw knuckles from various things, too, like working on those ducts at Flora's place. But you know, that's all part and parcel of working with your hands."

"In my business, we do everything possible to avoid breaking the skin. Too much chance of infection. A friend of mind once dropped a syringe, it pierced her foot and the next thing we knew she had flesh-eating bacteria. For all we do our best to keep things sterile, it's hard when you're working with sick people and bodily fluids. For a little while at least, the risk of exposure is very real."

"I hadn't thought about that."

She laughed quietly. "No reason you should."

He noted, however, that the farther they walked from

Flora's house, the more she looked around, as if expecting something to pounce at her. Once again, she was uptight. Dang, he hoped the sheriff or the chief could assure her they had a half dozen other complaints. Hell, even one more might be enough to make her feel as if she weren't on a shooting range with no idea where the bullet would come from.

The streets were quiet this morning. No kids in the park, although maybe their parents were busy at home, those who didn't have jobs. The rest? Well, Mom and Dad went to work and the kids went to the summer camp at the elementary school, where activities kept them busy. Older teens probably still hadn't gotten out of bed. He remembered those summer days where he and his friends would routinely stay up until the wee hours, then collapse until after noon. He was surprised his father hadn't objected. There was always work to be done in the shop.

He supposed he'd been indulged quite a bit. "I guess I had an idyllic childhood in most ways."

"Where did that come from?"

"Thinking back to summers where I could pretty much do what I wanted as long as I stayed out of trouble."

She flashed a smile. "No trouble?"

"No trouble. Like I said, boring."

"I don't think anything about you is boring."

He caught his breath, liking the way Haley had said that, then covered his reaction by quickly pointing. "See the corner up there, just past the courthouse square? That's the sheriff's office. Not much farther."

"It's okay. I'm enjoying the walk with you."

Another compliment. His head was going to swell. But he doubted that she was really enjoying herself, not when she was looking around like a soldier on patrol. Not when she quickened her step toward the sheriff's office.

He supposed some would think she was overreacting and unreasonable, but he didn't see it that way at all. Some things haunted people for a lifetime, and this woman was not lacking in grit. Just look at her career.

They stepped into the sheriff's office and were immediately greeted by a cloud of cigarette smoke. Velma, who'd been sitting at the dispatcher's desk since the dinosaurs roamed the earth, sat beneath a no-smoking sign and puffed away. If anyone had ever tried to get her to stop, they had lost the battle.

She made the worst coffee in the world. Famously bad. Even folks who'd never set foot in the station had heard about it. The row of antacid bottles behind the cups said it all. But despite everything, Velma had become a beloved institution around here. No one could imagine her ever retiring.

He watched as his cute nurse friend waved the smoke away from her face. She must find this awful. Remembering their trip to the market, he almost grinned.

"Velma? Gage around anywhere?"

"He's almost always in his office anymore," Velma answered in her cracked voice. "If I have to listen to him complain about paperwork one more time, I may dump the coffee urn over his head. Anyway, go on back. He's probably in there hiding behind a stack of paper."

"Don't computers help?" Haley asked as they walked down the short hall.

"Sure. But there's always a paper backup. Sooner or later, it gets moved to microfiche or something."

"Ah."

He rapped once on the door with the brass nameplate and heard an invitation to come through it.

Walking in with Haley, he heard Gage say from behind that stack of papers, "Close the door. Velma's been blowing a mega cloud today and Emma doesn't like it when I come home smelling like an ashtray." He lifted his head so they could see him. "Pull up a chair and tell me what I can do for you. Just don't hand me another piece of paper."

Roger laughed, but noticed Haley had begun to look tense. She didn't want to drag her story out again, but appeared to think she might have to. And she probably would, if they were to deal with the question that had brought them there.

"We were wondering," Roger said, "whether there have been any more reports of Peeping Toms."

Gage's dark gaze leaped to Haley. "No…" he said slowly. "If one had been reported, I'd have heard about it, either from my deputies or from Jake's police department. We share all information."

"No conflict there?" Roger asked easily, trying to take this slowly to be sure Haley could gather herself to explain the reason for her concern.

"Hell, no," Gage said. "Roger, you know Jake used to work for me. When the city got the funding and decided they wanted their own police department…"

He paused and glanced at Haley with his crooked smile, formed because one side of his face was covered with shiny burn scar tissue. "I think the city gets annoyed with me at times. I'm not famous for holding my fire, and I'm no politician. Power grab, I guess. Jake and I had no trouble working it out. Jake handles the town and I back him up when he needs it. Anyway, it was one of my deputies who responded to Haley's call because Jake's shorthanded at the moment. So much for budgeting when you overreach."

Roger had to laugh again. He might avoid it, but he still heard about the occasional power tussles around here. He didn't know how it worked in large cities, but a small place like this didn't seem to have enough power to go around.

"There's a concern here," Gage said after waiting a moment. "Why do you two want to know if there are other cases?"

Roger looked at Haley, wondering how much she wanted him to say and how much she wanted to say for herself.

Strain showed around her eyes and she didn't immediately speak, so he plunged in.

"Gage, maybe you remember hearing about the case in Gillette some twenty-five years ago? A little girl kidnapped out her bedroom window?"

Gage leaned forward, wincing a bit as he did so. He reached for a pencil and began to tap the eraser on his desk. "I heard something about it. That was before I signed on with this department." Again he looked at Haley. "I didn't live here until around that time. So I heard only a bit and I was kind of preoccupied with my own problems. So that happened to *you*?"

She nodded jerkily.

Gage swore quietly. "I am so sorry for you. Sorry that happened. Can I ask details?"

She began to speak hesitantly. "I don't remember a lot of detail."

"Hardly surprising, given you must have been traumatized." Gage waited patiently, allowing Haley to speak as much or little as she wanted.

Presently, she spoke again. "He always wore a ski mask. I think I glimpsed his face only once. I'm not even sure about that now. Anyway, I wasn't able to describe him in any useful way to the authorities or a sketch artist who tried so hard to drag any little detail out of me."

"That would be difficult for anyone," Gage remarked. "Not only á little kid."

"What I do remember was waking up to find a man standing beside my bed. It was dark, so at first I thought it was my dad. Then he grabbed me, slapped tape over my mouth and pulled me through the open window with him. That sticks in my mind. Then there was a car trunk. I remember *that* because I could smell the fumes. I was terrified out of my mind. After that, very little… I believe he touched me once or twice, but I can't say he was a sexual predator. For some reason, I've always had the impression that he wanted to try more, but it either didn't thrill him or he was too scared. It's all a blur anyway."

She closed her eyes and the room remained silent

except for some voices from the front office. Velma's, roughened from all her smoking, and possibly a deputy or two.

Haley opened her eyes. "Next thing I remember clearly was standing by a roadside all alone. I didn't know which way to go, or where I was, or if I was far from home. It was early morning. I was cold. And I just stood there, stunned or lost. I couldn't tell you. But still very, very frightened."

"I should think so," Gage remarked.

She nodded. "Yeah. After a while—it seemed like a century to me—a car came down the road. I started to run. I'd never actually seen his car, and that might have been him coming back for me. I stumbled into a ditch and got caught up in tumbleweed, then I heard this very nice lady say, 'Are you lost, sweetie?' She helped me out of the tumbleweed and into her car. I curled up in a tight ball, I was so afraid she was related in some way with my kidnapper. I didn't unfreeze again until we pulled up to the police station and a female officer came to get me out of the car and carry me inside."

Roger's chest had grown so tight with pain for her that he had trouble drawing breath. Her briefer explanations before hadn't prepared him for this look into the wounded soul of a five-year-old. Sure, he'd known it had terrified her, but something about the image of her standing alongside a road all alone, then running from help because she was so frightened… Yeah, that was vivid and disturbing at a deep level.

Haley had lowered her head as she'd spoken. Now Gage dropped his pencil and leaned back in his chair as if he had taken a blow. Roger felt pretty much the same way. A solid punch to the middle of his chest.

And none of it compared to what Haley must have felt, must be feeling right now.

Gage whispered something, probably a string of curse words he didn't want to say aloud. Roger had more than a few he'd have liked to use to turn the air blue. Because what could anyone do at this late date except cuss and call the guy who'd taken her all kinds of names?

"Pervert," Gage said finally. Anger sparked in his eyes.

Roger nodded agreement. "Pervert," he repeated.

Haley quickly wiped at her eyes. "Sorry," she said. "I thought I'd gotten past most of it through all the therapy I had afterward. Maybe not."

"Therapy," said Gage, "doesn't erase the scars. It helps us handle them. God knows, I had enough therapy myself after I lost my first family… Okay, thanks for filling me in. And don't feel bad because the peeper has stirred your memories. He has, hasn't he?"

Haley nodded.

But ask the important question, Roger urged her silently. Gage had just said there were no other reports. Was she going to walk around feeling as if she had been targeted? Could Gage say anything that would make her feel better? Or safer?

"You didn't come here to tell me about your kidnapping," Gage said with certainty.

"No," Haley answered in a smothered voice. "It occurred to me… Oh, it's crazy."

"I hear crazy in this office all the time. Shoot. I won't think any less of you."

She managed a wan smile. "If I'm the only one he's looked in on…what if I was his chosen target?"

Gage rocked, his eyes narrowing, his chair creaking beneath his movements. "Gotta oil this thing," he said almost absently. "I hadn't thought about that, Haley."

"I shouldn't have, either," she replied, her voice growing stronger. "It's been a long time. What's the likelihood this guy would be in this town, or that I'd even be a threat to him if he is? Zip."

Gage thought a moment, still rocking back and forth in his chair and occasionally shifting his weight as if his back hurt. "Okay, you want my assessment?"

"Please."

"Very unlikely the guy who kidnapped you would know you're here, or that he'd be here. I agree with that. But chance being what it is, I can't quite agree with *zip*. However remote, there's always a chance. But even so, I don't know why he should be worried even if he's living right next door to you. It's been so long, he probably looks nothing like he did back then and, anyway, I imagine he thought he'd gotten off scot-free when no descriptions or artists' renderings were ever in the media."

She nodded, relaxing visibly. "You're right. I'm worrying about nothing. I thought so, but I couldn't shake it."

Gage held up a hand. "Not so quick. While I doubt it's your kidnapper from so long ago, this perv might indeed have his sights on you. It's strange that we haven't had other reports, but it's possible he's been peeping without being seen. So that doesn't necessarily mean anything."

"Aw heck, Gage," Roger said.

Gage gave his crooked smile. "I have to be honest." Now he leaned forward, once again wincing. "Okay, patrols have been looking out for anyone lurking around at odd hours, but I'll tell them to pay better attention. Dismount and walk around if need be. Budget crunch means I haven't got anyone to spare to put on your house—"

Haley quickly interrupted him. "I wouldn't want that. It's bad enough like this without thinking I might deprive someone else of police support." She shifted on the chair and looked to the side. "Okay, I agree it's likely not my kidnapper. That would be too weird after all this time. But…let me know if anyone else reports this guy. I'd feel better, strange as that sounds."

"I understand." Gage nodded. "Yes, I do. But my folks can certainly be more alert. I have to admit, it's odd not to have a Peeping Tom turn up more than once. And sometimes they fixate on one person, but if they can no longer peek in, they move on to someone else. He may have moved on and his new victim might not have realized he's looking in on her. But if she becomes aware, I'll make sure you hear about it, okay?"

"Thank you. I'd really appreciate that."

After a little more casual conversation, Roger took her back out onto the street. He was surprised to see that the sky had grayed over. "Maybe we'll get some rain. It'd be welcome." Rare at this time of year, but he didn't know a soul who'd complain. "I suggest we go to Maude's and get a latte. Sound good?"

"Sounds wonderful." She actually smiled at him and he felt some of the tension in his chest let go.

Reaching out, he took her hand casually. He liked it when he felt her squeeze back. Man, it had been a long time since holding a woman's hand had felt so special.

"Maybe a little chocolate of some kind, too," he suggested. "Always good for the mood."

"My mood's improved since talking with the sheriff." They paused to cross a street. A one-traffic-light town, as it had been during her childhood. Traffic was light enough that they didn't have to wait long. "What happened to Gage? What he said about his family."

"Briefly? He used to be an undercover agent with the DEA. Somehow his cover got blown and his family was killed by a car bomb. To look at him, I would guess he wasn't far away when it happened."

"Oh, my God," she breathed. "Oh, my God."

"When he first arrived here, he looked…well, like murder. Folks called him *Hell's Own Archangel*."

"I can't imagine. God, the poor man. But he seems to have moved past it?"

"As much as anyone can." There was nothing else he could say.

The bell over the diner's door rang as he opened it and waved her to enter first. She always seemed a bit surprised by the courtesy. Maybe she didn't like it. He'd have to ask when the opportunity provided itself.

Inside they got a table at the window in the sunlight, away from the few people who were diving into their lunches. Maude made her usual stomp-and-demand appearance, wearing a white bibbed apron over her plain green dress.

"Lattes for two," Roger said. "Hey, Maude?"

"Yeah?"

"What have you got that's chocolate?"

For the first time in his life, Roger saw Maude smile. It wasn't much of one, but still recognizable. Was the battle-ax softening with age? Hard to believe.

"You reading my mind or something, Roger McLeod?" It sounded like a demand. "Would you believe I made some chocolate pudding pies this morning? With graham-cracker crust."

"Oh, my," said Haley, resting her chin in her hand and looking almost dreamy.

"Sugar-free one, too, for them that's worried about that stuff. The old sheriff, Nate Tate? He likes his piece of pie but he's become downright ornery about calories. I'm making all kinds of sugar-free pies now." She glared at Roger. "As you'd know if you ever ordered pie."

Roger grinned. "It seems I need to do more of that."

"You work hard enough you shouldn't have to be worrying about it," Maude grumped. "So two pieces, sugar-free?"

Once she had their agreement, she stomped off to make the lattes and get the pie.

Roger leaned across the table and covered Haley's hand with his. "You feel a little better?"

"I guess so. He's a nice man, your sheriff. He didn't make me feel silly."

"I'd have been astonished if he had. That man's seen a

lot in his time. What's more, I don't think you're silly, either. I wouldn't have suggested we visit him otherwise."

She moved her hand, twining her fingers with his. "You know, Roger, over the time I've been here, I've come to realize how much I missed you over the years. You were second only to Grandma in the reasons I loved to come here to visit."

He felt warmth flood him all the way to his toes. "I'm no big deal."

"Just a very nice guy who made my summers more fun. You never treated me like a brat who was in your way."

He had to grin. "Funny thing about that. I never thought you were in the way. We always had a pretty good time."

She smiled, and with the easing of her tension since she'd talked to Gage, it was the most relaxed expression he'd seen from her yet.

There was no clatter as Maude set the lattes in front of them. After all these years, Roger was used to the sound of coffee mugs slamming down, but for reasons known only to her, Maude served lattes in big paper cups.

The beverages, however, were followed by two slams as the clear-glass pie plates hit the table. Forks wrapped in napkins followed them.

"Oh, that looks good," Haley said, looking up at Maude.

"I made it, didn't I? And by the way, folks are hoping you plan to stay here in town." With that, Maude stomped away.

"Man," muttered Roger, "she's getting to be unpredictable. Is the sky falling?"

A lovely laugh escaped Haley, and Roger gazed into her beautiful blue eyes. Yeah, he'd been missing her for years, too. He just hadn't realized it.

Across the street, unseen by either of them, a man paused and stared through the window. He didn't like what he saw. Not at all. If the two of them were holding hands, it only increased the likelihood that Haley would hang around.

"Well, good afternoon, Mr. Metzger."

The sound of a woman's voice startled Edgar into turning sharply. He saw Edith Jasper with her Great Dane, Bailey. "Ms. Jasper," he answered almost sullenly. Man, he had to watch it before the whole town was talking about *him* and his sour mood.

"Where is Puddles?" the woman asked pleasantly. "Not sick, I hope."

"No, no. Just a little cut between her toes. Vet gave me some ointment and said not to take her on long walks for a day or two."

"What a shame! I hope the little dear is better soon."

"I hope so, too. She doesn't like it when I don't take her on long walks."

"If I didn't take Bailey with me, he'd probably dive through a window to follow. He's big enough to do it, too."

"I'm glad Puddles isn't."

"You have a nice day, Mr. Metzger."

He watched her stroll away, then shook himself

and moved in the other direction. He didn't want to be caught gawking through the window of Maude's. Since everybody could just walk in, there was no reason to stare, was there? No, he didn't want to be remarkable in any way.

But the two had gone to the sheriff. And now they were holding hands.

The combination made him nearly ill. Had he done something to give himself away? No, he couldn't have. But now with that hand-holding…

Hell, Edgar thought as he stormed away. He had to figure out how to get rid of that woman before much longer. One flicker, one half-formed accusation, and he'd be ruined. Even if they didn't get enough to send him to jail for life, in this town suspicion could kill you. People talked. A lot.

And now that someone had noticed he was walking around without his dog, it could be seen as unusual. He guessed he couldn't take Puddles out much for the next couple of days to uphold his lousy story.

Damn, he wasn't good at this. He ought to know by now. After he went to Alberta, far out of range, in a different country, and had managed to mostly stay out of trouble ever since. Well, except for occasional drunk and disorderly stuff, and a few brawls that were pretty much inevitable among oil rig workers. Tough men, they didn't take much lying down.

He'd cleaned up his act until Haley McKinsey showed up in his private little hidey-hole. She could cost him everything. *Everything*.

Yet he still hadn't figured out a way to deal with her. Or with Roger McLeod, as was becoming clear.

He cussed again, under his breath, and kept stomping his way home. He was afraid and he knew it. Maybe he wasn't thinking as smartly as he should. Maybe his head was as screwed up as when he'd stolen first the money, then the child.

That memory didn't give him a lot of confidence. And maybe that was what was stalling him, keeping him from devising a plan.

He headed home, determined to clean out mental cobwebs somehow. Either the woman or the saddler. He figured if he wiped out Roger McLeod, Haley McKinsey wouldn't want to stay in this town, house or no house. Especially since the two were starting to act like lovebirds.

Either way, he had to succeed or lose everything he'd worked for.

Chapter 7

Haley decided to let the sorting and packing go for the afternoon. The day had turned perfect, skipping the earlier promise of rain, and a gentle breeze blew, lightly ruffling her short hair. When she told Roger she wanted to spend some time on the porch swing, he nodded.

"Go for it. You've probably breathed enough dust since you got here to give you asthma."

"Not likely. Flora may have collected but she didn't let the dirt settle."

"Wait until autumn when some of the hayfields are turned under. The wind can carry enough dirt to make the sky go dark. Cleaning's a pain then. But, listen, I need to get back to the shop and take care of a few things. Will you be okay?"

She knew she'd been acting like a scared rabbit since

that awful night, but to have him ask if she'd be okay sitting on a porch swing in the bright afternoon sunlight embarrassed her.

"Of course I will," she said firmly. "This amount of sunlight should be a disinfectant for any creeps around."

He laughed then hopped in his truck, promising to be back in a couple of hours. "I'll bring dinner, so don't cook," he admonished her.

Well, that sounded nice, even with a chest freezer full of lasagna and goulash and casseroles. She settled on the swing and began pushing it gently with one foot, listening to the familiar creak.

Taking the afternoon off felt like a great idea. She'd been driven since she'd arrived and hadn't let up even when she'd decided she might well stay. There was still a lot to do, of course, but the pressure to deal with it had lessened.

Flora had been a reasonably neat woman, but the second floor was overstuffed, and the attic was full of things that might better go to an antiques store or auction. Whatever meaning they'd had to Flora, it was lost on Haley. The attachments they represented were gone.

Or maybe Flora hadn't found it easy to let go of things. People could be like that, always thinking they'd find a use for something someday. And then forgot about it or never did. The only dusty part of the house was the attic, so Flora probably hadn't been up there for years. No reason to go. She'd kept a bedroom upstairs ready for a guest, but the others weren't prepared and the closets and drawers were full.

It still amazed Haley that so much had been tucked

away in the house. As she'd opened each new area for exploration and decision, she'd been surprised that so much could be there. She ought to be used to it by now.

Catching movement from the corner of her eye, she saw Edith Jasper and Bailey coming down the sidewalk. Edith raised a hand, a handled shopping bag hanging from it, and waved. Haley immediately waved back, smiling. A visit would be nice.

A visit was exactly what Edith had in mind. She approached the front steps with Bailey. "Are you busy or do you have some time for a gab?"

"Plenty of time to gab," Haley answered. "I'm giving myself some time off."

"You should."

"Come on up. Join me on the swing, or we can go inside if you like."

"I'll take the swing. I frequently sat out here with Flora." She climbed the three steps and plopped down beside Haley. Bailey took the hint and settled beside her, his snout between his front paws.

"He's such a beautiful dog," Haley remarked. "But so big!"

"That has both advantages and disadvantages." Edie grinned. "He eats for his size. He also likes long walks and an occasional run in the park. Now, the walks are good for me, too, so I can't complain. But the running? My running years are in the past." She offered Haley the bag. "For you."

"Oh, thank you!" Haley looked inside. "Tea!"

"Flora's two favorite kinds. I decided whatever was

in the house couldn't possibly be fresh, and these might bring you some happy memories."

"How thoughtful." Haley smiled then held the open bag to her nose, drawing in the aromas. "The kitchen used to smell like this."

"Always," Edie agreed on a light laugh. "I hope you enjoy. And, didn't I promise to help you sort? I can rattle this old memory a bit for things I may have learned over the years. But since you're taking the day off, how about you set a time for me and Bailey here to show up. I bet this place is full of treasures."

"Most of them treasures I know nothing about. I'm torn between a need to clear space and the fear that I might throw out something important. I think the worry is slowing me down."

"Ah," said Edie, arching an eyebrow, "how would you ever know if it was important?"

That drew a laugh from Haley.

"What's more," Edith added, "what's the rush? Do you have a timetable? Do you need to get back to Baltimore?"

"I'll have to go back at the end of the month, if only to put in my notice."

"If?" Again Edith's brow raised.

"I know, I keep flip-flopping."

"Any idea what's causing the hesitation?"

Haley knew exactly what was causing it: the Peeping Tom. The uneasiness she couldn't quite escape, matched up against being able to live here near an old friend and the exciting idea of a new job. Part of her was truly ready for a change of scenery, and she loved this house of Flora's. Another part of her wondered if she'd ever be able to completely relax, though.

"Say," she said, lifting the bag, trying to be a good hostess—something she wasn't used to because she was too busy to entertain with any formality. Everything in her crowd back in Baltimore was ad hoc. "Would you like some tea?"

Edith cracked a loud laugh. "I drank it when I had to, which was when I was visiting Flora. I'm not a fan. I don't know about you, but when I smelled those at the store, it carried me back. If you're not a tea person, either, you won't offend me."

"When I was a kid, I drank it with her. I used to love her pretending to tell my fortune with the tea leaves in the bottom of the cup."

Edith nodded. "I remember," she said almost wistfully. "She used to drag that out once in a while so we could share a good laugh. I never took that cruise with a handsome stranger."

Haley had to giggle. "Well, I'll enjoy this from time to time in honor of Grandma. When I first got here, I tried to drink it. The whistling of that old teakettle was part of the pleasure for me. I felt almost guilty when I broke out the coffee maker."

"Times change, even in Flora's house." Edith sighed then leaned forward. "That man has been staring."

Haley swiveled her head as ice rushed down her spine, following Edith's gaze. She didn't see a man. "What?"

Edith shook her head. "Nobody special. And if he

was staring, he was probably staring at Bailey. That dog sometimes stops traffic."

"He *is* large," Haley agreed as she forced herself to return her attention to Edith, aware that her relaxation was seeping away. Damn, she couldn't give in to this. She'd had enough trouble adjusting to the idea that she didn't need to fear every little thing after her kidnapping. Did she want to backtrack? Of course not.

She gave herself a little shake. "You don't know who it was?"

Edith smiled crookedly. "I may have lived here all my life and there *was* a time when we were small enough that everyone knew everyone else, at least by sight. Then we grew a bit with the junior college and the now-defunct semiconductor plant. I can no longer say that I know everyone. Anyway, I didn't get a good enough look. Hate to say it, but I have cataracts and it's getting close to time to have them removed. What I saw was Vaseline-blurry."

"Oh, that must be awful!"

"Large-print books these days. Do you have any idea how annoying that is?"

"How come?" Haley was honestly curious.

"Not enough words on a page. Can't explain it, but I find it off-putting. I'd probably get used to it a lot faster if I didn't have light—literally—at the end of the tunnel."

"When's your surgery?"

"Three months. I'll make it that long." Edith shrugged. "Easily. Right now I can't drive and Bailey is loving it. I have to walk everywhere. I'm probably fitter than I have been in years. As to that man, I'm sorry I drew your attention. To be perfectly frank, I couldn't see well enough to be sure he was staring. He just didn't move for a spell. For all I know, he might have been studying a bug at his feet." She shrugged. "No real reason for anyone to stare at two women gabbing on a front porch."

"No." But Haley still couldn't shake the feeling that Edith had gotten it right when she'd first mentioned it. Something about the man had made Edith feel he was staring, even if she couldn't see very well. Oh, heck, she needed to stop this.

But suddenly the day didn't feel quite so beautiful. "Want to come in and we'll make tea? Or coffee? Bailey is welcome."

"Sure, but don't take it amiss if I run soon. I have to meet a friend. And you still have to name a good time for me to come help you sort."

Edith had just stood when an insistent beeping came from her pocket. "My alarm," she said. "Sorry, Haley, I've got to run. Shelley's picking me up to take me to the grocery and I don't want to keep her waiting."

"Of course. And if you ever need a ride…"

Edith smiled. "I'll call. And I'll call you later about our meet-up. You still have Flora's phone number, right?"

"I do."

Haley watched briefly as Edith and her gigantic dog headed down the street, then slipped inside.

Simple words, possibly mistaken, had killed the afternoon for her. Instead of diving in to more sorting, she put the kettle on and decided she'd have some green tea in honor of Flora.

A few minutes later, as she poured boiling water over aromatic green tea leaves in the flowered teapot, she suddenly realized the day was darkening.

Too early for that, she thought, glancing at the clock. Then a hollow boom rumbled through the house. Wow, the weather had changed fast. It looked as if the morning's threat of rain had returned. On the front porch, though, she didn't have a view of the sky. It wouldn't have taken much time for a heavy cloud to suddenly obliterate the sun.

Another roll lumbered through the house, still sounding distant.

There was a storm on the way.

Roger looked up from the cantle he was applying the first layer of leather to as the thunder rolled. He loved storms, loved their wildness, but his thoughts immediately turned to Haley. The bright lights under which he worked had made him unaware that the weather was changing. He hoped the deepening darkness he could see through the windows didn't make her uneasy.

Shaking his head with sudden impatience, he wanted to hurry this last bit of work and get back to her. He couldn't hurry it, however. This was an important part of the saddle and it had to be constructed just so for the rider's comfort. Slap-dashing the pieces of leather just wouldn't do.

Sighing, he ignored the next rumble and bent again to his task. The leather had been softened and stretched into just the right shape. He needed to apply it *now*.

He did speed up his pace, however. Sacrificing nothing of quality, he was still able to get the pieces joined before the rain started. He cleaned up quickly after hanging the cantle to dry and tighten, then headed out to his truck. He paused just as he locked the shop behind him, remembering that he had promised to bring dinner tonight. Dang.

He didn't mind the dinner, but he couldn't help wondering how Haley was dealing with the blackening afternoon. The clouds rolling in were thick and gloomy, maybe a little greenish, a color that always made him a bit uneasy. While they didn't often have tornadoes in this town, they were possible, and that particular color always made him wonder.

Shaking his head again, he climbed into his truck while still deciding what he should bring to her place. The truck stop diner was farther away and stuck mainly with simple foods that would appeal to a wide variety of truckers. Nothing like home cooking there.

Maude's was better for that. Each day she prepared a fresh soup, and while the steak sandwich seemed to be a county-wide favorite, she also made a mean meatloaf, super mashed potatoes and a variety of vegetables that were never overcooked.

Meatloaf, he decided. Rib-sticking, always juicy, and someday he was going to learn her secret seasonings. He'd eaten plenty of meatloaf in his day, often at church potlucks, and while there were many good ones, Maude's beat the bunch.

Given that they'd only had lattes and pie for lunch, he wondered if Haley would think he was trying to ruin her health. The thought almost made him laugh. She'd dug into that chocolate pie like it was ambrosia.

By the time he departed Maude's and headed for Haley's, he had a stack of foam containers that held everything from salads to meatloaf, all the trimmings and a couple of pieces of pie that Maude had thrown in because "Haley liked it."

That was not the Maude he'd grown up with. Of course, maybe she always had been. Her gruffness was familiar, her bluntness equally so, but he'd heard more than one person say that beneath that Gorgon exterior she had a good heart.

Maybe so. He'd seen it a couple of times today.

When he pulled up at Haley's he saw that all the curtains were closed. The air was fresh with ozone, and the stiffening breeze felt cool. He'd have opened every window in his house for this. Perhaps he could coax her into opening one or two with him there. This time of summer, a storm was a treat.

Haley had indeed zipped up the house because of Edith's remark about a man staring at them. Edith, though, had admitted she might have misinterpreted it and her cataracts obscured her vision. Haley knew a little about what cataracts could do. She didn't have any doubt that Edith might have been unable to see the guy well enough to know what he was looking at.

She only wished she could have seen for herself. But at some point she realized she was going over the top with this. It was just a strong thunderstorm, and if any stupid dude wanted to look in on her, she'd see his face.

So she opened the curtains in her kitchen and looked out. Did the greenish color of the light mean anything? She had no idea, but to her it looked more as if the world outside was deeply under water.

Thunder cracked again, more loudly, as she set about making some coffee for Roger. It was going to be a wild afternoon. She thought about going into Flora's bedroom to turn on the TV and check the weather forecast and then foreclosed the idea. She wanted to keep the curtains open in the kitchen and watch it happen. She didn't want to leave an uncovered window unattended.

She sighed and plopped herself at the table, wondering when Roger would arrive. She was developing a dangerous dependency, but she was also developing a stronger and stronger attachment to him. Heck, she was beginning to wish he'd touch her more often. One hug and a bit of hand-holding made her feel cared for, but it was steadily becoming not enough. She wondered how she could break down the barrier he seemed to have erected, or if she even should. She highly valued his friendship and didn't want to risk it.

Maybe he felt the same. Oh, hell. She was growing confused about everything. She wasn't used to all this uncertainty.

She tried to tell herself it was a growth experience, but in truth she wondered if she really needed it. Dealing with an old fear after all these years stank. Flip-flopping about where she wanted to spend at least part of her future seemed needless. After all, she had a complete and fulfilling life back home.

And she wondered how she'd be feeling right now

if that man hadn't looked in her window in the middle of the night.

Come on, Roger.

The coffee maker finished brewing with a final puff of steam. The tea she'd made had put a pleasant, familiar, heart-touching aroma in the air, but now the coffee overwhelmed it. She liked it. Flora's memory had visited a little while but now she was ready for her own pattern again.

Including, it seemed, a long, rolling boom of thunder that felt as if it went on forever.

Did storms get worse here? She supposed it was possible. There were mountains on both sides, but in between lay a large enough plateau to count as a plain. Winds could build, and maybe they poured down from the mountains on both sides until they created some kind of vortex. How would she know? She was no meteorologist.

Almost laughing at this fanciful and uneducated line of thought, she heard the front door open. Urging herself to remain put so as not to seem like a frightened rabbit, she waited until Roger walked into the kitchen carrying a couple of large brown shopping bags.

"Dinner has arrived," he said cheerfully. Then he sniffed the air. "I smell coffee. Do you mind that I brought lattes?"

"The day I turn down a latte will go on my calendar never to be forgotten."

He laughed, setting the bags on the table. "Maude noticed you like the chocolate pie, so she threw in a couple of pieces. Feels like this storm is going to get rough. You okay?"

"I opened the curtains so I wouldn't miss it."

She rose and went to help him remove the coffees and foam containers from the bags. "What did you do? Buy out all of Maude's stock?"

He laughed again. "Nope. A very plain meal. Meatloaf, mashed potatoes, salads, some broccoli…" His voice trailed off. She looked up and their eyes locked. Suddenly all the air seemed to have fled the room. She floated in a vacuum, unable to breathe as stronger needs took hold.

Before she could find a breath, before she could move another inch, he stepped toward her and pulled her into his embrace. "I can't resist," he murmured near her ear.

Oh, man, she didn't want him to resist. Then a sensation she had never experienced before flooded her. Everything inside her softened like melting butter. Every tension, every concern, faded away as he held her close to his strength and heat.

Around her he created a cocoon that closed out the world. She wanted never to emerge from it.

But then, almost reluctantly, he released her and stood back. Their eyes met again and his were smiling. "You're a nice armful."

Wow! She'd never heard that before and wanted to respond somehow. But he'd already turned to the table to finish the unpacking.

"We don't have to eat right now. The containers will keep it all warm for a while. But I suggest we not waste the lattes."

Just like that, the day went back to normal. Except for a boom that felt as if it shook the house. Windows rattled audibly and Haley quickly looked out toward the day. "It's going to be bad, isn't it?"

"Yup." He folded the paper bags and set them to one side. "I don't even need to check the forecast. While I was out getting our dinner, I had a good view of the sky. The storm is still building."

He placed one of the lattes in front of her seat and his own across from it. "Wanna open up a few of the windows before it starts raining? I don't know about you, but I love the way the air smells before a storm, and this place could use a good airing, don't you think? And since I'm here…"

She nodded. "That *would* be good. I've got to stop living like a troglodyte."

"First coffee before it cools down. I was surprised when I pulled up, though, to see you have all the curtains drawn again. You weren't doing it so much just recently."

"Yeah." She sighed. "I was sitting on the porch swing with Edith and her dog when she said some man down at the corner was staring at us. I looked, but there was no one there. Then she said she had some pretty bad cataracts and couldn't be sure what he was looking at."

"Didn't make you feel much better, I suppose."

She gave a quick negative shake of her head. "Are you getting sick of me yet?"

"Hell, no," he said forcefully. "Don't even think that. In fact, because I was concerned about you, I looked stuff up online. And you know what, Haley? Many,

many women who've been peeped on develop fears and the same kind of insecurity you're experiencing. Call it normal, because it is."

She looked at him, feeling herself soften again. He was such a good man. "Thank you, Roger."

"For what? I didn't do anything. Now drink, because a cold latte...well, it's not the same, is it? I suppose pouring it over ice like some coffee shops do would work, and if that's what you want..."

She laughed quietly and lifted her cup obediently. It *was* still warm and tasted delicious. "Thank you so much for this."

"You'll thank me for the meatloaf, too. Maude does a bang-up job. I'd like to snatch her recipe."

Another deep roll of thunder shook the house and Haley couldn't help but look toward the window.

"Amazing, isn't it?" Roger asked. "We're generally in the rain shadow of the mountains, so this is a treat."

"Rain shadow?"

"Yeah. When clouds come across the mountains, the colder air generally makes it rain over them. Often by the time they get to us, they don't have much to dump. It's arid here."

"I thought it seemed drier."

"Oh, it is. Which is why that fishing trip I took you on was such a flop."

The memory made her grin. "You were so disappointed. But we *did* find another place to fish."

"I know, but that was my favorite spot. A great place to spend a morning or evening daydreaming and waiting for a bite."

The rain hit suddenly and heavily. For the first couple of minutes, as it struck the kitchen window, it sounded like hail. Then it turned into sheets that almost completely hid the house next door.

"Well, I guess we're not going to open the windows," Roger remarked.

Haley didn't care. It wasn't as if she hadn't been opening the windows for a little while for the past several days. He was right, though, about the scent of the air just before a storm hit. She was sorry she'd missed it.

There was only one reason she had. A man who was probably not anywhere near. Damn, she needed to gather herself and soldier on. She was no wimp. She had to let Roger get his work and life back, and stop leaning on him so much.

But she said nothing just then. Dinner surrounded her in foam boxes, thanks to him, and she was sipping a warm latte that he'd brought to her.

She never wanted him to feel that she was tossing him out.

Conundrum. Double damn.

Edgar sat in his house, battling fear and frustration. It kept coming back to him that one time when that girl had fallen asleep after crying her eyes out, he'd taken his mask off. He'd quickly turned and pulled the mask back on, but he couldn't escape the certainty that she had seen him, however briefly.

He'd allowed himself to be lulled by the fact that absolutely no description of him had ever reached the press. No Wanted posters in the post office. He'd figured she either hadn't seen him well enough to describe him or that trauma had completely blocked her memory.

But if there was one thing he'd learned over his lifetime, it was that people never forgot a face even when the years had changed it somewhat. The eyes, the shape—he had no idea how it happened, but people he hadn't seen in decades could remember his face even if they couldn't recall his name. If Haley got one good look at him, it might stir her memory.

And the way she had stared at him when he was walking Puddles. She'd remembered *something*. Strides, too, were easily recalled. He knew that because he'd recognized people from the back based on the way they walked.

She showed no sign of wanting to leave town, and right then he wanted to bang his head on the useless brick surround of his equally useless fireplace.

Life had taught him how easily he could get muddled when he tried to deal with matters he wasn't used to dealing with. Familiar things, okay. He could teach kids all about drilling an oil well. About shutting it off. About handling a blowout. But getting rid of someone? No practice. No idea.

One thing he knew for sure, he had to be very careful. Killing both her and that damn Roger would unleash a manhunt that would force him to leave town and his rebuilt life. But he couldn't find a way to get the woman alone or to remove her in a way that wouldn't raise hackles all over this county.

Poison? He couldn't find a way to get close enough to poison a bottle of milk or a can of coffee grounds.

He'd been looking online to try to find a poison that would be fatal in a single dose, but what good was that if he couldn't get it to her?

A box of azalea leaves presented as a box of tea might do it; killing her over a period of days would leave almost no trace if they even figured out the flu symptoms resulted from poison. But how to get them to her? Cripes. And how to get azalea leaves anyway? No one grew them around here.

Maybe some other local plant.

Castor beans, he'd heard, could be used to make ricin. But he still didn't know how he could get it to her.

He needed to figure this out. Desperation was growing, driving him until he could barely think about anything else.

Puddles was getting desperate, too, pawing at his leg and whimpering. Finally, he rose and put her leash on, leading her to the back door. She could go out in that rain to do her stuff while he stayed under that small overhang.

Dang, when he'd tried to walk by one street over to see if Roger was still hanging there, he'd seen Edith Jasper sitting on Haley's porch with her. And that big dog of Edith's. God, he wouldn't want to tussle with that animal.

As soon as Haley's head had started to turn his way, he'd fled around the corner of a building. Edith had likely seen him and mentioned it, but since Edith's cataracts were known to many, he wondered if she'd even been able to see him clearly. Maybe not. He hoped not.

Puddles finished quickly and followed him back inside, shaking her coat vigorously. Water flew everywhere, but he didn't care. When you lived with a dog, you had to put up with a few things. No escape.

But he was beginning to feel like a man who had no escape available at all. He couldn't live like this.

That's when he started thinking about guns. If she'd just open a curtain where he could see her, he had no doubt of his marksmanship. Or if she'd just get on the road outside of town by herself, he could knock her into a ditch and cause her little car to roll. If she survived, she'd want to get the hell out of this place.

He liked the car idea. He could latch onto an old banger from the student shop at the high school, steal it and drive it after her. No link to him as long as he was careful to wear gloves. He'd heard that everyone touched the rearview mirror when they drove, to adjust it, and often forgot to wipe away their prints.

Yeah, he kinda liked that idea. But she needed to get out on some road alone. The state highway might be best because if he rolled her into the ditch at a high speed, she was less likely to survive.

He toyed with that idea, letting go of some of his desperation. That or poisoning. A gun fired in town would attract too much attention too quickly. Unless he could use it on the open road. How the hell did he get her out there on a road?

He could start by dragging Roger away from her, he guessed. Cause some kind of problem at the guy's shop he couldn't ignore and would have to fix. He knew Roger worked with flammable materials. A small fire. One that could be ignited without leaving evidence.

Using an electrical line that could spark, maybe. Then there were those containers of propane he kept in the back of the shop. Open one of them, wait long enough, and flicking on a light could set it off.

Yeah. Then Roger would be too busy to drool after Haley. Long enough to maybe get her out of that damn house alone.

He fed Puddles her supper, dried food with a few cooked chicken livers thrown in. She loved it. It made him feel good to watch her dig in with such evident pleasure.

But his mind wouldn't stop rolling around ideas. Apparently he'd been a fool to think he could scare Haley McKinsey away. Well, he'd been a fool in the past. No surprise there. He just couldn't afford to be a fool now.

The meatloaf was as wonderful as Roger had promised. Succulent, flavorful and not at all dry as so many she'd eaten in the past. Perfectly steamed broccoli and fresh salad were flawless accompaniments, although she left most of the mashed potatoes for Roger. He seemed to need the carbs. She wasn't working hard enough today to justify them, especially with a piece of chocolate pie in the offing.

The phone rang just as they finished cleaning up, and she answered it, hearing the voice of her friend with pleasure.

"What's with you, girl?" Della demanded. "We're missing you in more ways than one. Overwhelmed at work, and no coffee klatches to make up for it."

Haley felt herself grinning even though Della

couldn't see it through the phone. "I've been missing you, too."

"You could fool me. So when are you coming home?"

Haley hesitated. "I'm not sure I am."

Della fell silent for a moment. "You met a cowboy. The kind who used to be in those cigarette commercials."

"Gak," Haley answered. "Not him. He was a heavy smoker."

"Quit the evasions. You know exactly what I mean."

Haley *did* know exactly what Della meant. She almost laughed, because in a way it was true. "I ran into an old friend from my childhood. We're catching up."

"Sure. Old friends grow up. So what's happening?" Della let go of that *have-you-met-someone* line of questioning.

"I'm just realizing how attached I am to this house, for one thing. Some of my happiest childhood memories happened here."

Della sighed. "It's hard to let go of those. But, girl, you got a whole life here and a bunch of friends who are wondering if you're abandoning us."

"Abandoning? Isn't that pretty strong?"

"Depends on which side of this relationship you're standing on. Like I said, we miss you and we're talking about how you haven't told us when you'd be back."

It was Haley's turn to sigh audibly. "I'm just not sure, Della. I'm dealing with some stuff here, bad stuff from the past, and you could say I'm feeling pretty shaky. I'm having trouble making decisions."

"Hoo, boy. That's not like you. Maybe the biggest

favor you could do yourself would be to come back here at least for a while."

"Maybe." Della's voice was making Haley feel a bit homesick, but she could also feel herself digging in for some reason. She didn't want to be frightened away, she realized. She wasn't sure she'd ever be able to forgive herself for that.

"Well, on to other news," Della said. "I shouldn't badger you. But you need to know, Casey just got a positive mammogram."

"Oh, my God. For real? Have they run a second one?"

"Yup. She's scheduled for a biopsy early next week. Doc thinks it's early, but who can know for sure. She's scared to death but trying to hide it."

Haley closed her eyes, visualizing Casey, one of the bubbliest and most irrepressible people she'd ever known. "I'll fly back. I don't want her to feel like I don't care."

"I'm sure she'd understand."

Haley wasn't having it. "Would you?"

"Mmm-hmm." Della laughed. "But I'm selfish. Besides, nothing would cheer me up at my bedside after the biopsy more than to hear all about your cowboy."

Haley laughed. "Back to the cowboy, huh? I hope you're enjoying your fantasies. Tell Casey I'll be there Sunday as long as I can get a flight."

"You sure about that? Like everybody, you have your own problems to deal with."

"If I can get a flight, I'll be there. Casey is more important."

They chatted a few minutes longer and then said heartfelt goodbyes. When she turned off her cell phone, she found that Roger had put out the pie on the table.

He looked at her, clearly curious, but appearing to be reluctant to ask. "Old friend?" he asked finally.

"Current friend. Della, from back in Baltimore. She wanted to know when I was returning."

He nodded, keeping his face expressionless. "Sunday, you said."

"Yeah. One of my friends is facing a biopsy for breast cancer. I want to be there for her."

"Of course you do." He nudged the pie her way. "It's what a friend would do."

She grabbed the still-hot coffee and poured them mugs. "I couldn't stay away," she admitted. She sensed what he wanted to know, but once again couldn't answer firmly. The tug homeward Della had unleashed was very real. Leaving those people behind wouldn't be easy. Not even for a quieter life here. Not even with Roger, who had thus far not even remotely suggested he wanted anything more. A hug and a compliment meant little on the large scale.

But as she picked up her fork and poked it into the chocolate pudding and through the graham-cracker crust, she realized he was tugging on her just the way Della's call had. She *did* have reasons to stay, and Roger was certainly one of them.

But how to let him know that without being pushy? Or clingy.

He solved part of the problem for her. "Think you'll be coming back?" His green eyes had grown intense.

She nodded slowly. "Yes."

"Firm?"

"Yes."

He unleashed a long breath and smiled. "I'd hate to see the last of you now. You've become an important part of my life."

Her heart skipped several beats and once again heat poured through her. "Roger..."

He shook his head a little. "As long as you're coming back, there's no need to rush. Frankly, Haley, I want you to be sure about what you choose, and I don't want to apply any pressure. That wouldn't be fair."

Fair? How long had it been since she had thought about fairness? In the ER, she'd never seen anything she would call fair. Some incidents were less life-threatening than others, but none of it was fair. It wasn't fair that a mother had to bring a sick child in for what should have been routine treatment for a strep throat because she couldn't afford to go to a clinic. It wasn't fair to battered and bloodied bodies on the brink of death because of a gunshot or auto accident. No, fairness wasn't part of it.

Had it been fair when she'd been kidnapped from her bed to spend nearly three days in terror with a stranger? That her nightmares were plagued by a man in a ski mask? That men went to war and returned to be hammered by worse nightmares—nightmares she could almost understand from her experience as a nurse. At least she could usually help in the ER.

But that still didn't make anything fair. She ate another mouthful of pie and considered. He didn't want to pressure her to remain, but he seemed to want her to. Maybe she ought to think about what that might mean.

Especially since Della's call had made her aware that she had two lives now, and that Roger was her biggest reason for wanting to stay here. Della and the other girls would carry on without her just fine. They had a wide circle. So what tugged her back other than friendships welded under constant trial at work?

Oh, that was stupid. They were *friends*. Just as she was friends with Roger. That was nothing to be placed on a balance scale and measured. The only question she should think about was the kind of life she wanted now. And she wasn't at all sure she missed the big-city ER. From her one brief contact here about the possibility of joining the ER group that served the hospital, they'd told her, warned her actually, that she wouldn't face the same kind of constant pressure and adrenaline rush she got in the big city.

Even then, that hadn't sounded bad at all. She doubted she was addicted to an adrenaline rush but mostly passionate about helping people who were often in dire straits. She could do that here, too, if not as constantly.

A more relaxed way of life. That actually sounded inviting. Lately she'd been thinking more and more often that she might be getting a little worn out. Burned out. That wouldn't help anyone, most especially patients. Some nurses could handle it for their entire lives, but over the past six or eight months, she'd begun to wonder if she was one of them.

So many battered, bloody, torn-up bodies. The worst were kids. What had a child ever done to deserve being caught by stray gunfire while sleeping in his own bed? She identified with them more than she wanted to think about. Kids!

And their parents. Watching families gather around a gurney for the last few minutes they could grab with a dying family member. Standing there, often in blood because there wasn't time to clean it up. Because it didn't feel right to keep the family away at such a time. Yeah, they kept the kids away when the victim was a family member, but a wife? A mother? A grandmother?

So many of them demanded to see their loved one. With only a few minutes left, it felt brutal to keep them away, even though they would never forget what they saw.

Maybe not standard operating procedure in many places, but it was in the ER where she worked. Sometimes those families got the last few precious words they wanted.

So often they were "I love you."

She put her forehead in her hand and forgot all about pie and coffee. Those memories were stamped indelibly in her mind, although the number of them sometimes blurred together. It didn't matter.

"I love you." She whispered the words then realized she had actually said them. Her head snapped up to find Roger staring at her.

"I don't think that was meant for me," he said after a moment. "You turned so blue all of sudden. Worried about your friend?"

"Actually, I was thinking about what it's like in a busy ER. And how often the last words people say are

I love you. That speaks volumes, Roger. However they got there, no matter what they've done in their lives, they want to tell someone that they love them."

"Wow. That's kind of beautiful in a way."

"Yeah, it is. It sure as hell says something about what's important when we're dying. Maybe a good thing to keep in mind."

"And that was making you feel blue?"

"I guess it showed, huh? While I was thinking about the ER back home, I thought of how unfair life is. None of those people *deserved* to be there. It's amazingly random."

"I'm not sure everyone would agree."

"Probably not. It's different when you're actually dealing with the shattered bodies, though. Does anyone deserve that? I don't think so."

He nodded slowly then said, "I once heard someone say that if we got what we really deserved, we'd hate it."

It worked. He instantly lightened her mood. "Good point. One to keep in mind. But just another way of saying life is unfair."

"Is that what started you off?"

"I guess. I'm not used to thinking in terms of fairness."

"Left you at a young age, huh?"

"Guess so." She shrugged a shoulder and resumed eating her pie. "Maude either deserves a medal for this or she needs to be locked away. I haven't eaten this much pie in years, and this one is wonderful."

"So enjoy and don't feel guilty. Afterward, wanna go sit in the living room? Better than this table."

She nodded. "We do seem to spend a lot of time right here."

"Close to the coffeepot for addicts like me. Anyway, it should do you some good to get back home with your friends, and maybe in the meantime we can take care of the peeper."

"Oh, I'd love that." She was, however, determined not to let that fear override taking pleasure in Roger's company. Most of her time with him had been spent dealing with old fears and new fears. Surely he must be getting tired of it, though he indicated that in no way.

Yet each day reminded her of why she had enjoyed his company so much all those years ago when she came to visit her grandmother. A boy his age shouldn't have enjoyed the company of a girl so much younger. But he'd certainly seemed to, seeking her out with ideas about how to spend lazy summer afternoons.

As they entered the living room, she said, "Remember that time we rode our bikes out past the edge of town, near the train tracks?"

"And waited forever for a train that never came. Sort of like showing you my favorite fishing hole."

She laughed. "Yeah. And the next day we heard the train come through."

"Missed it by about twenty-six hours. Close, very close."

He chose the love seat that didn't match the ancient sofa, then patted the seat beside him invitingly.

So close, but with miles yet between them. Nevertheless, she sat, getting a whiff of man-scent and something more. Leather? He sure did smell good, whatever it was.

His nearness on the couch had a strong effect on her. Her heart began beating faster, and an aching hope arose in her. Hope that he would put his arm around her, hug her. Just a hug. Man, she needed that contact, especially with him. It was a long way to come from childhood.

But she was a woman now, with basic needs, and he was a man. Things had changed, shifted. She just hoped he felt it, too, and didn't have her categorized as a child after all these years.

He spoke. "Tomorrow night is my usual night to go to Mahoney's to play darts and have a few beers with my friends. Wanna go with me?"

Darts and beer. She liked the sound of that. She knew nothing about darts but she could cheer from the sidelines. Besides, it would put Roger in a different context, among his friends, rather than just with her. She wanted to see that. "Sure."

"Good." Then he astonished and gratified her by wrapping a strong arm around her shoulders and drawing her close to his side. The storm still raged outside, and she couldn't tell if the rain had lightened any, but the wind and thunder still made the house shake a little.

"It's fierce out there."

"Yeah," he answered. "If this keeps up, our dry streambeds won't be dry at all anymore, and they might rise over their banks."

"Will that be a problem?" God, he felt so warm and his arm around her felt like shelter. But it was awakening stronger feelings in her, feelings that made her want to turn to him and demand a kiss, a touch, and eventual consummation. When was the last time that desire had pounded in her blood like this? His nearness was making it impossible to remember.

Her universe had narrowed to Roger, his touch, his heat. Everything else slipped away as she slid into a different world, one where nothing could touch her.

"Not usually. Most of the ranches aren't that close to the creeks for that very reason. It's not easy to drain water when the ground is fairly flat, and it's not good for livestock to stand in water for long. Troughs are the usual answer. Or ponds sometimes. But most keep their houses and barns away from danger and running water."

"Interesting." It was. She hadn't thought about any of this. "Is there higher ground the cows and sheep can get to?"

"In a lot of places, yes."

"Good." But the word emerged almost breathlessly because he was turning to her and his arm was drawing her closer. Oh, man, hope bloomed in her like an opening rosebud.

Chapter 8

Roger wasn't sure this was wise, but he couldn't resist any longer. He wanted her, and he saw flashes in her eyes that seemed to answer his desire with her own.

He might be all wet. But he promised himself that the instant he felt any reluctance from Haley, he'd pull back. This woman was skittish, with every right to be. He'd seen her childhood nightmare spring to life because of that creep at her window, and whether the guy was like her abductor or not, he'd invaded her life in one of the worst ways possible.

Now she had two things that filled her with fear, and he couldn't blame her. Although he'd said nothing about it, it had horrified him to read how often a Peeping Tom moved on to violent action of some kind. Keeping her windows covered and locked would be no protection against someone who truly wanted to mess with her.

Her fear didn't seem trivial to him. He didn't think she was overreacting in the least, but now he had to hope that he didn't add to her discomfort. He'd been talking himself out of this for days now, and it seemed foolhardy to make a move right before she returned to Baltimore. What if she didn't come back because he'd made her so uncomfortable?

But to be brutally honest with himself, he admitted that he needed to know. He couldn't stand being on tenterhooks much longer. If she didn't return...well, he had his answer.

In the meantime, he was determined to do everything in his power to track down this voyeur who had troubled her. She deserved to know she was safe in her own grandmother's house even if she only came to visit a few times a year.

So he tugged her gently and was pleased at how easily she let him draw her close. Not an ounce of resistance. She seemed to melt into him, and not passively. No, she raised an arm and slipped it around his waist, pulling them together even more closely.

She murmured his name, barely a breath, but it felt as if it exploded inside his head. No rejection. None. He hadn't read her wrong, although it seemed amazing to him that after the emotional wringer she'd been going through that she could be willing.

Or maybe she was willing because she needed the escape. Or needed to reaffirm life in a glorious way. Whatever, he supposed time would answer those questions. The questions were sliding away on the drumbeat of his blood anyway.

Nothing mattered except Haley and how positively wonderful her curves felt against him. When he lifted a hand and tipped her face upward, her mouth was ready for him. Warm and soft, she welcomed him inside, tasting delightfully of chocolate and a hint of coffee. Practically a dessert.

A small, husky laugh escaped him as he pulled back an inch.

"What?" she asked drowsily.

"You taste like dessert."

Her smile had turned sleepy. "I like that," she whispered. "So do you."

Then the capacity for words almost totally escaped him. He dived into her mouth again, this time more strongly, encouraging her with his tongue along her lips, then inside her mouth, tracing the soft sides of her cheeks, tangling with her tongue and falling into a rhythm that mimicked sex.

When thunder boomed hollowly again, he barely heard it. If the windows rattled, it must have been the earthquake she created inside him.

Such moments should be savored. Every detail should be etched in the mind as if in crystal. Instead, everything blurred into a world of panting, tearing at clothes, at feeling the marvel of skin on skin.

He tried to slow down, to taste her breasts until that touch alone made her cry out. Instead, with her hands on his hips, on a couch that was too short, causing him to bend his legs up and her to fold her knees to welcome him, he found his way into her and his groans joined her moans.

Quick, hot as lava, sweeping them away on a tide of racing fire. When he exploded into her, and heard her answering cry, the world seemed to go black.

But neither of them had a thought left for the man who was plotting Haley's death only a short distance away.

"Holy cow," Roger muttered into her neck. They were sticky, sweat drenched, and now he felt both exhilarated and embarrassed. He had more finesse in him than that, but it had sure escaped him. He hoped Haley didn't hate him.

But her hands told a different story, running up and down his back, her body still quivering. "Roger," she whispered. "Oh, Roger…"

He needed to roll off her, he thought dimly. His weight must be crushing her. But there was only one way to roll, and that was onto the floor. A truly romantic ending to the best sex of his life.

"Damn," he mumbled.

"What?" she asked weakly.

"I'm too heavy. I need to move. Anyway, this love seat is barely big enough…"

"I don't want you to move. You're a perfect fit."

Those words sent another wave crashing through him. *A perfect fit.* Well, she had her knees pulled up. His feet, still in socks, were dangling off the arm of the love seat. Ha! He could just imagine the picture of them tangled like this.

"How did we get our clothes off?" she asked after a bit.

"Damned if I can remember."

A smoky laugh escaped her. "Me, either. It was like riding a whirlwind."

At the very least. Maybe a rocket to the outer reaches of the galaxy. Falling into the heart of an exploding star. And what poet had just lodged in his ordinarily prosaic head?

"This ain't gonna be pretty," he said finally. "But you need to breathe sooner or later."

Then, before she could argue, he rolled off her and hit the floor. Next thing he knew she was looking down at him from the couch. Her gaze wandered over him.

"*Pretty* might not be the right word," she said, "but *gorgeous*? Absolutely."

"You're the gorgeous one." Reaching up, he tugged her down until she fell on top of him. Ah, now it was right. They didn't just fit together but they fit together just so. The way they should. His manhood reacted to having her between his legs and he was sure she must feel it. Her face settled into the hollow of his shoulder but he could still hear her when she said, "Rerun?"

"You bet. Not on this darn rug, though. A cat might be happy sprawled on it, but I'm not."

"I've got a bed," she offered. "Several of them."

A low laugh rumbled in his belly, shaking them both. He ran his hands over her back. "You're starting to feel chilly. The storm has dropped the temperature, I guess. Want me to turn on the heat?"

It was her turn to laugh quietly, even as she snuggled

closer into his shoulder. "You just want to try out that new ducting you worked so hard on."

He grinned into the very dim light. "Maybe. But actually, darlin', I'm worried about keeping you warm. Heat?"

"I seem to recall a very nice comforter in my room. Most nights, it's been too warm. But tonight, to snuggle up with you in there? Sounds fabulous."

It did to him, too. He helped her up off the floor, then, almost like little kids, they hurried down the short hallway and into the bedroom. Haley pointed to the comforter folded on the chest at the end of the bed and, with a flap, he spread it out. Moments later, he dived in with her, and they cuddled, laughing.

This was the Haley he remembered from childhood. Despite her kidnapping, when they'd gotten together over those summers, she had been irrepressible. Whatever trauma she'd endured, she'd put it behind her, at least when she was with him.

He hoped she would be able to do that again, soon. He hated catching glimpses of the fear she was fighting and often trying to hide, the way her eyes appeared pinched so often.

Somehow, he and the cops had to catch the creep who had restored terror to her soul. He vowed to himself that, while she was in Baltimore, he was going to make time to keep an eye out. He knew the cops were trying, but there were only so many of them, and a guy ducking around in the dark could be hard to spot.

It did seem strange that there had been no other reports, though.

He banished the thought for now. He was curled up with Haley, temperatures were rising beneath the covers, feeling like a warm refuge against the world.

He also owed her something after that amazingly fast coupling in the living room. A slower, more delicious experience. Time to explore her until delight filled her every cell. Time for her to explore him, too, because he was certain the touch of her hands would drive him nuts with pleasure.

He began tracing her, first with his fingertips then with his palms. Her skin felt so silky and smooth, igniting a slow fire in him. But this time he wanted to luxuriate, to enjoy a lengthy chance to bring them to a fever pitch. With each pass of his hand, he felt a little responsive quiver run through her.

She was so perfectly shaped, he thought. Narrow waist, flaring hips, a nicely rounded rump. And her breasts…perfectly fit to his hand as if designed for his touch. Her nipples pebbled instantly and he brushed his palms repeatedly over them, listening to little moans emerge from her throat. Exquisite.

But she was unwilling to lie back and let him do all the exploring. Her hand began to wander over him, testing his back, his chest and belly, teasingly approaching his growing erection then pulling back.

When she found the small nipples on his chest, she made a sound of delight and began to tease him, first with her palms then with her fingers. An electric shock ran through him at her touches. He'd never felt that before. His lovers, a small sample to be sure, had been inclined to be passive. Maybe as a result of upbringing. But not Haley. She acted like a fully equal partner and it felt wonderful. When her teeth found one of his nipples, he reached his breaking point.

There'd be time later. Now he was so hot he felt he might explode. Lifting her beneath the covers, he settled her on top of him. As he filled her, she reared back, exposing her breasts to his conquest.

It was dark in this room, darker under the coverlet. Hands found all that eyes could not see. With him holding her breasts, massaging them in ways that caused her to sharply draw in breaths, he felt her begin to rock on him, never letting their hips separate, but pulling him with her on her journey.

Slowly this time, they climbed the mountain of satisfaction until they reached the very pinnacle. There, he teetered with her, hanging on to the last strand of his willpower, waiting to feel her moment of completion.

When she reached it, a cry escaped her—all the signal he needed. With a strong thrust, he buried himself as deeply as he could. Shudders racked him as her core tightened around him, claiming him as he was claiming her.

Then the night burst into a shower of fireworks.

Please, don't ever let this end.

It almost didn't. Waves rolled through him like breakers on the shore, again and again.

Then he relaxed into bliss.

They dozed together like spoons. Haley woke occasionally and savored the weight of Roger's arm around her middle, the warmth of his breath against her neck. She couldn't remember having felt this secure, if she

ever had. Wrapped in his strength, remembering the
lovemaking they'd shared...well, he was making her
feel precious. And that was something she couldn't remember feeling since early childhood, before the kidnapping, before her mother had ripped her from her
father because she hated the oil fields.

Her mother had probably also hated a lot of the men
working in them. Even after all this time, young as
she had been, Haley could recall the wolf whistles and
comments her mother had endured whenever she went
out. Grocery shopping had seemed like a chore to her,
and while the young Haley didn't understand what was
happening, she had felt her mother's tension. It started
growing from the moment she said they needed to go
to the store, strengthening the whole time they were out
and relaxing only when they got home again.

She remembered the doors were always locked, the
curtains often drawn to prevent passersby from looking in.

God, Haley thought suddenly, *I'm becoming my
mother. Buttoned up and fearing the outside world.*

"Haley?" Roger's drowsy voice reached her. "Are
you okay? I felt you stiffen."

"Just an unhappy memory and a look at myself."

He squeezed her, silent for a few seconds, then said,
"I don't recall when we ate. I think it was early. Anyway, I'm getting hungry. You?"

She allowed herself to feel something past her internal moment of shock. "A little."

"Then let me go heat up leftovers or something.
Maude always serves enough to feed an army. And while

I'm at it, I'll rescue clothes from the living room. You don't have to get dressed. In fact, please don't dress."

That pulled a small laugh from her. "Okay, but I'm not coming out there naked. I think I left the curtains open in the kitchen."

"Consider them closed." He let go of her with a reluctance that warmed her. "Clothes coming up, maybe a little light, and definitely some food."

He rolled out of bed and she drew the comforter to her chin, focusing on his scent that still filled the room, along with the aromas of their lovemaking. Then she caught a whiff of Flora, too, from the pillow on which her head was resting.

"Oh, Grandma," she whispered. "I miss you so much."

She heard Roger padding around in the living room and a glow from a lamp came through the bedroom door, to be followed by his large shape. He was wearing jeans now, she noted. She still hadn't really seen him nude. Next item on the agenda, she promised herself.

"Close your eyes," he suggested. "I want to turn on a lamp for you."

Through her closed eyelids she could see the glow from the bedside lamp as he turned it on.

"Come to the kitchen if you want," he said. "Or I can bring you a plate of something in here."

She sat up, holding the comforter to her breasts, ridiculous though that was at this point. She was greeted by the sight of a magnificent, powerful male chest. Her heart leaped. "You look good enough to eat, Roger."

He grinned. "We can look into that later, after real food. So, kitchen or in here?"

"Flora would hate me eating in bed. I'll come to the kitchen."

"See you in a few."

He turned, leaving her alone. Hating having him gone, she hurried out of bed, did a quick wash in the bathroom, and pulled on her terry-cloth robe. She even paused to slip her feet into the matching slippers. No fancy lingerie for her.

As promised, Roger had closed the kitchen curtains. For the first time, she noticed the wind was still blowing. "Some storm," she remarked.

He pulled his head out of the refrigerator long enough to look at her. "Still raining, too, but not heavily. So, meatloaf or meatloaf? Some mashed potatoes left. Have you ever noticed how mashed potatoes seem to be a necessary side dish for meatloaf?"

"I never thought about it, honestly."

"I am, right now. There's also part of one of the salads left. Shall we do a second dinner or should I hunt for something else?"

"Second dinner would be great." She slid into a chair at the dinette and watched him as he moved around pulling out items and readying them for warmup in the microwave. Delightfully, he whistled as he did it.

A man in worn jeans and nothing else making her a late-night supper. She could get used to this. He made her want to forget everything else in the universe and just drink him in.

His back rippled with muscles as he buzzed around. Not gym-built muscles, but work-made. Smooth, not bulging. She just wanted to run her hands over them but made herself stay put and not get in the way. Besides, it was nice to admire his narrow hips in those jeans, especially when he bent over.

Haley spoke. "Has anyone ever told you that you're scrumptious?"

He turned his head and smiled, those green eyes of his twinkling. "You know, I think someone just this very evening told me I was good enough to eat."

She had to laugh at that. God, she felt so wonderfully relaxed. Since the Peeping Tom, she'd forgotten how that felt.

And right now she didn't care about the creep who'd peered in her window. A sicko, probably incapable of doing anything except peering in a woman's window and getting off on it.

"You're scrumptious, too," he said as he began placing food-filled plates on the table.

Hardly a snack, she thought, but instead, a perfectly served full meal. "You trying to win brownie points by setting the table like this?"

He winked at her. "Every single one counts. No, we've had a very special evening, and if I knew if Flora kept any candles, I'd serve this by candlelight." He slid into the chair across from her. "I should put a shirt on. This is rude."

"Some might think so. Don't take away my view. As for candles, I never saw Flora use any and I haven't run across them anywhere."

"Yeah, she's got some candlesticks on the sideboard in the dining room, but I never saw any candles in them. Maybe she didn't care for them."

"Or was worried about a fire hazard."

The meatloaf was still succulent and the potatoes had survived being warmed up. She was just sorry they'd devoured all the broccoli earlier. The salad hadn't grown soggy, however, and she noted the way he pushed the small bowl toward her. "Eat up, health nut."

She flashed him a smile and didn't argue.

"So," he said while they ate, "you want to leave Sunday?"

"My thinking is to get there the night before her biopsy. I want to spend some time with Casey. This isn't an easy thing to wait for."

"I wouldn't think so. In fact, I can't imagine knowing some ugly, deadly thing might be growing in your body and having to wait to find out."

"I did once," she remarked. "Turned out to be nothing—they didn't even want to do a biopsy after the second scan. But waiting for the second check? Waiting for the radiologist's report? Being a nurse, I know all about false positives on mammograms. But not knowing for *certain* is tough."

He nodded. "*That* I can imagine." He paused for another bite of meatloaf and then asked, "You thinking about flying out of Casper or Laramie?"

"I'll check in the morning to see what's available. If it's Denver, it's Denver."

"I'll drive you, you know."

She felt anew that wave of warmth he caused in her. "You're a great guy, Roger. But you've been shorting your work because of me—and don't deny it. I'll drive myself. I won't feel like a fraidy cat on the road."

"You're not a fraidy cat," he said firmly. "Far from it. You've got good cause to be concerned. Now, eat up, because I want to take you back to bed."

Edgar was going nuts with the waiting. If this kept up, he wasn't going to be able to stay beneath the radar. Classes at the junior college would start up in two weeks, making it all but impossible for him to avoid the daytime streets.

Damn, Edith had seen him and, at the last second, he'd managed to skitter away as he'd seen Haley begin to turn her head. Close one. He needed to get rid of her, and soon.

Conviction was strongly growing in him that she would somehow identify him if given enough time. The fact that a five-year-old hadn't been able to give anyone a useful description of him didn't mean she'd ever forgotten him, how he moved or the time she'd seen his face briefly. Trauma had probably stamped that indelibly in her brain even if she'd been unable to describe him usefully.

There was always the chance that she wouldn't remember him at all, but he wasn't willing to bet his future on it. Frustrated, agitated, he decided he needed to do something that felt as if he was moving in the right direction.

Edgar liked the idea of driving her off the road, so he needed to keep a sharp eye out for the first time she headed out of town in her own car, alone. But if she wasn't alone, he could still take her out, and take that damn Roger McLeod with her.

Barring that, he needed to figure out another way

soon. How could he have guessed that McLeod and the cops would have clamped down so hard when he'd looked in her window and she'd seen him? But he'd had to be sure it was her.

Well, he was sure of that. Now he needed one additional plan, a plan for anytime she was alone. She'd have to be alone at some point. McLeod had a business to attend to. He couldn't keep letting his work slide.

The idea of breaking into Haley's house had been growing stronger, but McLeod was there again tonight. Were they cementing a relationship? If so, that was merely pushing him into a corner that would force him to act somehow.

He'd read online that castor beans could make a good poison. So if he could get into her house while no one was there, he could probably find a way to get it into a beverage. He figured he could get castor beans more easily than azalea leaves. Up here, anyway.

In the meantime…well, in the meantime, he needed to get a grip before anxiety and impatience made him do something as stupid as kidnapping her in the first place. He needed to feel that he was actually moving toward ridding himself of the threat.

Hell. No longer able to stay hidden in his own house, desperately needing action, he decided that, as soon as the rain let up, he was going to take Puddles out by the high school to look over the cars awaiting this fall's shop class.

He needed one that would be heavy and big enough to drive Haley's little compact off the road. He could even add sandbags for weight if he managed to get to it before he needed it. And he certainly needed to be sure it was an old enough vehicle to hot-wire because he was positive that if any of those vehicles could still run, there wouldn't be any keys in them.

The rain lessened to a drizzle shortly after eleven. He wouldn't draw suspicion by being out at this hour, unlike well after midnight. He gathered Puddles up in his arms, clipped the leash to her collar, and she expressed her excitement and gratitude by licking his chin.

Puddles made him feel wanted. Maybe the only being who did. He'd had friends among other oil rig workers over the years, but that wasn't the same kind of companionship. Dating hadn't worked well for him, either. Something always went wrong before too long. He often considered himself lucky, however, not to have a wife to please or listen to.

Puddles was the perfect companion. When he felt like sitting in front of the TV and watching sports with a few beers, she never told him to get off his behind. She never gave him "honey-do" lists or expected him to spend his free time doing what she wanted. Other than walks, and feeding, she was content to lie across his lap or at his feet. No, she wasn't demanding the way a woman would be.

So while he occasionally felt there was something missing from his life, he didn't miss it enough to want to put up with all the hassles of answering to another person. He'd always gotten his fill of that from bosses and coworkers.

Edgar was careful to select a residential street so that his pickup wouldn't stand out by being parked on school property. He pulled out the slim jim he carried under the seat of his truck and tucked it up inside his jacket. Then, when he was assured that no one else appeared to be around, he and Puddles went for the walk she awaited so eagerly.

Another thing about Puddles: if someone questioned him for being out at this hour, she was his answer. In fact, because of her, no one would question him at all.

The school was surrounded by a fence that hadn't been there a few years ago, since a crazy bomber had blown up the outside wall of the woodworking shop. These days there was even a gate across the entry of the traffic circle and parking lot, but it wasn't locked. It was more of a *Do Not Trespass* warning. Early in the morning, it was always unlocked to allow the school buses in and the student and teacher cars.

Getting by it was no problem at all. He was even careful to close it behind him. And still, walking around the school parking lot and athletic fields with a dog wouldn't attract any attention.

It seemed that walking a small dog made him appear inoffensive. No trouble at all, that man walking that little Yorkie. Ha. If they knew…

But they didn't know. He'd been so careful since taking the job at the junior college to follow the straight and narrow. Not a thing to nail him with, not even a joint or too many beers. The upstanding citizen.

Thinking about it, he almost laughed and nearly forgot himself enough to whistle. He'd built a life that would never draw a suspicion or question. Though he hadn't realized it before, he now was grateful because he wouldn't be anyone's first suspect in anything.

Two years of good behavior, even in this gossipy town, protected him.

Puddles had started to run in circles. Apparently she was in the mood to go full throttle, so he quickened his pace. He knew where the cars for the auto shop were stashed. If he didn't find a useful one there, he could always go to the college since they ran a course, as well, leading toward full certification.

He'd rather not go there. Too close to him and his job. Out here, he believed he was removed enough from the place to not even draw attention if a car turned up missing.

Everyone would believe some teen had stolen it for a joy ride, if he took it, and when it got involved in an accident, they'd believe the same thing. No reason to look at a college teacher who had a perfectly good vehicle of his own.

Yeah, maybe he wasn't so dumb at all.

Or maybe he was just wasting his time. Thus far he had no indication whatever that Haley was going to get on a road heading out of town. She seemed to have planted herself, a situation that was becoming as constantly annoying to him as a mosquito bite or a bee sting.

He reached the back lot where the shop cars were parked, and immediately spied the one he'd like to use. An old Suburban, probably a relic from the sheriff's office to judge by the brown splotches of paint on its sides and hood. He only needed to know if it was still able to run. He didn't need much out of the vehicle, just a few miles.

He pulled on a glove as he approached it, thinking he couldn't have asked for a better choice. The damn thing was heavy, built more like a truck than a car. When he reached it and pulled on the door handle, he had his answer. It was locked, which meant they didn't want anyone to steal it. So, it ran.

Well, that had been easy, he thought. Pulling the slim jim from under his jacket, he jimmied the driver's-side window. Yup. He could get in. So, bring a couple of gallons of gas, hot-wire it, and he'd be ready to go. He just needed a heads-up. Then he could steal this damn thing in the dead of night, park it somewhere out of sight. He doubted anyone would notice it was missing for a few days. The school had no full-time security of its own, but depended on sheriff's patrols to keep an eye out.

Nope, they wouldn't notice the Suburban was gone, not immediately.

Satisfied, he locked and closed the door. Then he took Puddles back the way they had come. She seemed to want to explore more, but he couldn't let her. He didn't want to be spotted out here by some patrol that might remember him when things started to happen.

Puddles had different ideas, of course. He imagined this place was full of new and interesting aromas. When he tugged on her leash, however, she came along obediently.

Back in his truck, he started the engine and turned toward home. Yeah, he needed to get those castor beans. From what he understood of them, if he managed to get a powder or liquid into her house, it could be quickly fatal.

But he didn't much care about fatal. What he wanted was her to be gone from this place, and he'd do whatever it took to cause Haley to leave.

He glanced over at Puddles and knew that nothing would make him give her up. This had become about more than just preserving his new life and living without fear. It had also become about the dog he loved so much. The threat must be removed, one way or another.

Thinking about it, he knew just where to get those beans. A neighbor on the next street over had the plants because she liked to fill display jars with them. She thought they were pretty. So he'd take a handful from the plants in her garden.

The next steps weren't out of his reach, but the scary part was that he could poison himself.

Hell, there was no guaranteed way, but scaring the life out of Haley would be good enough for him. Car or poison. He guessed he'd need to take a look into her mud porch when she wasn't around and hope he found useful bottles in there. In a liquid, he could put enough poison to kill her, and he wasn't about to screw around with making it into a powder if he could avoid it.

That could be dangerous to both him and Puddles. Nope, he wouldn't do that. But the liquid? Oh, yeah.

In the morning, after a delightful breakfast with Roger, who ran out to get doughnuts from the bakery, Haley got on her phone to see what she could do about flights to Baltimore at this late date.

All she cared about was getting in no later than Sunday evening so she could spend time with Casey. Otherwise, she had no reason not to be flexible.

She kept getting distracted, however, by thoughts of the night just past. Roger had taken her so far and fast that she still felt ripples running through her entire body. Her search of various travel sites kept falling victim to delightful memories of last night.

She hated to think she had to go away, even for a few days. That was dangerous thinking, however. Roger hadn't promised a single thing, or even hinted at a longer relationship. She needed to make any decisions about whether to return here or to Baltimore free of thoughts of Roger.

Not that that was likely to happen, she mused ruefully as once again her thoughts drifted and the travel app on her phone logged her out. When she caught it, she sighed. *Damn, girl, just pay attention. It's not that hard to make a plane reservation.*

Eventually she concentrated enough to finish. No convenient flights available from Casper, except into Denver. From Denver, she could fly directly to BWI. The question was whether she wanted the longer drive or the extra flight. The other question was whether she would get a return ticket. Overall, that would be cheaper, but what if she didn't want to come back? At least not right away, because she was certainly going to have to finish up with this house.

Shoot, she thought. The way airlines operated these days, you could either accept that you were going to be locked in with nonrefundable tickets it would cost a lot to change, or you could offer them your firstborn child to leave your return open-ended.

Well, she finally decided, she was going to have to come back here one way or the other, whether she came only to put the house on the market or to stay indefinitely. Loose ends on both ends of this trip would have to be taken care of.

And what if Casey received a positive biopsy for cancer? Haley would certainly want to hang around in Baltimore a lot longer.

After another twenty minutes, she realized she'd drifted into pleasant dreams of last night, and shook herself sharply. Time was wasting if she wanted to get to Baltimore *before* Casey's biopsy.

Finally, she bit the bullet, sacrificed more than she wanted to from her savings account and left her return open-ended. Done. She clicked the button to seal the deal, and before long her ticket and boarding pass showed up on her phone.

Modern convenience. However, she'd always preferred paper. Receipts seemed more real then.

She *did* take a few moments to write down her receipt number and flight information, and tuck it into her purse. Backup.

Maybe that came from her job, double-checking everything, making sure records were complete, verifying orders against labels. She certainly got persnickety about a few things. Almost OCD when it came to reading the contents of vials, solutions and bags.

Well, she'd get into Baltimore at a reasonable hour as long as she was willing to drive to Denver from here. A flight from Casper to Denver had been harder to find and arrival times for getting to Baltimore had been less than optimal. So drive she would.

She kinda liked the idea, too. It would feel good to be on the open road for a while, especially after feeling so cooped up because of that creep. She'd like to leave him behind for good.

But leaving Roger behind for good? Not so easy anymore. And definitely not easy if he wanted her to hang around.

Ah, heck. She felt as if she were being torn in two by competing desires. Life here was pleasant and would grow more pleasant with time. Especially if Roger wanted her. But she still felt strong ties with her home in Baltimore and her friends. Two parts of her were pulling in different directions.

Satisfied with her reservation two days hence, she felt a lot better. Rising, she opened the kitchen window curtains and blinked. It was as if last night's rain had washed the air clean, leaving the light brilliant enough to hurt her eyes.

Oh, she had to go outside. Tossing her fears aside as ridiculous—man, nobody would bother her in broad daylight—she picked a book from her grandmother's shelf and carried it out onto the porch with her.

Seated on the swing, she could see what an amazing blue the sky had become. Only now did she understand how much dust the air must have been collecting. It was gone now, the air clearer than glass.

Forgetting the book, she pushed herself slowly with one foot and simply drank in a gorgeous day. She could get used to this, too, she decided. Very used to it. A quiet morning, leaves on the tree-lined street rustling a little in the soft breeze, just warm enough not to need a jacket… Oh, yeah.

The day generated peace within her. Life had turned

from a horror show of fear and memory into beauty. Last night. Now this. She felt as if she were being showered with blessings. An awakening of sorts.

Maybe she had dozed off. She didn't know, but she was sure the light had changed a bit, as if the sun had moved. Then she heard a familiar click-click and looked around to see Edith walking Bailey.

"You're going to wear your shoes out," she called to Edith.

"That's all right. The doc says this dog will keep me alive to ninety, all this walking." She came to the foot of the steps, smiling. Bailey sat, tongue lolling as he grinned his pleasure in the day.

"I saw Roger earlier," Edith said. "He was hanging some large sheets of leather over his front porch railing. To dry out, he said. I dunno, that much leather might be worth somebody stealing."

"Around here?" Haley asked, patting the swing beside her in invitation. Edie immediately climbed the steps and sat beside her.

"Well, not likely. But some care needs to be taken." Then Edie laughed. "As if he hasn't been using his front porch railing for years as a drying rack. I'm getting a little old and crazy, I guess." She eyed Haley. "Are you liking it here? Are you going to stay with us? The church group is still hesitant to descend on you because they don't want to scare you away, and because they're not sure you'll stay anyway. Figure that one out if you can."

It was Haley's turn to laugh. "I won't try. At this point, I'm a little up in the air, Edith. Saturday night I'm driving to Denver to catch an early-morning flight back to Baltimore. One of my girlfriends is about to have a biopsy and I want to be there for her."

"But will you come back?"

Haley turned her head and looked at Edith. "You know, I want to. So unless something goes horribly wrong, I'll probably be back very soon."

"Good." Edith nodded. "I'll tell the gals to hold on to the casserole deluge until you come back. And I hope your friend is okay."

"Me, too. So Bailey's keeping you active?"

"You sound like a nurse," Edie remarked. "Hardly surprising since you are. But, yes, he's a big dog. I can't walk fast enough to please him, I'm sure. But with two walks a day, we must do at least four miles."

"That's impressive! I need to do that, too."

"I suspect you're getting quite enough exercise taking care of this house. I promised to come help you and I haven't. When you get back?"

"Absolutely." She wished she was as certain of her return as Edie seemed to be. She'd learned at a very early age that life could throw curveballs, however. If Casey turned out to be seriously ill…well, she wasn't at all certain that she'd feel comfortable returning here. Not while her friend would need all the help she could get.

"You're worried." Edie reached over and patted her hand. "Friends like you are a blessing. Your grandmother was like that to me. Flora and I went all the way back to childhood, and only my husband got in the way."

A surprised laugh escaped Haley. "Your husband?"

"Well, you know men. He had all these ideas about

dinner on the table when he came home from work, that the house needed to be clean, the kids looked after..."

Haley had to laugh again. "You're more of a free spirit?"

"Always was. Flora and I were a lot alike in that way. I don't think she was terribly sad when your grandfather died. Oh, she grieved, don't misunderstand me. He'd been a big part of her life for twenty-three years. The operative words, as they say, were *big part*. Flora didn't fit inside lines too well. Did you ever notice?"

"I never really thought about it. Maybe she showed me her more conventional side."

"It's possible. She could be conventional with the best when she needed to be. But there was a free spirit that always wanted to break out. If there's one thing I would warn you about in this town, it's that free spirits don't fit any better here, and there are few places to hide. It's gotten better with time, though. Much better. Unfortunately, Flora didn't benefit all that much when she was younger and tied to an apron, the kitchen and a kid."

"You felt sorry for her," Haley said, surprised. "But what about your own situation and kids?"

"God spared me kids and I divorced the dictator years ago. And Flora wasn't miserable. Don't misunderstand me. There was just a part of her that was caged like a bird. But she loved her son, loved her husband and made her own choices. Sometimes, like everyone, she might have wished she'd made different decisions. Don't we all?"

Haley thought about that as Edith rose at Bailey's insistence and resumed her walk with a wave.

Might have wished she'd made different decisions.

Boy, that was loaded. It was also plenty of food for thought.

How many decisions was Haley making by default? How many had she made because of a childhood trauma or because her mother had taken her away from her father at an early age?

And now that she had a forked path in front of her, she hesitated. Why? Why did she feel pulled in two directions? Yeah, she had friends back in Baltimore, but she seemed to be growing a few here.

Well, she'd go home to be with Casey and decide how much her perspective might have changed.

It was possible that home might not feel like home any longer.

It didn't take long for the gossip to reach Edgar. Oh, no. The church was having a bake sale, and he especially liked the cinnamon buns one of the women made. Every time they had a sale, he showed up to buy a dozen. They froze up well…if they lasted that long. He also felt comfortable there. The women, and a few men, recognized him and always made him feel welcome without pressing him in any way. He figured, too, that in this crowd he could melt away if he saw Haley.

It was while he was there that evening, staying out of the brightest lights as he walked along the display tables making his choices, that a conversation between several of the women caught his attention.

"Edith said to save up the casseroles and welcoming committee until Flora's granddaughter gets back."

Edgar's ears perked. *Gets back?* He sidled a little nearer, pretending interest in a rhubarb pie.

"Where's she going?" one of the other women asked.

"Back home, Edith says. She has a sick friend. Guess she's going to be driving out tomorrow night."

"That'll make Roger McLeod sad," another woman said wryly. "Since the girl got here, Roger's been practically tacked to her side."

The group laughed, a friendly sound, and Edgar moved on. Tomorrow night. His heart began to race and he hoped his hands didn't shake so badly that he dropped the foil pan of cinnamon buns.

His chance was right around the corner. Tomorrow night. Pleasure spread a smile across his face.

And on the off chance that she changed her plans and didn't leave tomorrow night, the liquid poison he'd made from those castor beans was ready. His backup plan, but still in place.

Yup, he wouldn't have to live in fear of discovery for very long. And tonight he'd snatch the Suburban. He knew an isolated gate along the state highway to stash it until tomorrow night, because no one would miss it before then.

All his ducks were in a row. Yes!

Chapter 9

Saturday morning dawned with the same brilliant light as yesterday. Haley and Roger enjoyed a simple breakfast after a delightful night together. She could grow used to that, Haley thought. Nights in his arms, mornings spent laughing and chatting over breakfast. He seemed to wrap her in warmth and a sense of security.

"Are you sure you don't want me to drive you to Denver?"

She shook her head but smiled. "I need to do this, Roger. Maybe it will help me get past my fears and make it possible to come back and be normal. I'd love to feel normal again. Or at least as close as I can get."

"I understand. If that's what you want, who am I to argue? But I'm going to miss you, darlin'. A whole lot. I

hope Baltimore and your friends don't snatch you back
there, but I won't ask you for a promise."

She wouldn't have been able to give it. Not yet. Not
until she'd gone back to her own life, however briefly,
to be sure she was ready to give it up. "Thank you. I'll
call and let you know when my return flight will be. It
might take a few days to be sure about Casey."

He nodded. "Keep in touch anyway."

Her smile widened. "And you get some work done.
I'd hate to think I had a hand in making your customers angry at you."

"They get mad at me and they miss out on the best
saddles in the West."

She had to laugh. "I'm sure they will."

He gave her a long, lingering kiss before he left,
making her promise to call when she got to Denver so
he'd know she arrived safely. "And when you get back,
you're going to come to my house and my shop and get
to know me better."

"Definitely." She was touched that he was speaking as if her return was a foregone conclusion. He *did*
want her back.

She dawdled a bit, enjoying recollections of their
night together, then shook herself into action. Since she
was flying, there was a limited amount she could take
with her, and since she had no idea how long she'd want
to stay, depending on Casey's situation, the choices became even more difficult.

Basic street clothes, she decided, plus some grungies
to hang around in the apartment she shared with Della.
The two of them and a bottle of wine or a couple of beers

could be a lot of fun when they had an evening on their own. So, something comfortable.

And pajamas. She almost forgot them because she certainly hadn't worn them the last two nights. A giggle escaped her, followed by a sigh and closed eyes as memories returned. Man, she got hot just thinking about Roger. All the ways he'd touched her. All the ways she'd touched him. She suspected her hands and lips would never forget the way he felt and tasted.

Ah, heck. She needed to get going. She didn't want to wind up driving into Denver after dark. Being unfamiliar with the city could make that problematic.

At last, a carry-on and a purse were ready for her to go.

She locked the house and stood in her driveway surveying the street. A beautiful, quiet street. Old trees fully leafed out, the sounds of children playing at the park two blocks behind her. So damn inviting. It was a bit like discovering a movie set, picture-perfect if a little worn around the edges.

Finally she climbed into her car and set out. Casey needed all her friends right now, especially if she got bad news on Monday.

This town didn't drag on for miles as did the towns and suburbs she was used to back East. No, it cut off pretty quickly and then she was on the open road, with ranch lands on either side and only an occasional commercial truck passing her, headed the other way. She would have expected more traffic on a Saturday but had to admit she hadn't learned the rhythms of life around here yet. Maybe people were busy catching up on chores with the help of their kids. Maybe grocery-store runs happened later in the day. Maybe parents were getting their kids ready for a new school year.

But Casper was a fair drive, too, and if people had wanted to shop there, they might well have left far earlier.

All of this was speculation, she reminded herself. When she returned, it would probably take her months to figure out the ebbs and flows of life in Conard County, certainly in town. The whole time she'd been here, the streets hadn't been very busy.

Having the road pretty much empty in front of her gave Haley an opportunity to enjoy the open plain on either side of her and the next range of mountains looming in the foreground. When she turned south to Denver, she expected the traffic to pick up.

She passed a large, white vehicle backed up to a gate that guarded acres upon acres of open land. She almost giggled when she saw deer in the pasture grazing alongside cows. She wondered what the ranchers thought of that. The cows didn't seem to mind.

In her rearview she caught sight of the brown-splotched Suburban pull onto the highway behind her, but it kept a safe distance. Probably someone headed home after fixing a fence or something.

She was making up stories, she realized, about things she knew nothing about. Amused, she wondered how she could fit them into a larger tale.

But with each mile she left Conard City behind, she felt the burdens of her fears lifting. That creep had really shaken her. Maybe he was the best reason for not returning.

But there was Roger. Twenty miles and he was already calling to her like an irresistible song. A siren's song, although weren't they supposed to be female?

Her mood was lightening and she giggled at herself. She felt so free, free of bad things. She had so much good.

There was her grandmother's house, a place she had always loved, a place filled with great memories and now filled with amazing ones because of Roger.

He'd always been special to her, a friend at all times. He was right up there beside Flora in her impressions of those summers. He'd contributed so much to a young girl who might otherwise have felt a little lost with no one her own age around.

He'd been older, but that hadn't seemed to matter to him. A very special guy even when he was young.

She just wished she could quit linking the Peeping Tom to the kidnapper in her childhood. Two different people with different aims. One had wanted to use her to get money. The other just wanted to get his unsavory jollies. A very different thing. She needed to sever that connection inside herself and treat each as an unrelated event.

She did, however, hate how much this new creep had reopened her past, making it fresh all over again. Maybe when she was at home with her friends, they could help her get past this.

Assuming, of course, that Casey would get good

news. She probably would. She was young, still, at an age where this shouldn't happen. As if that mattered.

God, was she trying to be a Pollyanna all of a sudden? She was flying back home because she knew how scary this had to be for Casey, and knew perfectly well that the results might be even more terrifying. Cancer was no respecter of age.

She was vaguely aware that the Suburban was still behind her. Didn't mean anything. Hadn't Flora told her the ranch hands like to spend free weekends at the roadhouses to enjoy a few too many beers and maybe stir up a little trouble? Maybe the driver behind her had finished his work and was looking for a watering hole. Vaguely, from her drive up here, she remembered there was one just a few miles ahead.

It had amused her to see how scattered those establishments were. They dotted the state highway here and there, and probably showed up on some county roads. They brought the alcohol to the ranchers and their help, not the other way around. Maybe it even reduced police involvement if there was a brawl.

Even as she had the thought, a sheriff's SUV came toward her. She wasn't sure she recognized the deputy at the wheel, but she caught the friendly wave and returned it. Another nice thing about this place. When was the last time a cop had given her a friendly wave back East?

Never. Another laugh escaped her as the tan vehicle disappeared over a rise in the road. The prairie was rolling now, getting ready to meet the mountains still far in the distance.

Then she heard an engine roar and it pulled her out of her wandering daydreams. The speed limit wasn't enough for the guy who'd been following her. Too bad, she refused to exceed the speed limit. She allowed her own speed to drop a little as he began to pass her.

But he didn't pass her.

She kept her hands steady on the wheel and glanced over. She couldn't see the other driver's face. It was shadowed beneath the brim of a cowboy hat.

Maybe he didn't have the acceleration to get past her. Fearful they'd meet an oncoming truck, she let up a little more, hoping the big Suburban would ease past.

But it slowed, too, pacing her.

Fear began to crawl into her throat, turning her mouth as dry as sand. What was going on? Maybe she should jam on the brakes to make sure he passed.

Just as she had the thought, she felt the impact as the Suburban slammed into her side. Immediately she had to grip the steering wheel hard to keep from driving off the road.

Her mind, still trying to grasp whether that had been an accident, had a few moments to feel a wave of relief as he dropped back a little. An accident.

But before she could decide how to respond, the Suburban swung over and hit her rear quarter panel hard. She could feel her tires skid sideways on the pavement.

Fighting with all her might, she tried to accelerate to get away.

Too late. One more slam and she was rolling, the world turning topsy-turvy.

The last thing she remembered was a sharp blow in

the side of her head as it hit something and the airbag exploding in her face.

Then the world turned mercifully black.

Mission accomplished. Satisfied that, dead or alive, Haley would want no further part of living out here, Edgar drove a few more miles down the road, turned onto a gravel county road that had little traffic except a couple of local ranchers, then parked nose-down in a ditch not a half mile from where he'd left his truck.

The sun felt hot on his back as he walked, but that was okay. He was used to it. When he got to his truck, he climbed in, started slowly so as not to leave tracks, and drove back to the state road. Instead of heading into town, he continued toward Casper. Going back to the scene could be incredibly stupid. He'd just have to rely on gossip to tell him how successful he'd been.

Roger started worrying as the afternoon waned. He told himself not to be ridiculous, that Haley would call when she got to Denver, but his fascination with the clock steadily grew until work became hopeless.

He performed mental calculations, estimating the drive time conservatively. Haley struck him as the kind of person who'd pretty much stick to the speed limit. It was Saturday. She might run into a ton of traffic, or very little.

He decided very little. Most folks who wanted to travel to Casper or some other large town today would have left last night or early in the morning to give them time to do their errands or enjoy themselves. But then there was that turn onto the interstate heading south. That would be full of trucks and traffic. She might have whizzed along or she might have been forced to slow down.

He told himself to cut it out. In the absence of news, there was no reason to think she had run into trouble. And if she did, if her little rental broke down, she'd probably have called him to tell him not to worry, she'd be late getting to Denver.

She didn't at all strike him as thoughtless and she'd promised to let him know when she arrived.

But time was passing. Surely, she should have reached the city by now. Or at least the outskirts of Denver, where she might have picked up something to eat. Yeah, that was a possibility. And with her planning to call from the motel tonight, why would she think to do it while having dinner?

He couldn't shake an uneasy feeling about it. Damn, he should have ignored her and driven her himself. At least then he wouldn't be wondering if she'd had a breakdown or something.

But she'd needed, wanted, the independence of driving herself and, after the last couple of weeks, he understood. She'd be proving herself to herself.

He hated that she seemed to be growing so impatient with herself because of the scars that creep had opened when he'd peered through her window, but he got it. Hate it or not, he got it. Haley's world had been closing in on her because of her past and the recent event. She needed to take it back.

Driving herself to Denver had probably been like

shucking a load of crap from her back. A sense of returning freedom. Good for her.

Not so good for him because he seemed to have developed a very strong inclination to protect her and worry about her. Not his right, but whenever had his rights been determined by whether someone granted them? He couldn't just order himself to stop caring.

Nor had the last couple of nights exactly freed him of his urges. Sex with her had been a splendid experience. Each and every time they had come together, he'd felt his universe tremble at its very foundations. He wanted her back. He wanted to take the chance that this time there could be a future.

Until Haley, he'd never even thought of picket fences and a crew cab on his truck to carry youngsters. Now those errant thoughts danced through his mind every so often, even though this wasn't a picket fence kind of town.

Man, he had it bad. He hammered the last tack into the saddle he'd been finishing, aware that his deadline was creeping ever closer. He'd been taking too much time off, but Haley was worth it. Anyway, being only human, he needed the time off occasionally.

His stomach rumbled, reminding him that he hadn't eaten since his breakfast with Haley. He could have cooked something for himself, but cooking for one held even less interest for him after the meals he had shared with Haley.

Well, he might have to eat alone, but at least he could do it at Maude's diner, where he'd fill his arteries with bad stuff and maybe run into an acquaintance to spend an hour with. Friday-night darts had been called off until school reopened because most of his friends had families and kids now.

He was far behind them and had never been in a rush to change that. Until, possibly, now.

Damn, he hoped Haley returned, that she didn't discover she'd missed her friends too much, or that she didn't want to return to the nightmare this place had become to her.

He locked up his shop, making sure everything was safely shut down, then walked around his house to his truck parked out front. He probably smelled like the glues and solutions he used, not to mention the leather, but so far not a soul had complained. Of course, he didn't complain when a bunch of ranchers showed up and smelled as if they had a bit of cow dung on their boots.

The city had changed over the course of his life, but it was still a town that existed largely for working folks who didn't smell like aftershave but more like livestock.

He liked it.

Just as he opened the door to his truck, a police car pulled up. It felt as if everything inside him froze. Either they were here to tell him they'd caught the Peeping Tom or...

He didn't want to think it.

Gage Dalton climbed out and limped his way closer. "Rog? There's no good way to say this. Haley had an accident about thirty miles out of town. She's in the emergency room right now."

"How...how bad?"

Gage shook his head. "I don't know. A trucker saw her vehicle rolled in a ditch. The fire department got her out of the wreckage. All I know is that she was unconscious and went to the hospital on a backboard."

"I'm going."

Gage nodded. "I thought you would. Want an escort?"

Haley was in a hinterland. Flashes came to her then succumbed to a peaceful darkness. The guy who'd run her off the road...she could see the side of his head... Searing pain, shoulder, head...and more darkness.

A vague memory of voices, the sound of screaming as she was tugged and pulled. One clear image of a concerned female face above her. Feeling something holding her head...

Weird feeling of being wheeled as if on ice beneath bright lights. Familiar sounds of voices and beeping equipment. A clear thought: emergency room.

Everything punctuated by darkness. She couldn't let the darkness win. She had to fight it. That determination pierced every slightly conscious moment she had.

Don't let go.

Someone calling her name loudly. "Haley! Stay with me!"

Oh, that was a bad sign, but the dark was so soft and inviting.

"Haley! Hang on. Stay with me!"

Why? Why bother? Sinking away felt so easy.

"Haley!" A different voice. A man. Roger?

"Haley, don't let go. Please. Stay."

"Unfair," she thought she mumbled, but couldn't be sure. Unfair to bring Roger into this. But the dark still reached for her and she didn't think she could fight it.

So easy...

Roger watched them wheel her from the bay to the MRI. He'd felt bad before in his life, like when his dad died, but this was far worse. Internally he felt like ice, except for his heart, which ached as if a big fist had squeezed it.

They still weren't sure how bad Haley was. Suspicions had been mentioned by medical personnel as he hovered outside the bay, listening, worrying, wanting desperately to reach Haley.

Finally, Mary let him in, a nurse he'd known almost his entire life, one of the previous sheriff's daughters. She'd encouraged him, hoping Haley would respond to his voice.

She'd responded, but only to mumble something he couldn't understand.

Now he stood there alone, staring at the detritus on the floor around where her gurney had been. She'd bled so much! It didn't help that Mary assured him that even superficial head wounds bled a whole lot. How was that to reassure him? Haley still hadn't opened her eyes.

Possibly broken ribs. Shoulder bruising, maybe broken collarbone from the seat belt. Legs bruised, possibly broken.

It was mostly her head. They were worried about brain damage.

God, he hated to even imagine it. What if she

couldn't be a nurse again? That might gut her. What if she didn't remember him? That would gut *him*.

He finally accepted the urging to go to the waiting room, and found he wasn't alone. Edith was there, without Bailey, and a couple of deputies he knew. Jake Madison, the chief of police, and a few of the church crowd that Roger didn't believe Haley had yet met.

But he hadn't been in that room for long when he realized they were there for *him*. To support him whether they knew Haley or not. And they'd all certainly known Flora.

He rubbed a hand over his face, loving this town and its people, then looked toward the deputies, Connie and Beau. He played darts with Beau. "What happened?"

Neither answered.

"We can't be certain," Connie eventually said. Careful cop.

But Roger only had to close his eyes to see the road. A sunny day, dry pavement, and a shoulder wide enough to keep anyone from straying into the drainage ditches to either side. It was the kind of road where a driver had to fall asleep at the wheel or be drunk in broad daylight to get into trouble, unless the pavement was slick.

"Something happened," he said finally.

Connie and Beau exchanged glances. "We have to check the car out before we can say anything," Beau answered. "She might have had a mechanical problem."

That was a possibility. Roger clung to it, fighting back guilt. He'd had no authority to tell her not to make the trip alone.

But what began to plague him more was remembering how he'd tried to dismiss the creep who'd looked into her window, tried to minimize it as a toothless threat. How he'd simply refused to let her make the connection she'd been trying to make at some level.

What was the likelihood that her kidnapper would turn up in this little town after all these years? Slim. So slim, the odds were incalculably small. He'd told her that.

What if he'd been wrong? What if the guy was here and feared she could identify him? What about the guy she'd stared at so hard the day they'd been out for a walk and had met Jake Madison? Even Jake had noticed the way she had stared.

Damn, what if her suspicion had been right and he'd helped her dismiss it?

He didn't think he'd ever forgive himself.

Edgar took a roundabout way home, feeling quite proud of himself. Puddles jumped up and down as if on springs when he walked through the door, and he snapped on her leash and took her into the backyard.

An untraceable vehicle, and he'd managed to drive the woman right off the road. In his rearview mirror, as if in slow motion, he'd watched her car flip and nearly disappear into the drainage ditch. With any luck, if she was still alive, it would be hours before they found her. Painful hours. Hours that should persuade her to go back to her former life for good.

He doubted the saddler would be enough to make her stay after that. She'd feel attacked. Much more so than when he'd peered in her window. He spared a moment to remember how she'd kept the curtains closed and the windows closed since the night he'd looked in on her. He'd scared her then. And now, today...

Yeah, he'd done a good job, and there was nothing to trace any of this back to him. Most likely it would be dismissed as an accident. But if they found the Suburban, all they'd be able to discover was that it had belonged to the school auto shop.

They'd blame some joyriding kid.

Once Puddles was done, he brought her back inside and gave her a few treats. Her tail wagged happily until she jumped into his lap while he drank a beer.

All was good. His own fears had already begun to recede. When the fall semester started, he'd be able to return to work without having to dread showing his face around town.

If she lived, maybe her brain had been addled, too. Concussions could do that.

Smiling, he reached for the remote and flipped on a baseball game.

He'd been smarter this time. Much smarter.

Roger thought he was going to wear a hole in the linoleum of the waiting room floor as he paced a tight circle. When they'd let him come into the ER bay to speak with her, she'd looked awful. Blackened eyes, swollen cheek, minor abrasions, and that was only the parts he could see.

He wasn't a relative. What if they wouldn't tell him anything at all? They might leave him here wondering forever about her condition. He didn't think he could stand it.

And, hell, he didn't even know who to call. Della? But who was Della and how could he get her phone number?

It may have been several hours, or maybe less, before Gage Dalton joined him. His sense of timing was shot now as he worried about Haley. Everything seemed to be taking forever, time was dragging its feet as if someone had put on the brakes.

And apparently time was taking long enough that all the people who had come to comfort him had taken their leave with gentle excuses, promising to return after dinner.

"Roger," Gage said with a nod. As always, he limped, and Roger suspected he hadn't spent a single day without pain in all the years since the car bomb. God, he hoped that didn't happen to Haley. That she'd come through this well, with no lasting deficits. No pain.

"Any word?" Roger asked without preamble.

Gage nodded. "Her MRI was pretty good. Some bleeding from a concussion, but not enough to worry about. They're a little concerned because she hasn't roused yet, but they expect that shortly."

Roger blew a long sigh of relief. "Thank God," he whispered. "What's the rest?"

"A broken rib, which is going to make her miserable for a while. A broken leg, which may make her just as miserable. They'll have to do surgery to put in a pin or something. No internal damage, thanks to the airbag, but…" Gage shrugged. "She may have a shoulder problem from the seat belt. They see some bruising. In short, she'll live, but she's going to need some help for a while."

Roger sank into a chair. His legs felt suddenly unsteady. "She'll get help. How much on the outside am I, not being family?"

Gage patted his shoulder. "I told them you were the closest thing she has to family, so it's a wink-wink situation. You'll be able to see her soon."

Roger nodded and looked at the floor beneath his feet. His hands, he noted, had bunched into tight fists. "What happened?" he asked again.

"We're towing her car in for an examination but..."

"But?" Roger's head snapped up.

"The scene investigator thinks someone may have sideswiped her. Accident, probably, but it could have been enough. Anyway, we can't know anything for sure until we go over the car."

"Okay. Okay." He felt as if emotions were roiling inside him, a bunch of them so mixed up he couldn't have named them. Relief, he guessed. Infinite relief. Then he remembered.

"Did anyone get her cell phone? She's got a friend expecting her in Baltimore tomorrow. She was on her way to the airport."

"I'll check. If it's with her belongings, do you want me to call?"

Roger pulled his thoughts into line. "What would be worse? Hearing the sheriff on the other end of the line or me?"

"Does she even know you?"

Roger realized that not only did Della not know him, but probably didn't know his name, either. He couldn't remember Haley mentioning it. Just some stuff about cowboys.

"No."

"Then I'll do it, Rog. I can tell her more anyway. What's her friend's name?"

"Della. That's all I know."

Gage turned away then looked back. "One of the nurses will come to get you. I lied a bit, said you were all but engaged." Gage winked with the unscarred side of his face. "I'll let you know what her friend says."

"Thanks, Gage."

"Unfortunately, I've had experience with making this kind of call."

Roger was sure he had.

Grateful he was alone in this waiting room, Roger resumed his pacing. He hadn't felt like this since his father's fatal heart attack over a decade ago. Waiting, endless waiting, on tenterhooks, trying to pray but unable to utter more than a few broken phrases as his mind whirled with worry. The doctors had fought for hours and failed to save his dad in the end.

This was different, he assured himself. Gage had said Haley was going to be fine, although in a lot of pain. Still, Roger knew he wouldn't feel any better until her eyes opened and he heard her voice again.

Damn, he should have insisted on driving her. Except what good would that have done if some reckless driver had sideswiped her little car, even with him at the wheel? Those subcompacts had no weight to them. Thank God, they had front airbags. But his truck might have been better.

Aww, hell, what good did it do to think about this now? There'd been an accident, Haley was hurt, and *what-ifs* weren't going to change anything.

Later Gage appeared with news. "Okay. Della, who's her roommate by the way, wants Haley to know she'll fly out on Tuesday or Wednesday." Gage consulted his pad. "Something to do with getting word about Casey."

Roger nodded. "Casey's having a biopsy on Monday. Another of Haley's friends."

"Okay, so Haley will have help, at least for a while."

"Not like I wouldn't do it," Roger muttered. God, had he said something so asinine? This day had taken a lot of out of him. "Good news," he managed to say.

"And final word. Haley's in recovery. They'll call you as soon as they move her to a room."

Roger nodded as the first real relief began to hit him. As he watched Gage take his leave, heading back to find out what he could about the accident, Roger wondered why he could feel relief but couldn't feel that the worst was over.

If any part of her didn't hurt, Haley couldn't feel it. Coming out of inky blackness, pain seemed to fill her universe. Every breath hurt in her left side. Every single one. Her leg felt heavy and useless, but she couldn't see. The visual world seemed to want to lag, but her hearing was already working. She heard stirring around her, voices talking, male and female. Maybe a groan or two, but she might have been the one groaning.

"She's waking," said a female voice.

Then she felt fingers pry her eyes open one at a time. "Good reflex," a male voice said.

She knew what that meant, even in her muzzy state. Her head ached, probably indicating a concussion, but if her pupils were reacting normally, then she hadn't suffered any severe damage.

"Can you hear me, Haley?" the man asked.

"Mmm." Even that little sound hurt to make.

"You'll need to breathe deeply even though it hurts. You have a broken rib. We don't want pneumonia."

Of course she didn't want pneumonia. Steeling herself, she sucked in a long, slow breath despite the shriek in her side.

"That's good. Do it as often as you can manage."

"How bad?" she whispered.

"One broken rib, a concussion, some lacerations and a broken leg. Nothing major, just painful."

Good. She didn't know if she said it out loud, but she tried another deep, gentle breath. Being a nurse, she knew what counted.

"Back?" she whispered.

"You mean your back? No spinal injury. You were one very lucky lady. But your left shoulder will probably hurt like the dickens when you wake up a little more. Seat belt."

"Collar?"

"Amazingly, you didn't break your collarbone. And

the airbag must have kept your head from rolling around too much when your car tumbled."

All good, she thought. All good. But the darkness was creeping back.

"Feel up to going to your room? You have a friend waiting."

"Yes." Friend? Della? She couldn't be here already. Roger? Oh, she hoped it was Roger. Then she let the gray gauze of surgical drugs carry her away again. So much easier than all the pain.

Chapter 10

Haley woke to night beyond the window of the room, hammering pain reawakening in what felt like most of her body, and a warm, large hand holding hers.

She blinked. Awareness, she thought, was over-rated. She couldn't prevent a *mewl* of pain escaping her lips.

"Haley?"

Roger's voice. So welcome. Reaching out to her like a lifeline. Gingerly she turned her head, seeking him. Only the floor night-light was on, but she could still see his concerned face. "Mmm."

"I was starting to get worried," he admitted. "Welcome back. The nurse said you didn't seem to want to wake up."

"Would you?" she mumbled.

"No, probably not. Feel that button control in your other hand? Morphine drip. You know all about that."

"Mmm." Yeah, she did, and the gray gauze of hiding in it sounded good right now. But she didn't want to sink away. Not yet. Not with Roger so close. "What…?"

"What happened?" He completed the question for her when she said nothing else.

"Car accident. Sheriff thinks someone sideswiped you. You're fine, you're gonna hurt, your leg has a pin in it or something, and you're supposed to breathe deeply as often as you can." He blew a breath. "I think I got everything, but the nurse will remind you, I'm sure. Oh, and your shoulder is going to add to your discomfort. Bruised from the seat belt."

Quite a catalog, she thought muzzily. But she'd seen auto accidents with far worse outcomes. She'd been lucky. "Roger?"

"Yeah?"

"Della?"

"Oh, yeah. Gage called her, told her what happened. She said she'll fly out on Tuesday or Wednesday to look after you, but she's going to wait on Casey's results."

"Good. Casey matters. Needs us."

"Yup. And you're gonna need Della, too. From what they're saying, you might need help for a while. You can definitely count on me."

She knew she could, and the knowing felt like a warm, soft blanket around her heart. "Thanks."

"Deep breaths," he reminded her gently. "Then go ahead and push your morphine button. Dang, woman, you don't *have* to hurt. And you don't have to stay awake. I'm not going anywhere."

"Get something to eat," she managed to whisper as the morphine began to flood her system. The gauze was back. The pain slipped away.

Haley was released on Tuesday morning. Roger took her home, along with a wheelchair. After a week she'd be allowed to get around on a walking cast, but right now she was under instructions to keep her leg elevated to prevent swelling.

That had made for some amusement getting into Roger's truck. She could bend her knee, but it was still awkward, and by the time he slipped her into the passenger seat, she was giggling and a bit flushed from the places he'd touched her all while trying to avoid doing so.

She had a bag full of items like a water pitcher and cup that she'd probably never use, hand sanitizer and some nonslip socks, which she'd always liked. Tucked in her purse was a supply of pain meds.

Because that rib hurt like hell. Her leg throbbed, but that rib... The doctor had told her they'd needed to wire it. Lovely. Well, that explained the small scar on her left side and the staple holding it closed.

All in all, she was feeling like one very lucky person when they arrived at her grandmother's house.

Roger wheeled her inside, promising a ramp if she needed one. "I can fix one up in a jiff."

"Does anyone say that anymore? Jiff or jiffy?"

He shrugged, flashing a grin. "Like I care? I'm dated."

She wanted to laugh, but that dang rib prevented it. "God, it feels good to be home."

"A place with food whenever you want it, coffee by the gallon, or tea if you prefer, and I even got you some ice cream."

"Hey…"

"No *hey*. You're recovering and you didn't eat damn near enough in the hospital."

She nodded as he pulled a chair out of the way and slid her leg and wheelchair up to the table. "Morphine kills the appetite."

"And you can justify the ice cream because it has lots of calcium to help your leg, and calories to make up for starving the last several days."

She smiled up at him. "Damn, you're good."

"I'm great with excuses."

He started a pot of coffee when she expressed a wish for some, then began pulling enough food out of the fridge for an army.

"What are you doing?"

"If you want a decent sandwich around here, you can get one from Maude easily enough. But I want more than decent. I went to Miranda's bakery to get some hard rolls, real hard rolls, and I hit the supermarket deli, such as it is, for cold cuts and cheese. The only thing I need to know from you is mayo or mustard or both?"

While she watched, he proceeded to build master-pieces on those rolls, and he hadn't forgotten a thing. There was lettuce and tomato, as well, which she absolutely loved on a sandwich. By the time he put one in front of her, she wondered how she'd wrap her mouth around it.

Before she could even try, her cell phone rang. Roger had set her small purse within reach and she grabbed for it, wincing as her rib objected. "Della," she said as she read the name on the display.

"Well, hi, girl, are you running marathons yet?"

"Not yet." Haley had to laugh. "I'm sitting at the kitchen table, with Roger, about to dig into the most amazing sandwich I've ever seen. How's Casey?"

"Great. Biopsy was negative, so she won't be needing the tissue squad for tear-wiping. I've booked a flight that's leaving this afternoon, and I'll be parking on your front step by noon tomorrow."

"Della, you don't—"

"I know I don't. I talked to that cowboy of yours. Roger? Sounds like a capable sort of guy, but you're getting me, like it or not."

Haley felt tears prickle her eyes. "Oh, Della."

"Now, don't you be crying. This is what friends are for, and besides, I'm a nurse. Your cowboy isn't. I need to set eyes on you. You've been through hell, girl."

She had, Haley thought. She guessed she had.

"Any idea what happened?"

"Not yet. Probably just a weird accident." But even as she said it, Haley realized that she didn't quite believe it. Couldn't quite believe it. The fear was back, even though pain meds were smothering it a bit.

"Yeah, well, we're gonna find out about that while I'm there or I'll know the reason why."

Another laugh escaped Haley. "You are a force of nature."

"You will be again, too, once we get you mended. Now put that cowboy on."

Haley handed her phone to Roger. "Della wants to talk to you."

"I'm not surprised," he said with amusement. He took the phone, saying, "Hi, Della. It's Roger." Then a long pause. "Yes, ma'am." Another pause. "I sure will. Believe it." Another pause. "Will do. But if I get hammered for it, you're on the hook. Right. 'Bye."

He handed the phone back with a grin. "She's gone to see Casey. And I have my marching orders. I guess she's forgotten you're a nurse, too. Breathing and all the rest of it."

Haley laughed. "That's Della. A fire-breathing dragon. As for me being a nurse, the instant I put on my invalid cap, I lost my nurse's cap."

"It sounds like it, at least as far as Della is concerned. Basically, I'm supposed to be a nag, but she's catching fallout from me if you get annoyed." His grin widened. "I trust you to know your orders, so mum's the word unless I catch you cheating. Ready to eat?"

Surprisingly, she was. The sandwich was a bit to handle, however, and Roger told her to just forget delicacy and manners and pick it apart however she needed to. "These meats aren't bad at all," she remarked.

"I didn't buy prepackaged. We don't have the most extensive deli, as I'm sure you've noticed, but what we have is good."

Once she had eaten as much as she could, Roger set

her up on the living room couch and moved an end table to be within easy reach. Beneath her leg, he propped a pillow and placed another one behind her back.

Before he returned with her glass of water, she had fallen asleep again. Healing required most of a body's energy, and she didn't battle it. At least the couch was comfy.

She awoke quickly to the sound of knocking at the front door. Her instinctive move to answer it sent pain rocketing through her, and a groan escaped her. She'd forgotten she was totally laid up.

But Roger was there. As if out of nowhere, he appeared to answer the door. "Hey, come on in, Gage. I don't know if Haley's awake—"

"I'm awake," Haley answered. "Didn't you hear me groan when I tried to move?"

"You've been groaning a bit in your sleep," Roger told her as he ushered Gage into the small living room and waved him to the goosenecked chair. "Coffee, man?"

"No thanks. This is business, not pleasure, unfortunately."

Haley heard that and desperately wished she could sit upright. Roger came to her aid with another pillow behind her back, but she still didn't feel properly positioned for what she suspected was going to be a serious conversation.

"About your accident," Gage said to Haley as Roger took a matching chair nearby. "We had some state investigators come in to look it all over. Haley, it was no accident."

Memory, quiet until now, came crashing back. The white Suburban, the man driving it, the way it had hit her. "No," she said quietly. "It wasn't. I guess I was blocking it, but…not an accident."

"You've been doped up since we pulled you out of the wreckage. Concussed. I'm surprised you remember at all."

"Yeah." She sighed, ignoring the protest her rib shrieked, and let her head fall back against the pillow. "The memory is vague, though. Some guy sideswiped me. I think I tried to slow down to let him pass, then…" She trailed off and furrowed her brow. "After that, I think I felt another bump, but then everything—well, mainly me—was flying and banging into things. I'm not even sure I felt the airbag deploy. I *did* feel the side of my head hit something."

Gage nodded. "Not bad, considering. You were side-swiped pretty strongly. A lot of paint gone from the side of your car. Then there were a couple of dents on your rear quarter panel. He hit you hard, and the only reason for that was to drive you into the ditch."

She gasped then ardently wished she hadn't. Another helpless groan escaped her, even though she tried to swallow it.

"Pain pill," said Roger, rising. "More than six hours."

"I don't want one."

"I don't care." He dashed from the living room to the kitchen and returned with the bottle of pills and a fresh glass of water. "If it makes you drowsy, I'll bring coffee. You're a nurse, but I'll repeat what the doctor said anyway. The pain meds work better if you don't wait to take them until you're really hurting." He tipped one out of the bottle and put it in her hand. "Don't give me a hassle or I'll tell Della tomorrow."

She'd have laughed if she had dared. "Good reason." She swallowed the pill obediently.

"Della?" Gage asked.

"My roommate from Baltimore. She's coming to keep an eye on me."

"A nurse," Roger elaborated. "That's more than I can offer."

"That's right. I talked to her." Gage nodded and shifted in his chair. "Okay, we know it was purposeful. Paint transfer says it was a white vehicle, but there was some brown on it, too. It had to be somewhat bigger than your vehicle."

"Not saying much," Haley murmured. "Yeah, it was bigger. Really big, like a Suburban."

"Suburban," muttered Gage. "Just so happens, the high school reported one missing from their auto shop lot yesterday afternoon. Now we just have to find it. Did you see the driver?"

Haley closed her eyes. "No. Not really. I only got a glance and his face was well shadowed by a cowboy hat."

Gage scrawled that in his notebook. "Can you remember anything else at all?"

She looked at him. "He turned out of one of those little side thingies, with a gate in the fence. Whatever they're called. He followed me for a while at a reasonable distance. I didn't think a thing about it. Not until he pulled up beside me. I thought he was trying to pass, so I slowed down."

"No other traffic?"

"I don't remember any. It happened so fast. I couldn't even figure out what happened when he scraped the side of my car. I think I wondered if he was drunk, but I'm not sure."

Gage nodded, added a few notes and then closed the pad and rose. He winced, and Haley felt a lot of sympathy for him.

"Coffee?" Roger asked again.

"Thanks, but Justin will be headed back to college in a few days and I've been making a point of getting home to have dinner with him and Emma in the evening. Maybe next week?" He looked at Haley. "I'll keep you posted. Thanks for your help. I'm pretty sure we're looking for an abandoned Suburban now. That'll help."

"If he left some traces."

Gage paused as he neared the door. "What's the first thing you do when you get in a car you haven't driven before?"

Roger thought about it for a second. "Plug the keys in the ignition and adjust the mirror."

"Exactly. You'll never believe how many thieves wipe down a car and forget to wipe the mirror. If we're lucky, this clown isn't any smarter than most."

Roger saw him out then remarked to Haley, "Fingerprints are useful only if they're on file. They'll probably have to catch the guy first."

Haley smiled. Her pain was beginning to ease and

that made her feel so much better. "It'll be okay. I can't imagine what the guy was thinking, but right now I don't much care."

"Good," said Roger. "That's why we have the police. Let them worry about all of it."

Edgar was once again feeling dumb. Driving by the McKinsey house, he saw light leaking through the front curtains and the saddler's truck once again in the driveway. Room for it now that there was no subcompact.

He tried to assure himself that this was only temporary. That as soon as she could travel, she was going to get the hell out of Conard County. She had to realize she had been attacked for some unknown reason, which surely frightened her more than when he'd looked through her window.

Yeah, another week or so, and from what he'd gathered from gossip, she wasn't going to be walking around the streets at all for a while. He didn't have to hide as much as he had been. He told himself the woman would be headed home before the fall semester started.

It would be okay. He kept telling himself that even as the drumbeat of *stupid, stupid* tried to run through his head. Better if she had died, but she hadn't. There was no way she could feel safe here now. No way.

And that's what he'd needed, wasn't it? For her to want to run away.

But as he tooled down the darkened highway, passing by the messed-up ditch where her car had landed, he saw something else that concerned him. In the distance, in the direction where he'd dumped the Suburban, there were flashing lights. Red, blue and yellow. They'd found the vehicle.

Okay. He'd planned on that happening eventually. Pretty soon they'd be questioning high school kids about taking a joyride. Nobody would look at him. Nobody.

Satisfied, ignoring the sickening sense that he might have screwed up again, he kept driving. The woman wouldn't be on the street for a while. If necessary, he could take a short vacation from town until she returned to wherever her home was.

She had to know that someone had tried to kill her. Only a lunatic would hang around for a repeat.

Chapter 11

Other than a few humiliating moments when Roger helped her into a comfortable nightgown and took her to the bathroom, Haley's night passed in a bit of fog-filled pain. The meds helped, but the dose wasn't strong enough to eliminate it, which was fine because she didn't care for the way the drugs made her feel. She preferred a clear head.

But when she expressed embarrassment to Roger for the intimate ways he had to care for her, he reared back a little and flashed his charming grin. "Like you weren't flaunting all of this to me just recently?"

One corner of her mouth lifted. "This is different."

"I suppose you tell that to your patients, too. So think of me as your practical nurse until I can have my way with you again."

That sounded delightful, but she suspected she was going to have to wait awhile. Damn.

Dreams bothered her that night. Her past and present intertwined until she dreamed that one monster was chasing her, following her through her entire life, seeking to destroy her. Whenever she woke with a start, Roger was right there. He'd spread his air mattress on the floor beside the couch, just inches away, ready to take care of her. If it was time, he pressed another pain pill on her, and made her take her deep breaths. At least she wasn't coughing. God, the thought of pneumonia and how that coughing would feel was frightening all by itself.

Then she'd fall asleep again, wishing that she could turn over. Not to be, not yet.

In the morning he brought her breakfast, eggs and toast and some bacon, with a tall glass of milk. Her appetite still wasn't great, but she noted that the aching and throbbing had eased. Not gone, but better. Better enough that she refused a pain pill. Roger was having none of it.

"One more, so you can rest up for Della. Then she can take over and you can argue with her."

She gave in.

The next thing she knew, she heard Roger speaking to someone, introducing himself. Then she heard Della's familiar and welcome voice.

"I swear," her roomie said, "I feel like the only raisin in a bowl of bread pudding around here."

Roger laughed heartily. "You're not, but I can understand why you might think that."

Then Della was bending over her, her deeply brown face and dark eyes both smiling and expressing concern.

"Victim," Della said. "Girl, that ain't you."

"Wouldn't have thought so," Haley answered, glad that she was truly waking up. "Oh, man, Della, it's so good to see you."

"Of course it is. Nothing like an old, old friend at a time like this. I gather Roger is an old friend, too."

"From childhood," Haley agreed.

"He'll do for a cowboy."

Roger had cleared away his air mattress and now pulled one of the chairs over for Della to sit on. He stood in the background, smiling.

"Now get back to work," Della said to him. "You make saddles, right? Someone must be riding bareback right now."

Roger laughed again, and Haley wondered how many more times they might have spoken since her accident. Della seemed pretty well filled in.

"I'll bring dinner over," Roger said as he prepared to leave. "Time for Della to meet Maude's steak sandwich."

"That does sound good. Now scat."

After the door closed behind him, Haley asked, "How's Casey doing?"

"Really good. Relieved, needless to say. She's going back to work tomorrow. She said to tell you she really missed dumping all her angst on you."

Haley started to laugh then caught herself. "I'll bet."

"Misery does love company. Anyway, she and the

others send their love, and Celeste sent a pillow. Let me get it for you."

"A pillow?"

Della headed toward a bag she'd left by the door. "Should have had the cowboy bring in my suitcase. Not like I can't handle it, but he needs to be put to use."

"Oh, please, don't make me laugh."

"You know me. A chuckle a minute." Della held out the deep blue pillow. "Celeste was making it for Casey, but the two of them decided you need it more."

Haley drew a deep breath, annoying her rib, but well worth it. Celeste, who loved to embroider, had cross-stitched one word in gold thread on it: *Hugs.*

"Aww, that's beautiful."

"Also useful if you need to cough. Now let me look at your discharge orders and, while I do that, you promise me you'll be a good patient."

Haley hugged the pillow, feeling loved indeed.

Edgar started thinking about the ricin he'd made from castor beans stolen from his neighbor's garden. It now sat in a small bottle on the highest shelf in his shed. Since he'd managed not to poison himself in the process of making it, he didn't feel quite so stupid. But how to get it into something in Haley's house?

What if she didn't leave? God, he was beginning to doubt his own plan for her. Dead. She was no threat to him if she was dead.

Driving cautiously past her house, he saw that the saddler had left. There was, however, another compact car parked out front. He'd have to wait until tonight, perhaps, to try the mud porch. But first he had to know the dimensions of what was going on inside. Who was there? Colorado plates on the car told him nothing.

Damn it! He pounded his fist on the steering wheel and prodded his brain into action. He had to take care of this mess before it became a mess for him. Poisoning her was the sure way to do it. From what he'd read, it might take a few days for her to die—the symptoms were often mistaken for another illness.

Or she might die within hours.

But he began to think it was the only way to save himself.

Then he had a brainstorm.

Edith had stopped by to check on her, giving Della a warm welcome to town, and promising the church group would bring over enough food that no one would need to cook.

"Well, that cowboy is bringing dinner tonight," Della told her.

"Roger?" Edie laughed. "Can't keep that man out of Maude's diner. Okay, I'll tell the crowd to start running deliveries tomorrow morning. It's so wonderful Haley has you to look after her."

"And the cowboy," Della added. "Seems awfully concerned."

"I think more than average," Edie responded. "Most men would be looking to take a hike into the mountains."

Haley enjoyed listening to the two of them talk and laugh, but Della had encouraged her to take another of the pills, so the gauze kept her happily quiet. Friends. There was nothing on earth like friends.

At some point during the afternoon, the front bell rang. "You just stay put," Della said. "I'll get that."

"Like I can move?" Haley asked. "When did you become a drug pusher anyway?"

"Only since you need it for another day or so. You won't heal as fast if you're knotted in pain, and you don't need me to tell you that."

"Yes, Nurse Ratched."

Della was still chuckling as she went to the door. Unfortunately, in her position, Haley couldn't see who was there.

"Sorry to intrude," said a man's voice. "But the gals at church thought you might like doughnuts for breakfast…"

At that instant, Haley's world collapsed in on itself. She recognized that voice. It pierced her. Then the world swam as she fainted.

"Stop struggling," Della said sharply. "Haley, don't fight, you'll hurt yourself."

"What happened?" Gage Dalton asked. Seeing him startled Haley but only in a flash. Terror dominated.

"I don't know. Some guy came to the door with a box of doughnuts from the church and when I turned around… Haley?"

Haley opened her eyes, welcoming the rush of pain that must have come from her struggles. "I need to go. Get me out of here!"

"Hold on, girl," Della said firmly. "What the hell happened?"

"That voice… Oh, my God, I know that voice!"

"What voice?" Gage asked.

"The man… My kidnapper!"

Della used some words she rarely used and suddenly Gage's scarred face swam before her eyes. "Your kidnapper?"

"Yeah." Now it was hard to catch her breath. Adrenaline burned in her veins and her rib hurt so much. Had she loosened it? That seemed irrelevant. The voice. The voice of so many nightmares, so much horror and terror. She knew that voice.

"Metzler?" Gage straightened. "I saw him leaving as I arrived. From when you were five?"

"Yes," she whispered.

"I'll take care of it. You don't move. Listen to your friend."

"Go, sheriff," Della snapped. "I got this. Haley, I'm going to call Roger."

Roger sounded like a bulwark against the storm. His strength, his innate power. Della could take care of her, but Roger could protect her.

She turned her face to the back of the couch, panting painfully, and feeling tears begin to flow.

It was happening again. All over again. The childhood trauma, the days—she never knew how many but it had seemed endless—when she'd been held captive by the sick man, and now here he was? Miles and years away from the crime? How was that even possible?

But she'd heard the voice. No mistaking it. It had haunted her most of her life, a recording at the back of her mind, ever ready to leap to the forefront if she let it.

He was here.

"Haley." Della. "Take this pill now. Hell, take two. The bottle says you can. Just don't fight me again."

The adrenaline left her like the popping of the balloon. A kind of hopelessness filled her. She swallowed the pills as if she were a child again, and part of her was, and then, as if by magic, Roger was holding her hand and saying, "No one's going to get near you, Haley. He'll have to get through me. You're safe. I swear I'll keep you safe."

She felt tremors ripping through her, each one a new kind of pain, but as she held Roger's hand tightly, she felt the medicine take hold, its gauze easing everything, even stopping the helpless tears.

"Darlin'." Warm lips against her cheek. "You're not alone. You'll never be alone again."

"Well, now," Della said, concern lacing her voice. "That's my kind of cowboy."

Then Haley let go. She had to. Reality had overwhelmed her.

By late afternoon, Haley had her self-control back. She awoke, was aware of pain, but it felt distant. Roger was there, and as soon as her eyes opened, he said, "Gage called. Edgar Metzger is in custody. You can relax."

"Della?"

"In the kitchen unpacking Maude's munificence. Since Gage called, I felt it was okay to run out fast and bring in dinner. Because Gage has the guy in a cell. Okay?"

More than okay. She summoned a smile. "They can hold him because of his voice? Because I recognized it?"

"Apparently so. Gage said to tell you they've begun questioning, Metzger isn't as bright as he may think, the FBI is coming and please don't eat the doughnuts."

She blinked. "The doughnuts?"

"I didn't ask why. I'm sure he'll tell us when he can. In the meantime, I put the box in a garbage bag for him to collect."

"Wow. That sounds serious."

"I guess we'll find out. Are you getting hungry? You haven't eaten enough to keep a finch going these past few days."

She was, she realized. An amazing sense of freedom was filling her, as if a cloud that had been hovering for most of her life was finally breaking up.

Della came in from the kitchen. "A ton of good down-home cooking awaits. Hey, gal, you want to eat here or try chairing your way to the table?"

"The table, please. I *so* need to change positions."

The two of them lifted her easily into the wheelchair and Della made sure the leg rest was securely locked. "A few more days and you can sit normally again." Before they moved, however, she pulled the sock off and checked Haley's foot. "A-OK," she said brightly. "Now, let's go dig into that feast."

It looked as if Roger had bought out the diner's entire menu, including the chocolate pie and some pecan pie. "I don't mind leftovers," he explained as he helped

Della serve. "And if I know that church group, you're going to be sick of tuna casserole by next Sunday."

Haley laughed cautiously. God, she felt good. Her two favorite people in the whole world to share dinner with, and that creep behind bars. Assuming it was him. But his voice…

The dark cloud made a brief return as she recalled the sound. She closed her eyes, testing two memories, one very old against one only a few hours old. Yeah, it was the same voice. The shaft of ice it had speared her with had been no accident. It was *him*, and she hoped they'd be able to tell her why he was so near to her after all this time.

Her eyes popped open. "Did he cause my accident?"

Roger answered. "Judging by what Gage said about not eating the doughnuts, that would be my guess."

"He wanted to kill me? But why?"

"Maybe," Della said, "because he was afraid you'd do exactly what you did. Identify him."

Roger nodded. "That would be my guess. I can't imagine any other reason. Assuming he's not just some nutjob. But you remembering his voice? That's the only way I can put it together. And remember, there's no statute of limitations on kidnapping. He can still be charged."

"But I can't prove it was him."

Roger shook his head. "Darlin', let's just wait until Gage tells us what's going on. All we can do is speculate."

He was right. And she loved the way he called her *darlin'*. She hoped he didn't say that to all the girls.

* * *

Haley spent the night on the couch again, with Roger nearby. Della took one of the rooms upstairs, making the two of them promise to call her if they ran into any trouble.

Morning came with bright sunshine and open curtains. Haley got into her wheelchair, feeling as if that sunlight pouring through the windows was bathing her soul. Warmth after a long, long night she'd learned to live with.

Until this moment. Never again.

Roger wheeled her out onto the porch and he and Della sat on the porch swing.

"Now, I like this," Della said approvingly. "You say you can get a position at the local hospital, Haley?"

"I checked when I got here because I thought maybe I'd want to keep Grandma's house. And, yes, they'd hire me."

Della looked thoughtful. "Maybe I ought to check for me. If the two of you could stand a roomie, that is."

Both Haley and Roger laughed. He assured her he'd be pleased if she decided to stay.

But before that conversation could go much further, a police vehicle pulled up out front and Gage climbed out. He was smiling and waved as he limped up the short walk to climb the porch steps. He welcomed Della to Conard City and asked if she'd be staying awhile.

"It crossed my mind to hang around on a permanent basis."

"You'd like it here."

Roger crossed the porch to get him a folding chair,

and Gage sank into it, wincing visibly. "Dang back," he muttered. "Okay, official business."

Haley tensed, her hands gripping the armrests on her chair. Part of her was eager to hear and part of her wanted to run from it. What if this wasn't the guy? What if he hadn't tried to kill her on the highway? What if...?

Roger leaned over from the swing and took her hand, squeezing it gently.

"Okay," Gage said again. "Mr. Not-So-Smart, also known as Edgar Metzler, should never take up lying for a living. He couldn't keep his own stories straight. By six this morning he was beating his head with his hands, telling everyone that the dumbest thing he'd ever done in his life was kidnap Haley. Then he admitted to being scared she'd recognize him, so, yeah, he'd run her off the road. And those doughnuts? Well, when we searched his house, we found a bottle of homemade ricin poison. Only one reason for that. You still got those things?"

"In a garbage bag, untouched," Roger answered.

"My God," Della breathed. "Ricin? Really?"

"Oh, yeah. That's what broke him. No earthly good reason for making that stuff."

Della shook her head. "If any of us had eaten those doughnuts, we probably wouldn't have survived. If we didn't die immediately, then I doubt the local hospital would have even known what to look for. It's not something that tops the list in an emergency room."

Haley nodded agreement, even as a cold breeze seemed to blow through her. "He might have succeeded."

"He might have," Gage agreed. "But he didn't. And like I said, he's not that bright. He kept tripping over his own lies until he'd boxed himself in and we finally got the whole story. The FBI is taking him away on federal charges, including kidnapping, and I'll be glad to see the last of him."

"So will I," Haley agreed vehemently. "No more nightmares."

It was truly over. After twenty-five years, it was over. No more fear. Maybe a few bad moments here and there, but at last she could be confident that creep wasn't still on the street. For the first time in ages, she beamed.

Della went upstairs early for the night, pointing out that she was still on East Coast time. Haley had returned to the couch for the night, and Roger pulled a chair close so that he could rest his elbows on his knees and hold her hand.

"I came so close to losing you, Haley."

She smiled at him, despite the ache in her leg and side. "Couldn't quite shake me off," she teased.

"I don't want to shake you off." He hesitated. "I know things have been a mess since you got here, but I need to tell you something."

Her ears perked, even as tension began to creep into her. Was this the kiss-off? Go back to Baltimore? It's been fun, but?

His grip on her hand tightened a bit. "I want you to know…well, if you want to stay here, then I want you to stay. Permanently. Because I'm in love with you."

Her heart nearly stopped. "Oh, Roger…"

He waved his other hand. "I get that you probably don't feel the same. It's been rough for you. Hell, I wouldn't blame you if you wanted to get as far away from this state as you could. I just needed you to know."

She honestly didn't have to think about it. Her heart filled with so much joy, she felt as if it might burst right out of her.

"I want an intimate wedding," she said. "When I can walk again."

His eyes widened, a laugh escaped him, then he leaned forward and gave her a long, deep kiss. "You got it, lady," he murmured. "You definitely got it."

Then he leaned in to kiss her again, and a glow of happiness filled her to every corner. "I love you," she murmured against his lips. "I think I always have."

* * * * *

Don't forget previous titles in Rachel Lee's
Conard County: The Next Generation series:

Conard County Watch
Conard County Revenge
Undercover in Conard County
Conard County Marine
Conard County Spy
Conard County Witness

Available now from
Harlequin Romantic Suspense!

Get 4 FREE REWARDS!

We'll send you 2 FREE Books plus 2 FREE Mystery Gifts.

Harlequin® Romantic Suspense books feature heart-racing sensuality and the promise of a sweeping romance set against the backdrop of suspense.

FREE
Value Over
$20

Love Harlequin romance?

DISCOVER.

Be the first to find out about promotions, news and exclusive content!

Facebook.com/HarlequinBooks

Twitter.com/HarlequinBooks

Instagram.com/HarlequinBooks

Pinterest.com/HarlequinBooks

ReaderService.com

EXPLORE.

Sign up for the Harlequin e-newsletter and download a free book from any series at **TryHarlequin.com.**

CONNECT.

Join our Harlequin community to share your thoughts and connect with other romance readers!
Facebook.com/groups/HarlequinConnection

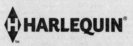

HARLEQUIN®

ROMANCE WHEN YOU NEED IT